*A Return to Servitude*

# A Return to Servitude

*Maya Migration and the Tourist Trade in Cancún*

M. Bianet Castellanos

University of Minnesota Press
Minneapolis | London

FIRST PEOPLES
*New Directions in Indigenous Studies*

Publication of this book was made possible, in part, with a grant from the Andrew W. Mellon Foundation.

Portions of this book previously appeared in the following publications. "Adolescent Migration to Cancún: Reconfiguring Maya Households and Gender Relations in Mexico's Yucatán Peninsula," *Frontiers: Journal of Women Studies* 28, no. 3 (2007); copyright 2007 by Frontiers Editorial Collective, Inc.; reprinted by permission of the University of Nebraska Press. "Don Teo's Expulsion: Property Regimes, Moral Economies, and Ejido Reform," *Journal of Latin American and Caribbean Anthropology* 15, no. 1 (2010). "Cancún and the Campo: Indigenous Migration and Tourism Development in the Yucatán Peninsula," in *Holiday in Mexico: Critical Reflections on Tourism and Tourist Encounters,* ed. Dina Berger Koecher and Andrew G. Wood (Durham, N.C.: Duke University Press, 2009).

All photographs were taken by and are reproduced courtesy of the author.

Maps were created by and are reproduced courtesy of Mike Foster, Cartography Lab, University of Minnesota.

Published by the University of Minnesota Press
111 Third Avenue South, Suite 290
Minneapolis, MN 55401-2520
http://www.upress.umn.edu

Library of Congress Cataloging-in-Publication Data

Castellanos, M. Bianet.
　　A return to servitude : Maya migration and the tourist trade in Cancún / M. Bianet Castellanos.
　　　　p.　　cm. — (First peoples — new directions in indigenous studies)
　　Includes bibliographical references and index.
　　ISBN 978-0-8166-5614-1 (hc : acid-free paper) — ISBN 978-0-8166-5615-8 (pb : acid-free paper)
　　　　1. Mayas—Mexico—Cancún—Social conditions.　　2. Mayas—Migrations. 3. Cancún (Mexico)—Social conditions.　　4. Migration, Internal—Mexico—Yucatán (State).　　5. Tourism—Mexico—Cancún.　　I. Title.
　　F1435.3.S68C37 2010
　　972'.65—dc22
　　　　　　　　　　　　　　　　　　　　　　　　　　　　　　　　　2010022657

Printed in the United States of America on acid-free paper

The University of Minnesota is an equal-opportunity educator and employer.

16　15　14　13　　　　　　10　9　8　7　6　5　4　3　2

*A mis padres*
*y a la gente de "Kuchmil"*

# Contents

# Acknowledgments

This book received the support of many people and institutions during the past two decades. I cannot name everyone here, but I would like to acknowledge the following. First, my greatest appreciation goes to the community I call "Kuchmil," especially the pseudonymous Can Tun and May Pat families and the migrants in Cancún for their generosity, kindness, patience, and insight. Their friendship enriched my life in more ways than I can say. *A Return to Servitude* is my testament to the dignity and spirit with which they embrace life, especially given such difficult times.

In Mexico, I was affiliated with the Centro de Investigaciones Regionales "Dr. Hideyo Noguchi," Unidad de Ciencias Sociales of the Universidad Autónoma de Yucatán. Its staff and faculty shared time, resources, and knowledge of Yucatán. I especially thank Dr. Alejandra García Quintanilla and Dr. Luis Ramírez Carrillo. Dr. Piedad Peniche, director of the state archives of Yucatán, and the staff of the Registro Agrario Nacional of the Secretaría de la Reforma Agraria and the municipal archives of Benito Juárez provided indispensable aid in the archives. Lic. José A. Bayon Ríos and Arq. Ricardo Alvarado Guerrero of the Fondo Nacional de Fomento al Turismo in Cancún; Carlos G. Nakasone Hisaki of the Cancún Convention and Visitors Bureau; Lic. Bertha Valderamma Iturbe of the Instituto de Fomento a la Vivienda y Regularización de la Propiedad; and Lic. Jorge Fregoso Toledo and Lic. Rodolfo García Pliego of the Municipal Government of Benito Juárez in Cancún provided information about tourism and economic development in the region. The staff of the Instituto Nacional de Estadístico, Geográfico e Informático helped me sift through Mexico's statistical data. Eladio Ramírez and Moises Espinoza shared information about the hotel industry. The late Eleuterio Po'ot Yah spent many hours patiently guiding me through the intricacies of Yucatec Maya language and culture; he was a dear friend whose intellectual curiosity and artistic talent are sorely missed. Dr. Ana Rosa Duarte Duarte and Dr. Byrt

Wammack cultivated my interest in documentary film and shared lively intellectual exchanges. *Mil gracias* to Adriana Bravo Jones, Rafael Bravo Solís, Liz Bravo Solís, Indira Chávez Cornejo, Madelín Murrillo, Wendy Somohano Sosa, and Miguel Brito Pedrero for their hospitality, friendship, and anecdotes about Mexican politics and economics.

Over the years, my fieldwork was generously funded by Stanford University's Department of Anthropology and Undergraduate Research Opportunities Program; predoctoral fellowships from the Ford Foundation, the National Science Foundation, and the University of Michigan's Rackham School of Graduate Studies; the University of Michigan's Department of Anthropology, Latin American and Caribbean Studies program, and Ford Seminar on Global Transformations; an International Predissertation Fellowship from the Social Science Research Council; a Fulbright Hays Doctoral Dissertation Fellowship; a University of California President's Postdoctoral Fellowship; and the College of Liberal Arts and Office of the Dean of the Graduate School at the University of Minnesota. I am indebted to the Mellon Mays Undergraduate Fellowship program and fellows for supporting this project since its inception.

While writing, I was aided by a number of institutions and people. I was funded by an American Fellowship from the Association of American University Women; a visiting research fellowship from the Center for U.S.-Mexican Studies and the Center for Comparative Immigration Studies at the University of California at San Diego; a Ford Foundation Postdoctoral Fellowship; a Woodrow Wilson National Fellowship Foundation Career Enhancement Fellowship; and the University of Minnesota. The Institute for Advanced Study at the University of Minnesota graciously provided me with office space.

The University of Minnesota has been my institutional home during the final phase of this book. My colleagues and the staff in the Department of American Studies warmly welcomed me and were extremely supportive. I especially thank Jennifer Pierce, Riv-Ellen Prell, and Rod Ferguson for their mentorship, friendship, and careful readings of portions of this work. For helping with the nuts and bolts of research, I thank Jorge May Pat, Ramona May Pat, and Horacio May Kauil and his wife, Mari. Elisa Chavarrea Chim, Teresa Miyar Bolio, and Mari González Menéndez transcribed the bulk of my interviews. Karen Carmody-McIntosh and Kelsey Weber provided research assistance as I revised the manuscript. I am grateful to Zulema Valdez for help with graphic illustrations, and I thank Mike Foster of the University of Minnesota Cartography Lab for the maps.

This project benefited enormously from the encouragement and advice of many scholars, friends, and teachers. I recognize Nancy "Rusty" Barceló, Victoria Bricker, Brenda Child, Kimberley Coles, Wayne Cornelius, Travis Du Bry, Katherine Fennelly, Donna Gabaccia, Walter R. Jacobs, Vanessa Litman, Michelle Madsen Camacho, Elaine Tyler May, Lary May, Timothy "Cage" McCajor Hall, Heather McCracken Cohen, Patrick McNamara, Valerie Minor, Ana María "May" Relaño Pastor, Jeffrey Pilcher, Roger Rouse, Jan Rus, Pauline Sanchez, Otto Santa Ana, Hinda Seif, Laura Selznick, the late Sharon Stephens, Edén Torres, Ben Vinson III, Tamar Diana Wilson, and Erica Wortham. For introducing me to the people, language, and culture of Yucatán, I thank James A. Fox.

As members of my dissertation committee, Mary Corcoran, Janet L. Finn, and Conrad Kottak gave freely of their time and ideas. I offer my deepest appreciation to Ruth Behar, my dissertation advisor, for her illuminating comments, her unflagging support, and for urging me to be a fearless writer. Robert Alvarez Jr. and Patricia Zavella gave me invaluable advice throughout the early stages of my academic career. Arlene Dávila and Patricia Zavella challenged me to think more critically about indigeneity, tourism, consumption, and globalization; their comments greatly improved this book. June Nash and Renato Rosaldo generously read the manuscript and gave valuable feedback. For reading portions of the manuscript in various stages, I thank Hillary Dick, Kale Fajardo, Ben Fallaw, Karen Ho, John Ingham, R. Diyah Larasati, Roger Magazine, Louis Mendoza, Ellen Moodie, Scott Morgensen, David W. Noble, Hoon Song, David Valentine, and John Walton. I was fortunate to share my work and receive discerning feedback from scholars at Bryn Mawr College; Macalester College; the University at Albany, State University of New York; the University of California, Los Angeles; the University of California, San Diego; the University of Colorado Denver; the University of Oklahoma; and the University of Minnesota. I am especially grateful to Lourdes Gutiérrez Nájera, Irene Lara, and Zulema Valdez for reading my work, for their unwavering faith, and for being generous confidantes.

I thank the staff at the University of Minnesota Press for its commitment to this book and for making the publishing process enjoyable. Richard Morrison was enthusiastic from the beginning, and my editor, Jason Weidemann, offered indispensable advice and editorial suggestions.

I express my deepest gratitude to my family in Mexico and the United States. For making me strong, I thank my parents Petra Chávez Castellanos and Alfredo Castellanos Verduzco, both of whom passed away before the completion of this project. My *compadre* Manuel Gutiérrez and my siblings, Elsa, Evelia, Efrain, Gumaro, Alma, Phillip, Ari, Fred, and Isabel, endured my long absences and accepted my fuzzy answers about what an anthropologist does in Cancún. I hope this book gives them a clearer picture of why I spent so much time in this city's shantytowns rather than on its beaches. My precious daughters, Sofía and Lucía, were born toward the end of this project; their delightful presence made adding the final touches to this book all the more pressing. Finally, I owe a special debt to David Karjanen for his unconditional love, infinite patience, and fabulous meals: thank you for making me laugh, cheering me on during the difficult moments, reading my work, contributing your intellectual comments to this book, and so much more.

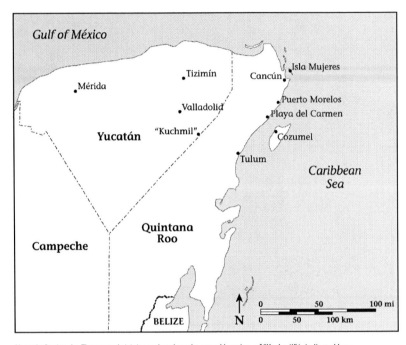

*Yucatán Peninsula. The general vicinity, rather than the actual location, of "Kuchmil" is indicated here.*

# Phantoms of Modernity

My first visit to Cancún in July 1991 was a respite from fieldwork. After six weeks learning the Yucatec Maya language and working on an ethnographic project on marriage practices in "Kuchmil," a rural Maya village that lacked indoor plumbing and running water, I longed to speak English and eat hamburgers at McDonald's.[1] In Cancún, I sunbathed by the pool of the luxurious Fiesta Americana Condesa hotel, snorkeled in the warm Caribbean, and haggled over prices in the artisan markets. Vacationing Mexicans and Americans crowded the streets and shops, while Maya migrants employed in hotels and restaurants attended to these tourists' needs. Tour guides advertised trips to the archaeological ruins of Chichén Itzá and the historic cities of Valladolid and Mérida. Compared to Kuchmil's poverty, Cancún seemed a tropical paradise. This blatant inequality sparked my initial interest in studying indigenous migration to tourist centers.

When I returned to Cancún one year later, I bypassed the markets and beaches and headed to the outskirts of town, where the city's migrant workers live in shantytowns. The expansion of these *regiones,* as the shantytowns are called locally, is correlated with Cancún's popularity. More tourists translates into more jobs, which attract more migrants. These migrants have overwhelmed the city's infrastructure because the municipal government cannot build as fast as people arrive. Lacking running water, a sewage system, and street lights, these neighborhoods represent a side of Cancún never portrayed in the glossy travel brochures, and thus, rarely seen by tourists. I ventured into the shantytowns to meet with migrant workers from Kuchmil. Sixteen-year-old Ramona May Pat, a resident of Kuchmil who had visited Cancún once before, was my guide to Región 74, the working class neighborhood where her brothers lived. Due to the long journey, Ramona's unfamiliarity with Cancún, and the danger associated with its shantytowns, Ramona's parents hesitated before granting her permission to accompany me, a single female traveler not much older than

Ramona. However, the savvy travel skills and moral rectitude I displayed convinced them I could be trusted to care for their daughter. I was one of the few people they knew who traveled alone by plane, bus, and train, but more important, they approved of my Mexican Catholic upbringing. The eight-hour journey from Ramona's hometown of Kuchmil began at four o'clock in the morning, the departure time for the only bus to pass through the area. In Valladolid, the commercial hub of southeastern Yucatán, we ate a breakfast of empanadas while we waited to embark on the five-hour, second-class bus ride to Cancún.[2]

In Cancún, Ramona relied on her memory and our cabdriver's knowledge of Región 74's unpaved streets to direct us to her brothers' apartment. Except that it was not the right place. According to Ramona, they lived near a soccer field, but the buildings along the park's borders, which served as her landmarks, had been repainted or expanded. Exasperated by her confusion, the cabdriver dropped us off at the park. We wandered through the dusty streets in the afternoon heat (a tropical forest was razed to build housing), asking those watching the soccer game if they knew where doña Ani, her brothers' landlady, lived. Ramona's brothers did not have a telephone and thus were not expecting us. In contrast to the commercial center of Cancún, there were no street signs or multilingual information kiosks where we could ask for directions. Since landmarks shift as fortunes improve or decline, it is difficult to orient oneself in the regiones. To make matters more confusing, people change residences at a faster rate than housing structures are built. Migrants may move every few months, to be closer to relatives and bus stops, to decrease housing costs, or to avoid danger. Finding people in this city at times requires door-to-door inquiries and long cab rides cruising unmarked streets and neighborhoods in search of "the palm tree" or local market intended to mark one's final destination. This sense of dislocation and process of erasure haunted Kuchmil residents' trips to Cancún, as well as my own efforts to visit migrants in their homes, and reflected the disorientation permeating a migrant existence. Although it did not deter them or me from visiting their kin, it sometimes made traveling a harrowing experience. To avoid this anxiety, Kuchmil residents usually traveled with someone familiar with the city's layout.

Eventually, Ramona and I found the apartment. Jesús had the day off, but Francisco was working. They lived on the second floor of a house that was undergoing renovation or had never been completely finished—I was

A hotel in Cancún's
Zona Hotelera and
working-class homes
in a new región.

not sure which was the case. Consisting of one large room, the apartment did not include a bathroom or a kitchen. The room was sparsely furnished with secondhand goods provided by the owner—a wobbly chair and a small children's table—and the few items Jesús and Francisco had acquired since moving to Cancún: a television, a stereo system, two bicycles, and the Christmas calendar given to them by the corner grocer. An outhouse in the backyard served as the communal bathroom. Occasionally and for a small fee, they ate their meals with the landlady's family. Jesús and Francisco were rarely home because they worked ten-hour shifts, six days a week, and sometimes took double shifts. Jesús was an electrician in a luxury resort, and Francisco worked as an assistant waiter in a three-star hotel.

During the past three decades, young indigenous men and women like Jesús and Francisco have migrated internally or internationally. This displacement is due to the agrarian crises that began in the 1960s and to reduced government support for small farmers, a result of the neoliberal policies of the 1980s and 1990s (Baños Ramírez 1996; Collier 1994/1999). For the Maya communities of the Yucatán Peninsula, Cancún is the principal destination. In the 1970s, these migrants were welcomed, even recruited, from the surrounding countryside to fill the vast labor supply needed to construct this tourist center. As Cancún expanded and gained international fame, the city attracted migrants from other regions of Mexico and foreign countries. Today more than half a million people live in this city.[3]

As a free-trade zone and urban center, Cancún is more than just a tourist town. This city not only is actively involved in the (re)production of transnational capital but also forms an integral part of the nation-state's modernization plan for rural, indigenous communities. Indeed, Maya migrants make up more than one-third of the city's population.[4] These migrants, many of whom arrive in Cancún in their late teens, work in hotels, in private homes, and in construction. Their minimum-wage salaries help support their families in the countryside, while their ancestral history and cultural practices comprise key tourist attractions. Given this involvement, *A Return to Servitude* considers the foundational roles indigenous peoples have played in the development of tourism, transnational spaces, and the modern nation-state. Spanning a period of fifteen years, it is based on an ethnography of a Maya community's migration experiences to Mexico's most popular tourist city, Cancún. How do migration and tourism alter and redefine what it means to be Maya in contemporary Mexico? As indigenous peoples participate in the deterritorialized social space of the migrant circuit, in which local identities and cultural practices risk being disassociated from their place of origin (see Appadurai 1990), how is community imagined and sustained among the Maya?

## Tracing Ghosts

Young men, like Jesús and Francisco, settled in Cancún and returned to Kuchmil every few months. While in the village, they spent their days playing impromptu games of basketball, soccer, and baseball; cruising on their bicycles; flirting with girls from the neighboring towns; and occasionally accompanying their fathers to the *milpa* (cornfield). At first, these men returned to recruit and escort their younger male siblings and cousins to Cancún after they graduated from the local *secundaria* (the equivalent of junior high school). But as they married and established families in Cancún, they persuaded their younger sisters to make this move as well. Eventually, Ramona and her younger brother Tómas joined Jesús and Francisco in Cancún. As young men and women have increasingly migrated from Kuchmil and the surrounding communities, the villages of the southeastern peninsula have been depleted of young people.

In light of these shifts, many of the residents of Kuchmil feel threatened by youth migration. They acknowledge the benefits of migration (e.g., greater access to salaried jobs, health insurance, and a more rigorous public school system), but they fear the changes experienced within their own communities, by the displacement of family members, the loss of children's labor, the increasing reliance on migrant wages, the shift in gender relations, and the rising social stratification among households in Kuchmil. Similarly, migrants are concerned with the transformation of community life. Leonardo May Kauil (Ramona's cousin) vocalized this concern after one of my visits to Kuchmil. "To me, *el pueblo* is disappearing. The people are gone. All of the people leave. When I return to my pueblo, there is no one. Everyone stays inside their homes. No one goes out to play. To me, el pueblo is disappearing."[5] According to Leonardo, what is at stake in this transformation are Maya cultural practices and, possibly, Kuchmil's very existence. As new forms of individualized sociality have replaced communally oriented social interaction, social relations between and within households have been fundamentally altered. And given falling prices for agricultural products, wage work in Cancún becomes increasingly more attractive. In spite of Leonardo's pessimistic prediction, community members and migrants are making a concerted effort to deter such outcomes. Yet Leonardo's fears are not unfounded. As indigenous peoples increasingly move from the countryside to urban spaces (see, for example, Collier 1994/1999; Fink 2003; Fixico 2000; Fox and Rivera-Salgado 2004; Grimes 1998), this mobility has been accompanied by debates among indigenous peoples and among social scientists regarding what it means to be indigenous once indigenous peoples no longer live in a particular place, wear "traditional" clothing, or speak indigenous languages.[6] The "disappearance" of indigenous communities is at the center of these inquiries. Historically, government policies and capitalist enterprises in the Americas have promoted the assimilation or eradication of indigenous peoples, resulting in their displacement and economic and political marginalization. Among academics, the consensus has been that the loss of these practices does not result in the demise of indigenous communities, but rather requires these communities to create new forms of identification and new types of relationships with each other, with the state, and with global capital (de la Cadena and Starn 2007; Hernández Castillo 2001; Little 2004; Nash 2001; Pineda 2006; Stephen 2007). This debate remains a central concern of local indigenous communities and serves as a linchpin to broader debates about the impact of neoliberalism and globalization, and the types of relationships indigenous people develop with the nation-state.

Within the last three decades, indigenous peoples have experienced a demographic and political resurgence (Cobb and Fowler 2007; Warren 2001). Rather than disappearing, they have denounced assimilationist policies and have demanded full citizenship within a pluriethnic society (Postero 2007; Rappaport 2005; Sawyer 2004; Stephen 2002). The 1994 Zapatista Rebellion in Chiapas and the 2005 election of Evo Morales, Bolivia's first indigenous president, offer compelling examples of movements that have gained international attention. Nonetheless, the majority of indigenous peoples, like many Maya communities in Yucatán, are not involved in constitutional reforms and mass public protests. But they suffer the social and economic consequences (e.g., poverty and displacement) of development projects and neoliberal reforms, like free trade.

In the Yucatán Peninsula, the Maya's reputation as "fierce" people and their struggle for autonomy in the mid-1800s resulted in state intervention based on "civilizing" projects as a way to incorporate the Maya into the body politic (Reed 1964; Sullivan 1989; Villa Rojas 1945). The postrevolutionary government relied on socialist reforms, like education and land reform, as a way to "liberate" Maya people from oppressive labor conditions (Eiss 2004; Fallaw 2001; Joseph 1982/1995) and to urbanize rural villages like Chan Kom (Redfield 1941; Redfield and Villa Rojas 1934/1990). These projects, however, did not necessarily improve the quality of life in the countryside; nor did they always acknowledge women's leadership roles within rural communities (Elmendorf 1976). By the 1960s, in response to the sub-subsistence nature of the agricultural economy, Maya people left their villages in search of wage labor. Through their follow-up studies of Chan Kom, anthropologists Mary Elmendorf (1976) and Alicia Re Cruz (1996a) show that even as migration fostered desires for alternative ways of living, it also produced tensions within and across households, and altered gender and class dynamics within rural families. Although Maya migrants have built families and established communities in Cancún, we know very little about their lives in this international resort. This book contributes to the extensive literature on Yucatec Maya communities by showing how this displacement alters consumption practices and notions of personhood, gender, and class within Maya households in both rural and urban spaces.

In so doing, this book investigates the limitations of imposing a model of modernity based on Western ideas and values on indigenous communities in Mexico. By tracing the tensions generated by the Maya's participation in state-led development projects (e.g., education, agrarian reform, and tourism), I reveal the *fantasmas* (phantoms) generated as a by-product of these modernization projects. Avery Gordon (1997) argues that studying phantoms is central to understanding modernity because ghosts draw attention to cultural practices and histories that have been denied, suppressed, or erased by modernity's violence. For Gordon, ghosts represent more than apparitions of dead people. A ghost, she argues, can be reinterpreted as a "social figure" that connects social structures to personal experience in ways that might not be clearly evident (ibid., 8). In a broad sense, a ghost's presence reminds us of what is missing, of what has been suppressed, of "that which makes its mark by being there and not there at the same time" within a structure of feeling (ibid., 6). Ghosts, then, direct us toward alternative interpretations or render visible new dimensions of social life. The "ghostly aspects" of social life are difficult to trace, as Gordon shows, but the process of articulating these hauntings can lead us to a clearer understanding of how social formations and systemic structures shape marginalized people's lives. Indeed, Latin America is haunted by the ghosts of its dirty wars, of its militarized border regions, and of its increasing gang and drug violence. They manifest themselves in the "disappeared" from Argentina, Guatemala, El Salvador, and Mexico.[7]

Following Gordon, I critique modernity by studying its phantasmic effects. I examine the hauntings afflicting the Maya and the Mexican nation-state as a consequence of war, slavery, oppression, and neoliberal policies. In Mexico, the primary objective of modernization projects is to assimilate indigenous communities into the nation-state. Becoming modern means shedding a Maya identity, becoming mestizo (mixed race or ethnically non-Indian), and adopting Western values and ideas of progress and development. Consequently, these hauntings take diverse forms. They manifest themselves through the "civilizing process" to which the Maya are subjected by the state and transnational corporations (chapter 4) and through the "poor talk" Kuchmil residents rely on to engage foreigners and the state (chapter 2). They can be found in the lingering presence of absent children, who were sent to indigenous boarding schools or who have migrated to work in Cancún (chapters 3 and 5, respectively). More recently, the devastation caused by Hurricane Wilma begat new ghosts and resuscitated old ones (chapter 7). A Return to Servitude examines how indigenous communities engage with this process of erasure and loss. Tracing these hauntings, Gordon suggests, "requires (or produces) a fundamental change in the way we know and make knowledge, in our mode of production" (1997, 7). In the case of the Maya, the fantasma serves as a metaphor for the disappearance and erasure of indigenous cultural practices, including language and forms of socialization, and for the sense of loss that results from the displacement of indigenous peoples. But in the process, this discourse evokes Maya cultural practices, histories, and strategies that counter the phantasmic effects of modernization.

Cultures rarely disappear overnight, but they can be written out of history, and hence, become fantasmas. Rosalva Aída Hernández Castillo (2001) illustrates this very process in relation to the Mames of Mexico. Forced by the state to adopt Western dress and stop speaking their language, they exited the historical stage of national memory in the 1930s, only to be included once again when national discourse embraced multiculturalism in the 1970s. Through a historical narrative, Hernández Castillo effectively argues against the current depiction of Mam communities as "closed-corporate communities" that have "only recently been 'hit' by capitalist development" (ibid., 233–34). Likewise, June Nash (1995) and Jan Rus (1994) have shown that the closed corporate nature of Maya communities was a defensive mechanism against further exploitation of their resources by elites. Hernández Castillo also criticizes the current institutional frameworks through which indigenous identity is constructed. Being Mam is far more complex than the typical ethno-linguistic definition assigned by the nation-state or the ethnic garb expected by international tourists. "It is important to acknowledge that the adoption of a Mam identity has not been 'a totally free and rational choice' but rather the result of wider social and political processes in the framework of relations of domination," like the war in Guatemala (ibid., 235). As such, being Mam involves a hybrid mix of multiple identities rooted in religious and political diversity, binational affiliations, gendered experiences, and linguistic differences, all of which people crisscross on a daily basis. Through such efforts, Hernández Castillo makes visible a fantasma of modernity.

Similarly, in her work with Mazahua communities in Mexico City, Cristina Oehmichen Bazán (2001) suggests that ethno-linguistic markers no longer adequately define indigenous identity. Many members of the urban Mazahua communities lost their language and donned Western dress as they became more involved in city life. As with the Mames, this loss did not mean that Mazahuas no longer considered themselves to be Mazahua, particularly since their structural position was not altered by the change in dress and speech. Oehmichen Bazán suggests that kin ties serve as the fundamental mode of social articulation for the Mazahua diaspora in Mexico and the United States by usurping dress and language as the primary marker of indigenous identity (there always exists more than one way to mark and construct one's identity). Another fantasma is resuscitated.

For Maya migrants who leave their village of Kuchmil as adolescents to find work in Cancún, being and remaining Maya requires an active refashioning of local notions of personhood and gender. Maya migrants rely on the symbols and goods of global capitalism as a way to fulfill social and labor obligations to their community, and perform personhood and gender in ways that conform to local understandings of what it means to be a man, woman, or child in Maya society. By tracing the circulation of goods, people, and ideas within this migrant circuit, I argue that these shifts in cultural and material expression enable Maya communities to negotiate and, in some instances, resist Mexico's neoliberal reforms, and resurrect the fantasmas of modernity.

## The Cultural Logics of Modernity

By examining the circulation of goods, money, and people within the Yucatán Peninsula, I also address recent anthropological concerns with tracing the multiple meanings and cultural logics of modernity. As a metanarrative of progress and development based on scientific reason and capitalist discipline, modernity has been criticized for being teleological, evolutionary, and unidirectional (Brenner 1998; Ferguson 1999; Hodgson 2001) and for ignoring the particularities of local histories, ideologies, and subjectivities (Napolitano 2002; Rofel 1999). These critics stress that in spite of modernity's telos, postcolonial and postsocialist nations and their minority populations do not experience modernity in the same manner. Similarly, I am concerned with tracing the multiple meanings ascribed to the circulation of goods, people, and capital within a translocality and what these meanings tell us about how alternative modernities are constructed. When I speak of alternative modernities, I am referring to the process by which people, as they actively engage with modernization projects and globalization, generate new ways of understanding and constructing what it means to be modern within local contexts. This is what Dorothy Hodgson calls the *"production of modernities"* (2001, 7). In the case of Mexico, state-led development projects like Cancún illustrate how this vision of modernity was enacted and reveal its limitations. Considering that indigenous peoples were targeted as the labor force for the construction of Cancún, I am primarily concerned with understanding how indigenous communities negotiated their integration into Mexico's vision of modernity and how this process transformed or reinforced Maya cultural practices.

Indeed, Maya communities in Mexico and Central America have a long history of engagement with and resistance to modernization projects and neoliberal reforms (Collier 1994/1999; Saldaña-Portillo 2003). In spite of sharing similar worldviews and forms of subsistence and social organization, Maya peoples' integration into processes of modernity and globalization has been marked by ethnic, class, regional, and national differences. As a result, how Maya people understand modernity and their role within it varies. We must be attentive to these differences and the oppressive and liberatory consequences they germinate. Yet, prior to the Zapatista Rebellion of 1994, scholars who studied Maya communities were more concerned with conducting "salvage ethnography" of "closed-corporate communities" and promoting indigenous assimilation in the name of nationalism, than with understanding Maya peoples' relations to modernizing and globalizing processes (for this critique, see Rus, Hernández Castillo, and Mattiace 2003; Watanabe and Fischer 2004). In contrast, recent scholarship has been intent on making these connections. Kay Warren (1998) shows that Maya public intellectuals who are at the forefront of the Pan-Mayan movement for self-determination in Guatemala are the products of local, national, and international alliances. Similar international alliances and quests for Mayan autonomy can be found in Mexico. June Nash (2001) suggests that Maya peoples in Chiapas have adopted the universalizing discourse of human rights with which to interrogate the predatory nature of neoliberal reforms. At the heart of these protests lies a fundamental clash over values, over which lives are valued, over governance, over social engagement, and over resource management. Moreover, through her corpus of work, June Nash points out that Maya struggles for self-determination and land rights are guided by a cultural logic based on an ethos of cooperation, moral obligations, and recognition of indigenous autonomy, which is distinct from modernity's emphasis on rational actors and free markets.[8] In the Yucatán Peninsula, Maya communities also find themselves clashing with a neoliberal rationality imposed from without, but that fails to recognize that social ties and communal rights matter and make survival possible in the unforgiving tropics. This book examines how alternative modernities are produced within this particular social and political landscape. In the process, it aims to contribute to research on Maya communities taking place in Chiapas and Guatemala.

James Ferguson (2006) cautions that this emphasis on plurality ignores the rise in global inequality and its effects on poor countries. He urges anthropologists to pay attention to "modernity's decomposition," which produces "relatively fixed global statuses and a detemporalized world socio-economic hierarchy" (ibid., 192). Indeed, this stasis is evident in Cancún's reconstruction after Hurricane Wilma (October 2005). Cancún was rebuilt into a new, more modern version of itself. This makeover was an effort to remake modernity by displacing "surplus" populations and tearing down its failed ventures. In the process, however, it further reinforced and escalated previous inequalities. By documenting these hauntings and their gendered, racial, and class dimensions, I unearth modernity's homogenizing and exclusionary practices.

Just as similar cultural logics of modernity have been imposed on Maya communities (even as they are experienced differently across these communities), the projects intended to discipline and modernize indigenous communities are markedly alike. Tourism has been hailed as a key model for economic development in Maya communities. Recent scholarship has begun to consider the merits of this approach. Through his study of Pisté, the Maya community neighboring the archaeological site of Chichén Itzá, Quetzil Castañeda (1996) provides a critical analysis of the collusion between Maya people, tourism, and anthropology to create an ahistorical and fixed representation of Maya culture. He reminds us that as Maya peoples participate in and combat modernizing projects, they may also be complicit in essentializing their own culture for a global marketplace. Lisa Breglia (2006) demonstrates that these tensions become even more pronounced as countries, in their quest to become modern, have begun to divest themselves of patrimonial sites. Scholars have also looked at how indigenous peoples who work in tourist sites experience and make sense of the global. Walter Little (2004) examines how Kaqchikel Maya handicraft vendors strategically deploy cultural identities to make a living in Guatemala's tourist economy. For these vendors, who travel back and forth between their communities and tourist cities, Maya identity is not fixed or homogenous, but is informed by gender and cultural differences. Similarly, Alicia Re Cruz (1996a) reveals that tourism and male migration produce clashing views over the symbols, rhetoric, and practices defining ethnic identity and socioeconomic status within the Maya community of Chan Kom. In sum, this compelling scholarship signals that tourism is a modern site of contestation.

Building on these works, I attend to national and transnational efforts to transform the corporeal and intimate lives of indigenous peoples through an analysis of the gendered, racial, and class aspects of tourist work. Consequently, this book focuses on the last three decades (1970 to 2006) of tourism development in the Yucatán Peninsula. It examines how Cancún came to be equated with modernity, how this tourist center has shaped the political economy of the peninsula, and how indigenous communities engage with this vision of modernity. More important, the book examines the practices of everyday life within the broader political, economic, and social structures of tourism and free trade and demonstrates how indigenous and rural communities experience, resist, and accommodate transnational capitalism. Specifically, I address the tensions experienced by young tourist workers as their indigenous bodies are disciplined for the sake of national progress and profit, and as they rely on consumption and remittance practices to reinforce notions of belonging and kin ties across time and space. Tourism and increasing social stratification within indigenous communities (an outcome of migration) have created conflict among Maya peoples about how to define tradition, community, and progress. At the same time, it is through this active engagement with modernity and its resources that indigenous communities are able to maintain their sense of indigeneity and community across a deterritorialized social space.[9]

## Exporting Culture

Since its inception, Cancún has been portrayed as a "deserted island" and "pristine" tropical paradise located in the land of the ancient Maya.[10] This narrative not only erases any presence of Cancún's original occupants, but also adopts spatial metaphors deployed by pioneers and missionaries and their colonial regimes to justify colonization (Redclift 2005). Visitors are invited to "discover" Cancún (with all of its modern amenities) and the surrounding archaeological cities. This ahistorical myth continues to be perpetuated in the popular imaginary by newspapers, tourist guidebooks, and the city of Cancún.[11] These popular narratives, however, overlook tourism's significance to national development plans and international development projects. Tourism is a global industry. Impoverished countries seeking to diversify their economies and development agencies seeking to improve these countries' fortunes turn to export production and services because they are cheap alternatives for economic development. Countries package their poverty and lack of industry as tourist attractions (Enloe 1989). Thus, popular explanations of Cancún's origins disregard the amount of planning, labor, and money—the power—necessary to build an international tourist center in an impoverished region.

For the Mexican government, tourism formed part of the postrevolutionary nationalist cultural project intended to unify a fractured nation and modernize the nation-state.[12] This project involved creating a national Mexican identity rooted in Mexico's pre-Columbian and colonial past and folk culture. To showcase these national treasures, the Mexican government funded the excavation of archaeological zones and their conversion into open-air museums of Mexico's past. The presence of numerous archaeological sites, beautiful colonial cities, and "typical" indigenous villages eventually transformed the Yucatán Peninsula into a site for heritage tourism—tourism that promotes the consumption of a nation's cultural heritage (e.g., cultural traditions, archaeological sites, historical buildings, landscapes, etc.) by a domestic and foreign audience[13]—and into an integral component of the nation-state's tourism plan.[14] Yet, the success of tourism as a development model required more than the presence of antiquities. Beginning in 1927, the federal government invested heavily in its local infrastructure (e.g., roads, hotels, airports), changed its migration policies, and created ministries and associations to promote tourism abroad (Berger 2006). To increase the number of tourists within Mexico, the administration of President Miguel Alemán Váldes (1940–46) attempted to "modernize" tourism by shifting the focus from heritage tourism to beach tourism—a type of tourism that promotes "sand, sun and sea" activities (Saragoza 2001). Such a transformation was expected to increase foreign exchange, allow for the commodification of Mexico's natural beauty, and cater to the growing Mexican middle class.[15] Insufficient funds, the Great Depression, two world wars, and a lack of organization, however, limited the growth of Mexico's tourism industry (Saragoza 2001).

From the 1940s to 1960s, Mexico's economic model was based on import substitution policies that supported the domestic ownership of the manufacturing industry, and the commercialization and industrialization of agriculture, by increasing tariffs on imports and subsidizing national companies. The resulting economic success, labeled the "Mexican miracle," began to wane by the early 1960s. The Mexican peso was overvalued, revenues generated by Mexican consumer goods declined, trade was down, and the budget deficit began to increase. These problems were compounded by mass rural-urban migration resulting from the displacement of small farmers by commercial agriculture; and by the United States government's cancellation of the Bracero Program, a guest worker program, in 1964.[16]

In the late 1960s, the Mexican government considered export production in the form of *maquiladoras* (assembly plants) and tourism as the solution to its economic problems. Export production offered the opportunity to capture foreign exchange and develop the country's peripheral regions, which were predominantly rural and poor (Clancy 1996;

Dachary and Burne 1998). The initial construction phase of Cancún, financed with a $21.5 million loan from the Inter-American Development Bank (IDB) in 1972, was intended to divert rural-urban migration from Mexico's core to its periphery by creating service jobs in an economically depressed region and was considered the most effective way to modernize the periphery without requiring extensive capital investment (Tancer 1975). To facilitate this process, the highway system was expanded, and in 1973, the entire territory of Quintana Roo was declared a free-trade zone (Martí 1991). Created to attract foreign investment, free-trade zones offer subsidies and reduced tariffs and regulations to international corporations. Mexico's federal government invested $25.6 million funneled through Fondo de Infraestructura Turística (National Trust Fund for Tourism Infrastructure, or INFRATUR), an agency created in 1969 and administered by Mexico's central bank to oversee the planning of tourist poles and secure private investment, and which later became known as the Fondo Nacional de Fomento del Turismo (National Fund for Tourism Development, or FONATUR) (Clancy 2001; Maldonado Torres 2000).[17] To decrease risks for foreign investment, FONATUR also built, expanded, and administered a hotel chain (under the name Nacional Hotelera, and later, Presidente) in tourist poles (Clancy 2001). Hence the development of tourist centers like Cancún followed the trajectory of export-processing zones in Mexico's northern border. Both were heavily subsidized by the nation-state and considered by developed and developing countries as projects that would modernize postcolonial nations by improving their technology and infrastructure, and stimulating job growth. In addition, Cancún's location within an indigenous region gave the tourist industry access to cheap labor and indigenous bodies for display and tourist consumption.

Cancún served as the model for four tourist centers: Los Cabos and Loreto in Baja California Sur, Ixtapa in Guerrero, and Huatulco in Oaxaca. Tourism, along with assembly work and oil, has become one of Mexico's leading exports. Unlike these other industries, what is being exported via tourism is the idea and narrative of service and leisure (Clancy 2001; Madsen Camacho 2000). Although export-processing zones include tourist sites, studies of export-processing zones primarily focus on assembly work (e.g., Iglesias Prieto 1997; Fernández-Kelly 1983; Lugo 1990; Ong 1987; Salzinger 2003). Yet, workers in the tourism industry experience many of the same problems faced by women and men working in export-processing zones dedicated to assembly work. Jobs in tourism, as in the maquiladora industry, are characterized by low wages, repetitive motion, attempts to control a worker's sexuality, limited job promotion, a lack of economic security, and a reliance on racialized bodies. Thus Cancún's thirty-year history provides clear examples of the benefits and problems of relying on tourism as a model for national and regional development. And, in light of Hurricane Wilma, which damaged much of Cancún's infrastructure and hotels and left thousands of migrants without employment, a reappraisal of this development model is needed.

## Cancún as a Translocality

Over three million visitors arrive annually to vacation in Cancún.[18] These tourists are greeted at the airport in Spanish, English, German, and Italian. They shop in open-air markets filled with intricately designed gold and silver jewelry and with crafts representing images of ancient gods that vendors claim to be of Mayan origin, though most iconography is Aztec. They buy clothing in air-conditioned malls from international clothing stores, such as Benetton, Ralph Lauren, and Zara, and stock up on snacks and liquor at any of the three Wal-Mart supercenters. They stay at luxury hotels designed to replicate Maya pyramids and ecological parks that form part of international hotel chains like the Global Hyatt Corporation and Grupo Posadas[19] (the largest hotel corporation in Latin America, which includes the Fiesta Americana hotels) and are located along miles of pale sandy beaches and the warm clear turquoise waters of the Caribbean Sea.

Not surprisingly, a major component of a migrant's work experience involves dealing with tourists and foreigners, regardless of whether they work in a hotel or not. For example, although most Maya women work as maids in private homes, their employers are predominantly foreigners. More important, a migrant's livelihood is dependent not only on making tourists happy, but also on the presence of transnational corporations (see Gregory 2007). Thus, understanding indigenous migration in Cancún entails broadening our lens beyond the framework of the nation-state. Indeed, Cancún is the product of a concerted effort by public and private interests, including presidential administrations (which escalated under Luis Echeverría, who pushed for funding for the project and purchased land in Cancún), the Banco de México (Mexico's National Bank), and Mexican investors like Grupo Alfa and later Grupo Posadas, to rebuild the national economy (Clancy 2001). But it is also the product of trans-national economic ties with international banks, like the IDB, and trans-national corporations. I am not suggesting that the nation-state is no longer relevant, as some studies of globalization propose. Rather, I attempt to answer Arjun Appadurai's call for ethnography to interrogate "the nature of locality, as a lived experience, in a globalized, deterritorialized world" (1991, 196). I do so by analyzing the link between transnationalism and the circulation of commodities, people, and ideas within the local context of the Yucatán Peninsula and within the national context of the Mexican nation-state.

Much of the work on transnationalism focuses on the movement of people across national boundaries (Basch, Glick Schiller, and Szanton Blanc 1994; Levitt 2001; Smith 2005). Initially as a critique of theories of immigrant assimilation models, *transnationalism* was defined as "a process by which migrants, through their daily life activities and social, economic, and political relations, create social fields that cross national boundaries" (Basch, Glick Schiller, and Szanton Blanc 1994, 22).[20] However, recent critiques of transnationalism point out the need to go beyond an approach that privileges bodily movement (e.g., Guarnizo and Smith 1998). Sarah Mahler (1998) suggests that transnational practices can be constructed and maintained without crossing national boundaries, as is evident by tourism and the flow of money, ideas, and things (see also Brennan 2004; Perez 2004; Smart and Smart 1998). Therefore transnational practices can create transnational spaces. In her study of the Dominican tourist town of Sosúa, Denise Brennan (2004) considers Sosúa a transnational space because it has a long history of local-global interactions. More important, Brennan argues that "transnational spaces not only are sites of new economic, cultural, and sexual possibilities but also are locations which can reproduce existing inequalities" (2004, 45). Similarly, the tourist city of Cancún, through its confluence of foreign and native people, transnational corporations, Western ideologies, and rising inequalities, also represents a transnational space.

In an effort to link the local with the global, I refer to Cancún as a transnational locality, or a translocality. Arjun Appadurai defines such spaces as

locations [that] create complex conditions for the production and reproduction of locality, in which ties of marriage, work, business, and leisure weave together various circulating populations with kinds of locals to create neighborhoods that belong in one sense to particular nation-states, but that are from another point of view what we might call *translocalities*.[21]

Building on Appadurai, I adopt the term *translocality* to discuss places that may not be directly engaged with transnational migration, but nonetheless are sites engaged in the circulation of foreign bodies, global commodities, and transnational capital. These historical and spatial processes produce a transnational experience in a local setting with its own local effects. For Maya migrants, what it means to be a Maya person in Cancún and their natal village becomes refracted not only through local indigenous conceptions of gender and personhood, but also through the broader processes of transnationalism and modernity. Although indigeneity may be presumed to be the antithesis of the global, it is constituted through the transnational. Through a description of this translocality, I examine how indigenous people participate in transnational practices from below and how these practices help them reimagine the nation and their role within it. I suggest that alternative approaches to modernity allow these communities to resist integration into the workforce and body politic (see Napolitano 2002; Rofel 1999), and to refuse to be relegated into fantasmas. Moreover, this book engages with the ways nation-states and global economic systems shape indigenous community formation. Specifically, I am concerned with the ways globalization, through migration, transnational tourism development, and neoliberal structural adjustments, influence indigenous notions of the self, family, and community.[22]

## Migrating East

The recent emphasis on studies of transnational Mexican migration in the social sciences ignores the continued economic, political, and social importance of internal migration within nation-states, particularly Mexico. But internal migration provides an economic and social safety valve for agrarian communities that lack strong ties to the United States, and resources to cross the U.S.–Mexico border. Just as some migrants choose not to go north, many others, like Jesús and Francisco May Pat, move east.

From 1940 to 1990, rural-urban migration increased dramatically in Mexico. The Mexican government's declining investment in small-scale enterprises over this fifty year period, in addition to the decline in land redistribution after the 1940s, the establishment of the United State's Bracero Program in 1940 and its cancellation in 1964, the industrialization of the 1960s, the growth of tourism in the 1970s, and the increasing inflation after the debt crisis of 1982, stimulated this rural exodus (Arizpe 1975, 1981; Collier 1994/1999; Fernandez-Kelly 1983; Grindle 1986; Lomnitz 1977). People fled to cities in search of wage work to supplement or replace subsistence farming. As a result of development projects like Cancún, rural-urban migration to tourist zones in Mexico's peripheries has grown exponentially since the 1970s. Both Mexican nationals and foreigners are attracted by the dollar-based economies of Cancún and the Riviera Maya, the area encapsulating one hundred miles of coastline sandwiched between the tourist sites of Cancún and the biosphere reserve Sian Ka'an.[23]

Like many mexicanos from the central states of Mexico, Yucatecans have been migrating to the United States since the initiation of the Bracero Program (Adler 2004; Cornelius, Fitzgerald, and Lewin Fischer 2007; Fortuny Loret de Mola 2004). These immigrants, however, primarily originate from the north and southwestern regions of Yucatán. In contrast, in spite of their acute interest in the United States, the people from southeastern Yucatán, which until recently was more physically isolated than the north and southwestern regions, migrate primarily to the neighboring state of Quintana Roo, not to the United States. Considering that Kuchmil migrants could make significantly more working in the United States, why don't they migrate north? Immigration scholars Alejandro Portes and Rubén Rumbaut (1996) claim that people migrate as a result of relative, not absolute, deprivation. The very poor, they argue, do not have the resources and the knowledge to migrate. "Those at the bottom of the social structure not only lack the means to migrate, but often the motivation to do so because they are less exposed to the lure of consumption styles in the developed nations and are less aware of the work opportunities in them" (ibid., 13). On the contrary, television, radio, and everyday talk quickly broadcast information about the goods, lifestyles, and economic opportunities in the United States to the general public, even to those residing in the remote regions of Mexico. Francisco confessed that if he could come up with the $2,000 necessary to cross the border with a *coyote* (smuggler of humans), he would not need to emigrate.[24] Rather, he could use this money to start his own business or for a down payment on a plot of land. While the residents of Kuchmil may not have the financial resources to get to the United States, they definitely have the knowledge and, in some instances, the social capital, because they work in an international tourist center. Foreigners have offered them jobs abroad. But their connections to the United States are tenuous compared to their established social networks in Cancún and the Riviera Maya.

Other important, noneconomic reasons keep Kuchmil migrants from becoming emigrants. Crossing the border loses its appeal when the risk of jail time and even death are considered. Why face these risks when one can find a job quickly in Cancún? One earns less in Cancún, but this move requires minimal risk and its proximity makes frequent visits home possible. In addition, strong family ties and obligations bind indigenous peoples to the Yucatán Peninsula. Established social and family networks facilitate continuous migration to Cancún. By remaining in the peninsula, migrants can return home as often as their work schedules permit, send remittances and goods, and receive visitors from Kuchmil in their homes in Cancún.

In 1997, migrants made up half of Quintana Roo's population (INEGI 1999). Nearly half of the migrants in Quintana Roo were born and lived in the state of Yucatán prior to their arrival (INEGI 1999, 29, 320).[25] Cancún's population has multiplied in size since it was transformed from a small fishing village into a tourist center in 1972, catapulting it into becoming the fastest growing city in Mexico (Van Bramer 1997, 6). Over half of the migrants living in Cancún arrived within the last decade (INEGI 1999, 31).[26] This increased migration, however, did not cause the total disappearance of agrarian communities; slightly less than one quarter of Mexico's population continues to work and live in rural communities, despite the Mexican government's efforts to industrialize the nation and exploit the resources of its subsistence base (Zapata 2005). Farmers who have access to *ejido* land (communal landholdings), like the residents of Kuchmil, are able to eke out a living from small plots (three to four hectares); justifiably, they are hesitant to cut their ties to their land and lose control of their labor by becoming full-time wage workers in the city. Instead, they participate in seasonal or temporary migration to supplement their existence. Thus agrarian communities are tied to larger regional and global economies like Cancún through the participation of subsistence farmers in wage labor and migration (Re Cruz 1996). Correspondingly, agrarian communities play an important role in Mexico's development as sites for the reproduction of the labor force at home or abroad (see Burawoy 1976).

Through an ethnography of an internal migrant circuit, I aim to provide the context for a comparative analysis of the relationship between internal and international migrant circuits and thereby contribute to the rich literature on transnational Mexican migration (De Genova 2005; Hondagneu-Sotelo 2001; Durand and Massey 2004; Smith 2005). To do so, I engage with many issues similar to those faced by mestizo and indigenous immigrants. I analyze how indigeneity shapes migration patterns, remittance practices, the settlement process, and natal community development, all issues relevant to indigenous immigrants (Adler 2004; Fox and Rivera-Salgado 2004; Stephen 2007; Velasco Ortiz 2005). In so doing, I bring migration theories into conversation with tourism studies.

## Who Are the Maya?

With a population of 759,000 in 2005, the Maya constitute the second largest indigenous group in Mexico.[27] Since this figure only accounts for Yucatec Maya speakers ages five and up who self-identify as Maya, and does not include Maya communities, like those in Chiapas, who speak other indigenous languages derived from the Mayan language family, the actual number of Maya is much higher.[28] Maya people make up significant portions of the population of the states of Yucatán and Quintana Roo, 39.7 percent and 26.1 percent, respectively, both of which form part of the four states with the largest number of indigenous speakers in Mexico (INEGI 2000b).

Although they acknowledged that they were descended from *los antiguos* (the ancient Maya), Kuchmil residents did not claim an indigenous identity as Maya. Historians and anthropologists point out that *Maya* is not a homogeneous, stable ethnic identity, but rather has been constituted over time by state policies, ethnopolitics, racial hierarchies, and the global economy.[29] Initially imposed by Spanish colonizers, this ethnic identification continues to be perpetuated by intellectuals and the international media. Some rural and urban Yucatecans adopted this term as a conscious form of self-identification following the internationalization of indigenous movements in the 1960s (Hervik 1999). However, many Maya people today use self-referents based on class, dress, and linguistic markers, rather than ethnicity. In the 1930s, Robert Redfield and Alfonso Villa Rojas (1934/1990) observed the use of the self-descriptive terms *Maya* and *indio* (Indian) in the agrarian village of Chan Kom. In Kuchmil, however, residents use the terms *Maya* and *antiguos* to refer to their ancestors, specifically those who built the pre-Hispanic cities that dot the Yucatecan landscape, but these terms were rarely used to describe themselves. In Kuchmil, identities are fluid, localized, and situational. Residents refer to themselves as *campesinos* (peasants), *óoȼilóob'* (poor people), *macehuales* (workers), mestizos, and *de Kuchmil* (to be from Kuchmil). But I did not hear Kuchmil residents and migrants self-identify as *indio* because this term was considered pejorative.

As a result of their encounters with foreigners and Mexicans from other regions, such as Chiapas and Oaxaca, Kuchmil migrants in Cancún adopt the identity of *mayero* (someone who speaks Maya) to differentiate themselves from other ethnic groups and linguistic speakers and to create a sense of ethnic solidarity. According to Wolfgang Gabbert, in some regions, *mayero* can refer to "anyone who speaks Maya, irrespective of descent or social status" (2004a, 111). But among Kuchmil migrants, this term did not solely hinge on speaking Maya, but was used specifically to refer to a particular ethnic and class position and social experience within a particular setting; that is, a migrant of Maya descent who may or may not speak Yucatec Maya, but who was raised by campesinos in the countryside. Kuchmil residents and migrants speak Yucatec Maya fluently.[30] Spanish, however, was spoken most frequently among men, children, and migrants and less frequently among older and younger women in Kuchmil. When Mariela Can Tun (see chapter 1) explained to me the definition of a mayero, she jokingly commented, "Since you speak Maya, you are a mayera!" Of course, we both knew that this identification hinged not just on speaking Maya, but on being a mayera, a social position rooted in race and class distinctions. In spite of these concerns, I use the term *Maya* to situate my work within the extensive anthropological literature written on this group of people.

## Romance and Revelation: On Methodologies

This book is based on an ethnographic study of the migrant circuit formed by the agrarian Yucatec Maya village of Kuchmil, Yucatán, and its migrant community in Cancún, Quintana Roo. The notion of the circuit captures the constant circulation of resources and people between Kuchmil and Cancún (Rouse 1991). I spent thirty months doing ethnographic fieldwork over a period of sixteen years (1991–2006), twelve months of which occurred concurrently from September 2000 to September 2001.[31] Over this time period, I conducted interviews, gathered economic data, researched archives, solicited migration narratives, collected labor force participation data (through a survey of the hotel industry), and engaged in participant-observation in the Kuchmil-Cancún migrant circuit. To protect the privacy of my informants, I use pseudonyms for the names of the people and places mentioned here, with the exception of elected officials, cities like Valladolid and Cancún, and hotel managers and staff who wished to be publicly acknowledged.

I began fieldwork at an impressionable age, when I was twenty years old. My introduction to Kuchmil occurred during the summer of 1991. Anthropologist James A. Fox considered this community as the perfect place for me to learn Yucatec Maya and to conduct an undergraduate research project on Maya adolescent sexuality and marriage practices. My ideas of anthropology were very romantic, due in part to my limited life experiences, to the history of the Incas, Mayas, and Aztecs to which I was exposed during high school, and to the classic Mayan ethnographies I read during college. While I did not expect the people I would be studying to be unaware of mainstream Mexican politics and society, I did expect them to know very little about the United States and to cling to "traditional" rituals and customs, including idealized gender roles. After all, the paved road leading in and out of Kuchmil had just been built the year before I arrived, not enough time, I thought, to alter "ancient" traditions and practices. I was advised to pack long skirts in order not to offend the natives' sensibilities, pants to ward off mosquitoes, a water purifier, rain boots, and exotic medicines, like antivenom to protect me from the poisonous reptiles that inhabited the region.

My romantic visions were quickly shattered. My first evening in Kuchmil, I was graciously invited to a dinner of eggs scrambled with tomatoes and served with warm thick tortillas and bottles of Coca-Cola and orange Fanta (a subsidiary of the Coca-Cola Company). At night, we watched dubbed versions of the syndicated programs *The Wonder Years, The Simpsons,* and *The Avengers.* To my surprise, residents had been drinking Coke and watching foreign television for years. Eventually, as I gained the women's *confianza* (trust), I was barraged with requests to wear shorts because they knew I was holding out on them. "All *gringas* wear shorts. We want to see you in shorts," they asserted. This knowledge was not a fact gleaned from television, but from personal experience. I was promptly informed that all Kuchmil families had a relative living in Cancún or Playa del Carmen, the international tourist sites of the Mexican Caribbean, where *they* could observe gringos at play. These encounters dismantled my beliefs that I could go "native" because of my Mexican heritage (my family hails from the state of Colima) and phenotype (I have dark skin and black hair). Although I consider myself more Mexican than American and have never considered myself to be a gringa (growing up in the United States, this word indexed "whiteness"), by calling me a *gringa* (an English-speaking foreigner), they marked my otherness and called attention to the uneven power relations in which our relationships were embedded.[32] This reading of my person—being marked "white" and foreign, regardless of my skin color, ethnicity, Spanish language fluency, and nationality (I traveled with a Mexican passport)—exemplifies the transnationality of this locale.

Although I enjoyed doing ethnography, living in a rural village took its toll on my health. After a near death experience during my first visit to Kuchmil, I planned never to return. However, memory has a way of tricking the body. After I recovered from the giardia, fever, and ear infection that weakened my immune system, I was anxious to spend time with the friends I had made in Kuchmil and to complete my project on Maya adolescent sexuality. Since then, I have returned to Kuchmil almost every other year. I have seen children grow up, get married, and become parents. I have celebrated the births and mourned the deaths of community members. As I traveled between Kuchmil and Cancún, I was entrusted with ferrying goods, money, and letters back and forth. Indeed, I have spent more time with the residents of Kuchmil this past decade than with my own kin.

These encounters resulted in a gradual recognition that indigenous communities in Mexico were deeply integrated into global capitalist markets and culture (Behar 1993; Kearney 1996; Nash 1993, 2001; Wolf 1982). Maya residents of rural communities provided much of the labor for the construction of international hotels along the Riviera Maya. They spent the last three decades cleaning for and attending to international tourists, and the anthropologists, entrepreneurs, and their families who make a living selling an invented Maya culture to these tourists (Castañeda 1996). Kuchmil residents cultivated honey sold to European markets and sewed *huipiles* (an embroidered shift traditionally worn by Maya women) for American Barbie dolls, foreign tourists, and regional consumption. In addition, they spent the last century helping archaeologists from both national and foreign universities excavate the ruins of their ancestors' ancient cities, and working as key informants of "Maya culture." Consequently, I do not attempt to resurrect "Maya culture," but rather aim to remind us of the complex lives indigenous peoples live today.

I visited Kuchmil frequently between 1991 and 2006. With each return, the community, which was at first incredibly suspicious of a young woman traveling unaccompanied by family, learned to trust me a little more. Over the years, political fissures began to show and the depth of the antagonism between families became palpable, exacerbated by rising class stratification. However, these tensions were not revealed until a decade after my first visit. At this point in time, each faction tried to convince me that their platform represented the community's best interest. Similarly, Kuchmil families publicly supported traditional gender roles, even as these roles were strained and, in some cases, transformed by migration. Thus these revelations generated more questions than answers and made me doubt whether one to two years of intense fieldwork was sufficient time to understand the dense texture of people's lives. As I began to ask new types of questions, I benefited from the hindsight and trust I gained from my continuing presence in Kuchmil. As a result, I consider longitudinal studies an invaluable resource. Thus my commitment to long-term fieldwork has left a deep imprint on this book.

The reflexive turn in anthropology made it commonplace to read about the physical and emotional trials and tribulations of fieldwork (see, for example, Behar 1993; Grindal and Salamone 1995/2006; Nordstrom and Robben 1996; Rabinow 1977). What we do not talk about enough, however, is what is at stake for communities involved with anthropologists. Initially, the residents of Kuchmil were invested in presenting their community as peaceful and united politically. As I became known as the anthropologist who always returns but who has limited influence on the Mexican government, this presentation became no longer adequate for the type of relationship they wished to establish with me. Nor did it sit well with me. I have spent the last sixteen years traveling to Kuchmil because I could not imagine ending my ties with a community that has invested so much of their time and energy in me and in my research. They have waited a long time for this book and the questionable benefits (and possible privations) that may come with an international audience. I hope it meets their expectations and, through its tribute, helps Kuchmil advance its dreams and future prospects.

## Guide to the Book

Chapter 1, "Devotees of the Santa Cruz," introduces two prominent families in Kuchmil, the May Pats and the Can Tuns, whose children serve as the central actors in the book. These families' accumulated experiences span the history of Kuchmil, the Mexican Revolution, and the construction of Cancún. Here I provide an overview of the main issues affecting families in Kuchmil, such as the rising cost of health care and durable goods, diminishing corn yields, and competition from imported U.S. produce after the North American Free Trade Agreement (NAFTA). These concerns with global affairs, along with rural residents' increasing access to education, motivate Maya migration to Cancún.

Chapter 2, "Modernizing Indigenous Communities," provides a historical overview of Maya communities in southeastern Yucatán. It examines early development policies implemented by the postrevolutionary Mexican government to incorporate indigenous peoples into the nation-state. I focus on two historic programs implemented in Kuchmil, the national land redistribution program known as "agrarian reform" and the Cultural Missions. In 1931, Kuchmil, in conjunction with three neighboring communities, received an ejido grant. Land redistribution in the form of ejidos delineated the geographic boundaries and homogenized the social and political structures of rural and indigenous communities. In Yucatán, agrarian reform aimed to quell Maya people's resistance to government intervention. This chapter documents how land reform transformed how community was imagined among Maya families in southeastern Yucatán. The Cultural Missions, an adult education program, intended to convert the peasantry into modern citizens by promoting literacy, nationalism, entrepreneurship, and personal hygiene. Both programs generated new ways of organizing social and economic relations in Kuchmil. In the process, they influenced the community's response to future modernization projects, like Cancún.

Chapter 3, "Indigenous Education, Adolescent Migration, and Wage Labor," examines the roots of Maya migration to Cancún through an analysis of the role education played in restructuring indigenous community life from the late 1960s to the present. Like in the United States, boarding schools, referred to as *internados,* served as key institutions through which the Mexican government could assimilate indigenous peoples. In the 1960s, the Mexican government established boarding schools (elementary through junior high school) to educate and transform children from isolated rural and indigenous communities into rural leaders. Twenty-eight children from Kuchmil, primarily boys, attended these schools. However, in contrast to state expectations, the majority of these children did not return to Kuchmil. Instead, these children became the first cohort of migrants to work and settle in Cancún. Thus, indigenous boarding schools prepared youth for low-wage jobs, rather than farm work, and spurred a wave of adolescent migration to Cancún. This chapter analyzes the internados' civilizing mission and examines the emotional and financial toll this separation placed on Maya families.

Chapter 4, "Civilizing Bodies," focuses on migrants' experiences working in Cancún. It looks at how tourism development alters the social landscape of the Yucatán Peninsula by changing local conceptions of work, labor, and gender. I address the process of social transformation migrants have experienced in Cancún, participating in wage labor and settling in outlying shantytowns, beginning in the 1980s through the present. Tourist sites located in free-trade zones rely on subsidies, reduced tariffs, lax regulations, and cheap, migrant labor to attract foreign investment. Like maquiladora workers, hotel workers are also subject to new production practices dependent on docile bodies. To become "good" hotel workers, migrants from the countryside underwent a "retraining" process that involved a reworking of attitudes, approaches to work, and perceptions of class and gender.

Chapter 5, "*Gustos*, Goods, and Gender," traces the flow of goods, people, and money between Kuchmil and Cancún. Given the emphasis on consumption in the global economy, I look at what migrants consume in relation to what they give. In spite of Maya migrants' relative poverty, they sent remittances to their families in Kuchmil. Remittances include both money and expensive durable goods like stereos and televisions. This chapter examines the cultural logics attached to these goods and what these meanings tell us about the transformation of Maya social relations. Here I discuss how Maya migrants used consumption and remittance practices to mediate the contradictory roles they experienced as they participated in Mexico's modernization projects. Thus providing remittances allowed both male and female migrants to maintain their standing within Kuchmil's moral economy despite the distance. Correspondingly, what people give and consume informs their changing conceptions of citizenship and belonging.

Chapter 6, "Becoming *Chingón/a*," questions the linear narratives of progress and development underscoring migration theories by analyzing the new forms of subjectivity that arise as migrants participate in a service economy. In the case of Kuchmil, as Maya migrants adopt new attitudes and behaviors to succeed in the tourist trade, notions of personhood shift to accommodate these new practices. Maya migrants appropriated the Mexican discourse of being *chingón* (an aggressive, astute person) as a way to maintain a sense of agency in Cancún and to critique the global economy. Becoming chingón provides Maya migrants with the attitude necessary to live within an increasingly economically polarized world that tends to relegate indigenous people into fantasmas, rendering them socially invisible in these metanarratives, but always present in low-wage servitude. Through this discourse, migrants articulate an alternative vision of modernity.

The final chapter, "The Phantom City," returns to the two families introduced at the beginning of the book. Based on fieldwork conducted in 2006, it assesses how their lives, cultural practices, and sense of place have been altered (or not) by tourism, transnationalism, national politics, and natural disasters like Hurricane Wilma. I conclude by reconsidering tourism as a development model for indigenous communities in Mexico. Although tourism creates jobs, the bulk of these jobs are low-wage, short-term, and dependent on the stability of global markets and the fickle tastes of tourists. For many migrants, tourist work does not provide greater economic security than agricultural work. Yet, it continues to serve as one of the key industries on which Mexico, and many other countries, has staked its economic progress.

## Conclusion

Whenever I tell students, tourists, and strangers that I study Maya migration, they assume I am speaking of the dead, not the living, Maya. This experience is revealing. First, it tells us about how little exposure most people in and outside of the United States have to indigenous peoples. Yet, most people have heard of or even been to Cancún. Second, it acknowledges the limited knowledge of anthropological research in today's world. Everyone assumes that I am an archaeologist, not a cultural anthropologist. *A Return to Servitude* bridges this gap and corrects this misconception by bringing together, through an ethnographic lens, the world of contemporary Maya culture with that of tourism and leisure. This book shows that these worlds are highly dependent on one another—in the case of Cancún, one cannot exist without the other. This is not surprising given that much of the growth in future employment worldwide is projected to be in the service economy. Through its comprehensive analysis of the service industry and its reliance on docile, ethnic bodies, this book calls into question an economic system based on privilege, social hierarchy, and exploitation. I hope it encourages us the next time we travel to local and distant places to take the time to thank and acknowledge the people who make our beds and serve our food.

Tracing the fantasmas rendered (in)visible by these encounters illuminates the tensions and fragility of modernization projects for indigenous peoples and for nation building. More important, through these resurrections, I attempt to dispel ideas of dead and disappearing Indians. The lives depicted in the following pages engage with global issues relevant to all of us, like the current economic and health care crises, neoliberal policies' push toward privatization, and the devastating impact of natural disasters. But they also invoke the fears and negative consequences that come with such transformations and that disproportionately affect indigenous and impoverished peoples in the global South.

# Devotees of the Santa Cruz: Two Family Histories

"Only the *monte* was left behind by the people, who long ago, left their pueblos—*los grandes montes*. They [the hacienda owners] gave them *libertad*, freedom, so they began to come here to cultivate the forest. That is how the people began to arrive here," explained don José Can Pat.[1] Born in 1910, the first year of the Mexican Revolution, don José was the oldest resident in Kuchmil and the son of don Francisco Can Chi, the first settler in Kuchmil since the Caste War of 1847, a civil war fought between Yucatecan elites and Maya peasants and farmers in southeastern Yucatán. Spurred by their devotion to the Santa Cruz (Sacred Cross) and by its prophecies of victory, the Maya rebels, known as the Cruzob Maya, resisted the Mexican army until the early 1900s. Although the Cruzob Maya allowed devotees of the Sacred Cross to remain in this hostile region, the war destroyed a majority of settlements in southeastern Yucatán. Kuchmil was located in this battle zone.

In the late 1890s, don Francisco Can Chi,[2] a Maya peasant and follower of the Sacred Cross, ventured into this disputed territory because he needed land on which to make milpa.[3] He set up temporary shelter near the *cenote* (sinkhole) of the Postclassic site of Kuchmil.[4] His relatives joined him, eventually, and two other extended families from the town of Xi'ikah, located near the commercial city of Valladolid. The new residents of Kuchmil designated Santa Cruz as the patron saint of their village, who protected them from aggression by the Cruzob Maya. Considered a symbol of freedom from oppression and *esclavitud* (slavery), a reference to the period of peonage experienced by the Maya during the 1800s, religious devotion to the Sacred Cross remains strong to this day throughout the southeastern peninsula. The community of Kuchmil holds a festival for the Sacred Cross each spring. This history of resistance has influenced how residents of Kuchmil think and talk about their community, and its place in the region and the nation-state.

I spent time with every family in Kuchmil. This book is based on stories culled from each family. Nonetheless, I focus primarily on the lives of two families, the Can Tuns and the May Pats. These families' experiences, which span the history of Kuchmil, the Mexican Revolution, and the construction of Cancún, are representative of the events, encounters, and sentiments experienced by the residents of Kuchmil. Since these two families form the spine of this book, I provided a brief history of their lives in this chapter. For a family tree, see the appendix.

## Close Quarters

To help one of the poorest families in Kuchmil, James Fox arranged for me to live with the Can Tuns (don Dani Can Balam and doña Pati Tun Pech) during my first visit to Kuchmil. Another student, Pauline Sanchez, was placed with the family of the *comisario municipal* (the elected leader and representative of the community who organizes community works and distributes government resources during a three-year term). I paid the family a small fee in exchange for partaking of family-prepared meals and sharing the front house, which served as the sleeping quarters for the Can Tuns' six children: Nícolas, Mariela, Jovana, Eduardo, Fátima, and Mario. The children and I slept in hammocks that crisscrossed the length of the wood house. Lime-washed cardboard lined the interior walls and shielded us from cool weather, while a tightly woven thatched roof protected us from rain. At night, rodents scurried through the roof beams, creating a ruckus with their shrieks and frenzied movements, and causing a light rainfall of thatch, dead bugs, and rat droppings to cascade on us while we slept.

During the day, the hammocks were stored away to provide space for socializing. The only furnishings in the house—a religious altar, a Singer pedal sewing machine, and four wooden chairs—were placed against the wall, as was the practice in most Maya homes. Two of these chairs were allocated for me to place my duffel bags of clothes and supplies, a signal to my elite status. The height, doña Pati explained, would prevent stains from the dirt floor and would protect them from rainwater that occasionally seeped into the house. The size of families and design of housing structures—oval shaped, measuring 20 feet by 10 feet, and lacking interior walls—made privacy nonexistent.[5] We slept, worked, and hung out in one room. To give me some privacy, don Dani added a curtain to close off one end of the house. However, I typically used this retractable "wall" as a clothesline for my laundry when it rained.

The kitchen was adjacent to the front house. Although electricity was available, doña Pati prepared all meals over the open fire of a three-stone hearth, located at one end of the house. The cost of purchasing a stove and the gas with which to cook was too prohibitive. In contrast to the front house, the kitchen walls were not insulated to allow smoke to exit. The smoke also formed a thick layer of soot on the roof, which preserved the thatch from damage caused by bugs and mold. The kitchen was sparsely decorated with a dining table, two *káan-čeʼobʼ* (wood stools), a low wood table next to the hearth where doña Pati made tortillas, and a small table on which clean dishes and cooking utensils were stored. Pots hung from ceiling hooks. The pans and dishes were proudly displayed because they were gifts from Nícolas that he purchased while working in Cancún.

Doña Pati prepared two meals a day: lunch and dinner. For breakfast, we ate a small loaf of French bread and drank Tang, hot chocolate, or coffee. The meals during the summer months were simple, primarily beans, tortillas, and fruits and vegetables in season (chile, tomatoes, watermelon, avocados, and oranges). Families rationed their food to ensure they could feed their families until harvest time in October. I was hungry all the time. And it seemed everyone else was, too. Whenever I left my residence, local children followed me around and begged for money to buy candy and Sabritas (a brand of potato chips) from the local stores. The local commercial stores did not sell meat or fruits and vegetables. Rather, they sold the goods provided by the companies willing to venture into this region, mainly the manufacturers of potato chips, cookies, carbonated sodas, and candy. To supplement the family's lean diet, I purchased dried goods (rice, beans, lentils, pasta, and potatoes) weekly in Valladolid. Few families owned refrigerators, with the exception of the local stores whose freezers were provided by the Coca-Cola Company. On the rare instances when meat was available for sale, the news spread quickly. This happened only once during the eight weeks I spent in Kuchmil in 1991, but over time, the sale of meat would become more frequent. In this instance, Pauline and I walked several kilometers to a neighboring village to find the source of this sale before the meat ran out. We returned triumphantly, carrying one kilo of meat from a slaughtered ox, snugly wrapped in a plastic bag.

## A Motherless Child

Because of their dependence on rain-fed agriculture, all families in Kuchmil are poor. But some are poorer than others. In 1991, the Can Tun family was nearly destitute. Don Dani Can Balam, the forty-year-old patriarch of the family and the grandson of don Francisco Can Chi, broke his arm. As a result, he was unable to work in his cornfield for several months. As a subsistence farmer, don Dani did not have extra money with which to pay for someone else to cultivate his cornfield. His nineteen-year-old son Nicolás, the only son strong enough and knowledgeable enough to do farm work, was working in Cancún at the time. Nicolás sent money, but it was not enough to feed seven people. Eventually Nicolás returned to Kuchmil to help his father cultivate his milpa, but he arrived too late in the season to plant much corn. The Can Tuns survived the year by consuming corn left over from the previous harvest, by selling their livestock, by accepting gifts of corn from kin, by borrowing money to purchase corn, and by housing an anthropology student.[6]

Although kin surrounded don Dani, his relatives could only spare a few hours here and there to help him out. In Kuchmil, households remain independent of one another, cultivating their own milpa, fruit trees, and vegetables; tending their own animals; gathering their own firewood; and acquiring their own cash. Upon marriage, daughters are expected to leave the household, while sons usually build their homes next door to their father's house.[7] This proximity guarantees a mutual reciprocity between the households of father and son, while the distance created by the tradition of exogamous marriage symbolizes the physical expansion of a family's social network. Extended-kin networks exchange resources, money, and social support on a steady basis, but each household determines the extent of the reciprocity, regardless of blood ties. The ejido provided a system around which communal labor was organized, making it possible for families to choose which biological ties to strengthen. Similarly, among Kekchi Maya communities reliant on subsistence farming in Belize, Richard Wilk points out that "ties between kin tend to be fragile" and "neolocal residence is quite common" because households are more dependent on their community for contributions of labor (1989, 307). Biological kin ties, then, did not guarantee solidarity, particularly when passions, deceptions, and quarrels play central roles in the drama of life.

According to don Dani, his poverty was rooted in the early death of his mother. His father remarried quickly because he needed someone to care for his four young children. Unfortunately, don Dani's stepmother was not kind; she beat the children, favored her own children over her stepchildren, and convinced her husband to withhold financial help to his children from his previous marriage. As a result, don Dani and his siblings learned at an early age to become self-sufficient. Don Dani's eldest brother moved in with an uncle in Valladolid and found work to pay for his room and board. To avoid an arranged marriage with an elderly man, an alliance supported by her stepmother, his older sister eloped with her boyfriend and moved to his village. Don Dani and his older brother preferred to remain in Kuchmil because the ejido system guaranteed them a *solar* (house plot) and access to farmland.

Don Dani married Patricia Tun Pech from the neighboring village of Chan Sahkay. Without the aid of his father, he could not offer her a lavish *muhul* (bride wealth) or even a house in which to live. However, Pati, as Patricia was affectionately known, was enamored with don Dani's dashing ways and beautiful singing voice. She convinced her parents to let her marry him after don Dani built a house made of thatch and wood saplings. Over the years, he added two other wood structures, one to be used as a kitchen and another to be used as the sleeping quarters for their expanding family. Doña Pati filled their solar with potted plants of medicinal, edible, and decorative value, and raised pigs, chickens, and turkeys. In rural communities where meat is scarce, livestock serves as a form of wealth, because these animals can be sold for cash.

Inspired by his grandfather's religious devotion, don Dani became an esteemed *rezador católico* (Catholic prayer leader). According to don Dani, his grandfather knew how to read and write, skills necessary to learn the series of prayers. "I believed he learned while a slave [on a hacienda]," explained don Dani. "He knew all the prayers by memory just like a rezador." To explain the provenance of his own devotion, don Dani recounted his grandfather's first encounter with spirits. After don Francisco moved to Kuchmil, he would hunt occasionally in the monte. It was during a hunt that he came across the remains of the town of Ke'eldzonot, with its crumbling colonial Catholic Church built next to a cenote. As a rezador, don Francisco felt obliged to hold a *novena* (session of ritual prayer) in this holy, abandoned site. He kneeled down to pray. Once he finished the first prayer, a chorus of "Ave María Purísima" echoed throughout the church. The voices belonged to the spirits of those who had died in Ke'eldzonot.

These spirits advised don Francisco to remain kneeling and to continue praying. Otherwise, they would disappear. As don Francisco continued with the novena, the church filled with voices of spirits who accompanied him in prayer, and sang along with his incantations. "Ave María Purísima," they again responded. On his return trips to Xi'ikah to see his family, he told his relatives and friends about the church, but he concealed his encounter with the spirits because this story would attract settlers. It was this connection to the divine, along with his respect for his grandfather that inspired don Dani's religious devotion. Like his grandfather, don Dani's piety helped secure his leadership position in Kuchmil.

It was for his skills as a *sobador* (a healer and bonesetter) for which don Dani was most recognized throughout the region, however. In contrast to most sobadores in the region, he did not learn how to treat ailments by serving as an apprentice. Rather, he thanked divine providence for his gift. In Maya society, dreams impart divine and mundane knowledge (Burns 1983). Don Dani recounted that through his dreams, he learned the healing properties of herbs and roots, how to set bones, and how to massage the *tíip'-te'* (an organ beneath the belly button) into its proper place. The Maya of Yucatán believe that the root cause of gastrointestinal illnesses and bodily aches and pains is a misalignment of the tíip'-te' and of the body's organs (Villa Rojas 1980). The sobador reinstates the body's equilibrium through full-body massage. While these jobs provided don Dani with social capital, neither generated much income, because he typically charged twenty pesos (the equivalent of $2 in 2001) for his services. Because of his religious fervor and healing skills, the community acknowledged don Dani as a local leader.

## Farmwork Is Not Enough

In spite of physical improvements to his home and his expanding livestock, don Dani remained poor for many years. Like most farmers, he cultivated two hectares of ejido land each year. To convert the peninsula's rocky terrain and thin top soil into farmland requires intensive labor. Although two hectares produce enough corn to feed a family until the next harvest, barring no natural disasters (e.g., locusts, hurricanes, drought), they do not generate a surplus that can be sold for profit. Not surprisingly, the wet summer months are fraught with hunger and illness because these months occur right before the harvest. Most families, like don Dani's, have run out of corn and beans from the previous harvest and must purchase corn to feed themselves. In order to produce a surplus, campesinos must cultivate at least four hectares of land, which requires additional labor. Yet, few families can afford to hire extra hands. For those who manage to cultivate more land, profits are minimal due to the low price of corn. In 1991, the price of corn was pegged at one peso (thirty cents) per kilo in Yucatán. The North American Free Trade Agreement (NAFTA) affected these prices. In 1996, the Mexican government phased out tariffs against U.S. corn imports, ten years earlier than mandated by NAFTA.[8] A decade later, competition with the United State's highly subsidized industrial corn producers depressed prices to two and a half pesos (twenty-five cents) per kilo.[9] By 2009, the price had risen slightly to four pesos (twenty-nine cents) per kilo.[10]

Hence, a family's survival in the Mexican countryside depends on more than access to farmland. Cash is needed to pay for electricity; to cover medical and travel expenses; and to purchase food, clothes, electronic goods, and school supplies. To generate income, women raise livestock, cultivate crops like chile, and sew huipiles for regional and tourist consumption. Through these activities, women make a limited contribution to family income; the sale of produce and huipiles generates, at most,

*An ejidatario works in his milpa.*

*A Maya woman walks to the cooperative mill to grind corn for tortillas.*

ten extra dollars monthly. Moreover, women's poor health increases families' expenses. Because of their sedentary lifestyles and nutritional deficits, women in Kuchmil tend to get sick more often than men. They suffer from diabetes, high blood pressure, infected gall bladders, and seizures, all of which require medical treatment. The Can Tuns' poverty was compounded after doña Pati was diagnosed with a chronic gall bladder infection. The family could barely afford the cost of her medicine and doctor's visits. Although a neighboring town had a government-sponsored Centro de Salúd (health clinic) that provided free health care for small rural towns, families in Kuchmil rarely frequented this clinic because the doctor-in-residence charged for his services, a practice that was illegal but common in rural areas.[11] Since access to cash is limited in Kuchmil's subsistence farming economy, medical bills or natural disasters can devastate a family's resources.

During such crises, Maya families rely on extended-kin networks for economic support. Don Dani's case, however, shows that not all blood ties bind households in reciprocal relationships. To expand their kin networks, families establish fictive kin through *compadrazgo* or ritual co-parenthood during religious and secular rituals (e.g., religious festivals, baptisms, and graduation ceremonies) (Mintz and Wolf 1950). The designation of *compadre* and *comadre* is used to cement existing reciprocal relations, including blood ties (Lomnitz 1977). Considering that many of these fictive kin are also subsistence farmers facing similar economic hardships, rural households turned to their children for help in alleviating this stress.

## The Politics of Migration

By the time don Dani held the political office of comisario municipal in 1994, his family's economic circumstances had improved. Many people accused him and his wife of getting rich during his tenure, which deeply offended don Dani and doña Pati, who considered themselves poor. If it were not for their children who sent food and money from Cancún, don Dani explained, they would have had a difficult time feeding themselves.

In 1992, to help alleviate her family's poverty, Mariela, the Can Tuns' eldest daughter, who was eighteen, found work in Tízimin, a city several hours north of Kuchmil, by bus. She worked as a live-in domestic servant and earned $60 a month, a quarter of which she sent to her parents. With Nicolás remaining at home, the only cash available came from Mariela's wages. That year, seven of the fifteen young women from Kuchmil sought wage work in neighboring cities. Initially, I was told these women went to "wash their brothers' clothes" in Cancún or to help a relative living in Valladolid or Tízimin, but when I visited these women, they proudly informed me of their employment (Castellanos 2007). Most worked primarily as domestic servants. In 1996, nineteen-year-old Jovana moved to Cancún after she married. She was followed one year later by seventeen-year-old Eduardo. Jovana worked as a domestic servant and Eduardo worked as a bartender at a nightclub. Their remittances made it possible for the Can Tuns to accumulate durable goods and to pay for travel. Eventually, by postponing marriage so she could work longer, Mariela funded the construction of a concrete-block house for her parents, which she converted into a small grocery store in 2005. As more young men and women migrated in search of wage work, their wages supplemented the local household economy of petty trade, penny capitalism, and sub-subsistence farming.

## Finding a New Home

In 1998, to diminish the political fallout from don Dani's term as comisario municipal, the Can Tuns moved to Cancún for one year. When I visited Kuchmil that summer, I had to find another place to stay. I thought this would be an easy problem to solve because during my first visit to Kuchmil, every family invited me to stay in their home. To my surprise, and in spite of my offer to pay for food and shelter, the first family I asked turned me down. I later found out from Julia, the daughter of this family, that as a result of my near-death experience in 1991, they were afraid that their food would make me sick. Julia exclaimed, "We didn't know what gringas eat! What were we going to feed you?" To avoid another negative response, I turned to the only other family remaining in town that had housed a gringo—the May Pats, who hosted James Fox during his visits to Kuchmil. They welcomed me enthusiastically. However, they refused to accept any money in exchange for their hospitality. But I finally convinced them by reminding them that with these funds they could fix their leaking kitchen roof.[12]

The May Pats (don Jorge May Cituk and doña Berta Pat Kauil) lived in one of the stone houses along the main plaza of Kuchmil. Their house consisted of three rectangular rooms and an attached kitchen made of wood and thatch. Not surprisingly, it was one of the most spacious homes in Kuchmil. Used as an all-purpose family room, the main room was filled with bookshelves, a sewing machine, and a large desk where the children did their homework. The rooms on both sides of the family room were used for storage and as sleeping quarters. I shared one of these rooms with Nora, their thirteen-year-old daughter. This room stored the family's seeds, fertilizer, and bicycles. The room had its own door, which was usually kept open, but I appreciated the possibility of privacy. Don Jorge and doña Berta slept in the other room, while their sons slept in the kitchen. During the day, the stone walls and roof prevented the breeze from cooling down the rooms. To avoid the heat, the family spent most of the day in the large kitchen. At night, however, the tile floors kept the room cool, which made it easier to fall asleep.

## A Scholar of Maya Culture

Even within a village the size of Kuchmil, social differentiation exists, although it manifests itself in subtle ways. The May Pat family provides an example of a family as respected as the Can Tuns, but financially better-off. Don Jorge's grandfather, don Pablo May Poot, arrived in Kuchmil soon after don Francisco informed him of the fertile soil and the ancient cenote that contained fresh water in this area. Like don Francisco, don Pablo and his wife, doña Rogelia Cocom Pol, escaped peonage during the Caste War. They, like many Maya *peones* (workers) and peasants, including don Jorge's mother's family, hid in a cave for months to protect themselves from the wrath of Maya rebels and hacienda owners, and from being conscripted into battle by the Mexican army (see Martos 1996). Heeding the rumors of the rebels' antagonism toward mestizos, including Maya with Spanish surnames, don Jorge's mother, doña Lupe, changed her last name from Pacheco, her father's Spanish surname, to Cituk, her mother's Maya surname. After much of the region was abandoned, both families fled to Xi'ikah where their relatives lived. Since they did not have access to land in Xi'ikah, they moved to Kuchmil. They brought with them their cherished *chan* Santa Cruz, a miniature replica of the miraculous talking cross.

Unlike don José, don Pedro and doña Lupe were extremely supportive of their progeny. After their son Jorge married Berta Pat Kauil of Chan Sahkay, they helped him purchase a stone house that belonged to Jorge's uncle, who was moving to Quintana Roo to be closer to his children who

were studying in its capital. Stone or concrete-block houses are highly desired in Kuchmil, because they offer better protection against hurricanes
that plague the region. In stone houses, however, the smoke from the
open fire gets trapped inside and stains the walls. Consequently, don Jorge
added a large kitchen made of thatch palm and wood saplings to the back
of the house.

Initially, don Jorge cultivated two hectares of land. As soon as his sons
were old enough to help with farm work, however, don Jorge cultivated
more land. By 1991, he was cultivating seven hectares of milpa annually.
When don Jorge's two eldest sons migrated to Cancún, their remittances
made it possible for their father to hire day laborers during the most intense periods of work. By cultivating more land—up to twelve hectares
in 2004—don Jorge had plenty of corn to feed his family and was able to
sell corn for cash. (In 2005, Hurricane Wilma severely damaged his cornfields.) Don Jorge invested this extra income in his cornfield and his children's education. More important, when doña Berta was diagnosed with
diabetes in the 1980s, these surplus funds prevented her illness from bank-
rupting the family.

In contrast to don Dani's religious fervor and vocation, don Jorge was
a teacher and a scholar of the Maya language. Trained by the Instituto
Nacional para la Educación de los Adultos (INEA; National Institute for
Adult Education), don Jorge taught the analphabetic elderly residents to
read and write in Maya. He also taught his seven children (Jesús, Francisco,
Ramona, Tómas, Cristián, Nora, and Andrés) to read and write in Maya
years before the elementary school instituted a bilingual education program in the early 1990s. Don Jorge and his children reviewed and revised
the Maya version of the interview guide I created to collect census and
economic data from each Kuchmil household. Tomás also served as my
research assistant in 2001.

Don Jorge served his third term as comisario municipal from 2004 to
2007. Don Jorge belonged to the opposition camp that questioned don
Dani's leadership capabilities, and continues to retain control of local politics. As an educator and seasoned political leader, the community regards
don Jorge with great respect. Being more economically stable, don Jorge
and doña Berta stressed their poverty less than other families, but they did
emphasize, and indeed, rallied for government support of local activities
and programs. Like don Dani and doña Pati, the May Pats were active participants in local and state-organized activities and programs.

Like the Can Tuns, the May Pats have benefited from their children's migrations. In 2001, their four eldest children lived in Cancún, while the three youngest studied in Kuchmil. Jesús, the eldest son, owned and operated a grocery store in Cancún with the help of his younger brother, Tomás. Francisco worked as a waiter, and Ramona, although trained as an accountant, stayed at home taking care of her son until he was old enough for her to leave him with others, at which point she entered the labor market. Their remittances were allocated toward the hiring of additional labor in the milpa, toward their mother's medical expenses, and toward their younger siblings' education.

## The Kuchmil–Cancún Migrant Circuit

Almost one half of households in Kuchmil include migrants in Cancún. Although migration to this city is a relatively recent phenomenon, migration has served as a long-term strategy for survival in the countryside (see Farriss 1984). In addition, as cash via seasonal or permanent wage labor has become central to the local economy, migration has served as a way to gain access to wages. However, who migrates, when they migrate, and where they migrate is contingent on the structure and necessities of the household (as is evident by the experiences of the May Kauils and the Can Tuns) but also on local gender ideologies, the political economy of the region, and the social networks developed within and beyond Kuchmil.

Since the 1970s, land erosion, chemical toxins, environmental degradation, droughts, and disease have increasingly diminished milpa production yields. As a result, Kuchmil farmers have relied heavily on wage work through migration to supplement their income. Despite being located equidistant to the capital of Mérida and the urban site of Cancún, both of which are a two-hour first class bus ride away from Valladolid, the inhabitants of Kuchmil do not migrate to Mérida, but rather to the international tourist city of Cancún. Mérida has become saturated with migrants from the surrounding countryside (Baños Ramírez 1989), while Cancún and the Riviera Maya continue to offer higher wages and more job opportunities. Of the twenty-nine households in Kuchmil, thirteen households include members who migrated to cities on a long-term basis, principally Cancún. The kin ties (biological and fictive) that bind Kuchmil residents to each other provide all households in Kuchmil with access to economic support from migrants in Cancún.

Migration from Kuchmil is best understood as occurring in four waves. The first wave of migrants (1970–1979) were typically married men between twenty and forty years of age who received a primary school education and participated in short-term or seasonal migration. These migrants continue to participate in temporary migration up to the present time, but temporary migrants no longer make up the bulk of people leaving Kuchmil. At least a third of the *ejidatarios* (ejido members) continue to migrate seasonally or for short periods of time to participate in wage labor in the Riviera Maya.

By the early 1980s, a shift in the demographics of the migrant population occurred. Age and education distinguished the second wave of migrants from the first. Between 1980 and 1990, the majority of the migrants were men who were not married, were between the ages of fifteen and twenty-two years, and had graduated from junior high school, high school, and professional schools that were located far from Kuchmil. At this time, few girls were educated beyond the sixth grade. Hence, few women migrated during this time period. These migrants disliked, or were not taught, subsistence farming; were eager to occupy positions in the service industry, occupations that they considered to be "easy" labor compared to farm work; and permanently settled rather than participate in temporary migration. These youths sought work as waiters, domestic servants, and bartenders in Cancún's service sector. Jesús May Pat and Nicolás Can Tun formed part of this migrant flow to Cancún.

Because of their higher educational background and their willingness to remain in Cancún, the Kuchmil residents who migrated in the 1980s reaped the benefits of this city's construction boom. With time, these migrants earned job seniority, which gave them the right to long-term contracts that facilitated occupational mobility within the hotel industry. As a result, many of these migrants became financially successful, earning about $1,200 in monthly income. They worked as head chefs, accountants, bilingual receptionists, electricians, and entrepreneurs. Even the few migrants who continued earning the minimum wage salary of $160 per month acquired long-term contracts with hotel corporations that offered job security in exchange for financial security, an important achievement within an industry riddled with low-wage short-term contract jobs. All of these migrants accumulated enough capital (social and economic) to purchase the land on which they built their homes. Since most of these migrants were men, few women benefited from this new economy, unless they married a male migrant. Eventually these migrants helped new migrants settle in Cancún by providing housing, information, resources, and access to employment contacts. For example, Jesús May Pat helped his brother Francisco find a job in Cancún.

The third wave of migrants (1991–2003) was also educated, but at the newly established *secundaria* (a secondary school covering seventh through ninth grades) in the neighboring village of Ke'eldzonot. Ramona May Pat, Eduardo Can Tun, and Jovana Can Tun graduated from this school. More important, although men continued to dominate this flow, women, including those with little schooling like Mariela Can Tun, increasingly participated in migration during this period. Life in Cancún in the 1990s, however, was more difficult than the previous decade because of a decline in construction and a shift in tourism. Overdevelopment had led to increased competition. Cancún's emphasis on all-inclusive tour packages, and reliance on "spring breakers," resulted in sending fickle tourists south in search of the "early" Cancún: places with fewer tourists, empty beaches, and a more exotic feel. Tourists were not the only ones heading south. Many experienced workers, like Jesús and Francisco, who became frustrated by a lack of social mobility in Cancún or were fired as a result of new corporate management policies, found work in the luxury hotels and ecological resorts located south of Cancún along the Riviera Maya. Even as wages stagnated, prices escalated, and land became scarce, migrants continued to flood the region. Kuchmil migrants, who moved to Cancún during this period, worked in more vulnerable and less economically stable positions as stewards or busboys, assistant bartenders, assistant cooks, maids, and domestic servants. In 2001, men earned $110 per month, excluding tips—significantly less than established migrants. Female migrants, however, earned between $217 and $326 a month working as domestic servants in private homes. Women's participation in an unregulated labor market provided them with a fixed standard wage, unlike the wages in the hotel industry that increased with experience. Tips, which improve as one moves up the hotel labor hierarchy, bolstered incomes by providing between $100 and $300 in extra monthly income.

These wages, however, no longer had the same purchasing power in Cancún. At least two-thirds of a migrant's salary was spent on rent. A room measuring four meters by four meters cost $40 in monthly rent in the early 1990s. By 2001, this cost escalated to $110, nearly one month's salary. To decrease living expenses, recently arrived migrants pooled their incomes with more established migrants. Consequently, migrant households, like most working-class Mexican households, were typically comprised of two couples or an extended family (Rothstein 1992). In 2001, of the twenty-seven migrant households established in Cancún, fifteen families owned the land on which they built their homes, seven households built their homes on a relative's land, and five households rented housing. This book focuses on the migrant community of 105 inhabitants, which included forty-five migrants (twenty-seven men and eighteen women) and their immediate families, although their extended kin network was much bigger. In light of the ages of this demographic, this book is centered on the migration experiences of young adults.

Since the year 2003, Kuchmil residents, in response to the changes in the political economy of tourism, have once again altered their migration strategies. In this fourth wave of migration (2003 to the present), Kuchmil youth now migrate at an earlier age, as young as eleven years of age, in order to improve their repertoire of job skills. They spend summer vacations living with extended kin in Cancún and working in the construction and service industries. Part of the income they earn through these "apprenticeships" is given to their parents and the rest is allocated toward school expenses. These migrants, however, settle in Cancún after completing a postsecondary education. In 1997, the government built a *colegio de bachilleres* (a three-year college preparatory or vocational degree program, or COBAY) in the neighboring town of Ke'eldzonot. Because of the proximity of this school and the scholarships it offers, the majority of Kuchmil's youth, both male and female, attend the COBAY. Its recent graduates include Mario Can Tun and Nora and Cristián May Pat. By continuing their education, these youth likely will meet the hotel industry's expectation for employees to complete a high school education at minimum. Even with this diploma, however, migrants continue to enter the work force at the bottom of the hotel labor hierarchy. In response, several young men and women, such as Mario Can Tun and Cristián May Pat, are now seeking a university degree.

Cancún attracts over three million visitors annually, but this flow is concentrated during the winter months, and is threatened by competition with the recently constructed tourist poles of Loreto and Huatulco (INEGI 2000a). This dependency translates into an unstable labor market. The busiest months of the year occur between December and April, with business slowing down progressively during the fall months. To decrease expenses during the low tourist season, hotels reduce their short-term contract staff from September to November, all the while requesting laid-off employees to return in December when the season picks up again. As a result, the city and countryside have developed a symbiotic relationship in which the countryside serves as the site for the reproduction of the labor force (see Burawoy 1976). Employees who did not save enough money to ride out the low season return to their villages of origin to work alongside their fathers, or work in their own milpa (e.g., Re Cruz 1996a). Fortunately, the agricultural calendar overlaps with tourist flows. The low season occurs during the harvest of the milpa, a time of plenty when villages offer *primicias* to their saints to thank them for a bountiful harvest, and thus have enough food to feed returning migrants.

## Expanding Community

This circulation of people, goods, and ideas has transformed Cancún and the Riviera Maya into an extension of the Maya community in Kuchmil. While tourists may not be aware of Kuchmil's existence, everyone in Kuchmil is aware of Cancún. Buses and *combis* (cooperative mini-vans) depart daily for this tourist center. For the May Pats and the Can Tuns, traveling to Cancún has become part of their routine. Similarly, in spite of working and residing in Cancún, their migrant children actively participate in political, economic, cultural, and social activities (e.g., festivals, life cycle ceremonies, elections, and village meetings) that take place in Kuchmil. With the growth of the migrant community in Cancún, whose population is almost equal to that of Kuchmil, Maya ceremonies and rituals no longer solely take place in Kuchmil. They are now being celebrated in Cancún. It is this exchange that is at the center of this book.

## 2

# Modernizing Indigenous Communities: Agrarian Reform and the Cultural Missions

In 1998, to track Kuchmil residents' births, deaths, marital statuses, and educational backgrounds, I created a formal household survey question-naire.[1] As I scheduled appointments and walked around with my survey and tape recorder, the residents, who had willingly answered my infor-mal questions in the past, hesitated to participate in a formal survey and have their words recorded. Recalling their ancestors' experiences after the Caste War, a few residents suspected that I was a government spy. In the early twentieth century, the Mexican government relied on military occu-pation to gain control of the southeastern territory occupied by Maya reb-els, but after encountering much resistance, it turned instead to teachers and public health officials to assimilate the rebels (McCrea 2002; Ramos Díaz 2001).[2] In 1932, to ease suspicions of espionage, anthropologist and teacher Alfonso Villa Rojas disguised himself as a merchant when he first ventured into the region controlled by the Cruzob Maya (Villa Rojas 1978). In 1935, a letter of introduction from archaeologist Sylvanus Morley, who was considered a friend and ally by the Maya rebels, made it possible for Villa Rojas to end this pretense. Regardless, he noted that on many occasions, his informants became suspicious when he recorded conversa-tions with a pencil and paper (ibid., 32). Not surprisingly, Maya commu-nities in this region continue to consider strangers, especially those affili-ated with the government, to be spies (Martos Sosa 1994; Sullivan 1989). In Kuchmil, I was frequently asked if I worked for the Mexican or U.S. government because people assumed that only government officials car-ried clipboards and tape recorders and asked intrusive questions. To ease these suspicions, I rarely recorded interviews, with the exception of life histories and ritual events that community members requested I tape and videorecord.[3] I denied rumors of espionage, allowed people to read the Maya and Spanish translations of my survey, and, during informal meetings, clarified its purpose—to gather information about the demographics and economic activities of the community for my research project only. Due to these practices, residents agreed to participate in my project.

This negotiation process hints at the tensions generated by Mexico's colonial legacy and modernization projects. As an outsider who carried a tape recorder and asked personal questions about people's lives, I was associated with a history of colonial and postrevolutionary government intervention. It is this history that I examine in this chapter. The Maya communities that exist today are a product of these tense and conflictive relations. I trace the policies employed by colonial and postrevolutionary governments to incorporate indigenous peoples into the body politic. By resurrecting the ghosts of these past encounters, I examine how these policies (re)organized indigenous peoples' lives and whether they fostered a sense of community among Maya peoples or impeded its growth. Considering that indigenous communities are not static and bounded objects, but rather are constructed in relation to, and in reaction to, broader historical processes and institutions,[4] I discuss how Maya peoples responded to and incorporated these programs into their own understandings of community. I specifically focus on two prominent programs in which Kuchmil participated: (1) the national land redistribution program known as agrarian reform; and (2) the Misiones Culturales (Cultural Missions), a program intended to transform the peasantry into modern, literate citizens. I examine how these programs reorganized Maya life and influenced Kuchmil's response to future modernization projects.

## The Epoch of Slavery

In southeastern Yucatán, the Caste War of 1847, more than the Revolution of 1910, profoundly shaped Maya people's social and political memory (and continues to do so).[5] They speak of the period before this war as *la época de esclavitud* (epoch of slavery), a reference to the period when Maya peoples, including Kuchmil's forefathers, worked in peonage on haciendas (country estates similar to plantations). Few sources exist that provide historical accounts prior to 1847 of life in Maya villages like Kuchmil that were directly affected by the war (for an exception, see Rugeley 1996). I rely on oral histories and secondary sources to depict what life was like for Kuchmil's residents during Spanish rule, the early national period, and the Caste War.

To maintain political and economic control of the Maya's labor, tribute, and souls, the Spanish colonial government and the Catholic Church forcibly resettled native peoples in large towns through the imposition of the *encomienda* system (tribute grants) and the formation of haciendas, both of which required a large workforce (Roys 1957, 10).[6] New towns or new sites were established to relocate people who previously lived outside the sphere of influence of the Church and state. One of these new sites included the pre-Hispanic village of Ke'eldzonot, located near Kuchmil (Roys 1933/1967). By 1832, 2,517 Maya and Spanish settlers resided in Ke'eldzonot.[7] Kuchmil's lack of a census for this time period and its proximity to Ke'eldzonot—an estimated distance of several kilometers—makes it likely that the colonial inhabitants of Kuchmil (if any existed) were counted as residents of Ke'eldzonot. Since forced settlement fragmented patronymic kin lineages and tore apart extended families (Chamberlain 1948), many Maya fled the villages and towns into which they were conscripted by the elite and escaped into the Yucatán Peninsula's sparsely inhabited forest in the "frontier zone" bordering British Honduras, where *terrenos baldíos* (virgin land) could be claimed by anyone willing to clear the land (Rugeley 1996). Individual households cultivated their cornfields, with the occasional help of extended kin. Communities remained small and communal because the use of swidden (slash-and-burn) agriculture required families to move every few years. During Spanish rule, "community" was most likely located at the level of the nuclear family and extended kin group (Farriss 1984).

During and after the conquest, migration became a survival strategy for Maya peoples (Farriss 1984; Roys 1957). After Mexico gained independence from Spain in 1821, plantations of tobacco, rice, cotton, and sugar, and sugar refining, livestock ranching, corn cultivation, and smuggling formed the primary modes of commercial production in southeastern Yucatán (Martos Sosa 1994, 68; Rugeley 1996, 149–50).[8] At this time, although many Maya lived and worked on sugar and cattle plantations, many also remained clustered in small units made up of villages and parishes. To escape government control, they fled to the forest. Don Victor Can Pech explained, "*Por esclavitud*, everyone was gathered, was taken. They ran. Long ago, it is said that the people ran. They hid in the trees. That is when all the people left, why they left here so long ago." These forced migrations resulted in the reconstitution of indigenous communities.

Under the newly independent Mexican government, native peoples experienced greater inequity. The Mexican government failed to uphold the rights and protections granted to the Indian pueblos under colonial rule. As a result, the communal lands of the Indian republics were encroached on by private developers (Rugeley 1996). Uncultivated forest was quickly transformed into grazing land for livestock and into ranchos (ranches) and haciendas for the mass production of corn, sugar, cotton, and *hene-quén* (the cactus from which hard fiber used to make rope and twine is harvested). As they lost access to virgin and communal lands, subsistence farmers were forced to enter into peonage with these commercial enterprises. To make matters worse, Maya *batabs* (political leaders), who had previously served as cultural brokers between peasants, elites, and the Church, lost prestige and influence as the Yucatecan elites directed their attention and monies toward securing independence from Mexico (Rugeley 1996). Taxes imposed on poor peasants by the Church and the state further exacerbated these problems.[9]

Like the colonial government, the Mexican state and the Church failed to effectively integrate many Maya communities. First, Maya leadership remained strong in southeastern Yucatán due to the distance from the state government in Mérida and to the strong Maya traditions of private land ownership, peasant entrepreneurship, and political leadership (Rugeley 1996). In addition, cases of sexual abuse of female parishioners further exacerbated anticlericalism among Maya peasants (Sullivan 1989). The Maya also resented the dues imposed by the Church because they were based on a caste system in which natives were required to pay higher taxes and fees for services such as baptisms and weddings than mestizos did (Bricker 1981).

In 1847, bolstered by this discontent and by access to money and weapons from the smuggling trade with British Honduras, Maya batabs of the frontier towns of Tihosuco, Chichimila, Tepich, and Tixcacalculpul organized their own insurrection against the Yucatecan elite and the Mexican government. Yucatán's geographic isolation from the central government's army gave the Maya rebels a great advantage because reinforcements could only be sent by boat from Veracruz. The war dragged on for two years as the Cruzob Maya steadily gained control of the peninsula, but this changed abruptly due to the agricultural cycle. When the season to plant corn arrived, many rebels returned home. Winning the war would not matter if they had nothing to eat in the upcoming year. The reduced rebel army was easier to defeat once military support from the Mexican army and artillery, food, and financial support from Mexico, Cuba, and the United States arrived (Reed 1964, 103–4). By 1853, the Yucatecan army had recouped most of the contested territory, with the exception of the independent territories of the eastern peninsula that were home to the Cruzob Maya. The Caste War severely disrupted life in southeastern Yucatán. In their efforts to survive the war, many Maya peasants deserted their milpas, while others, like don Francisco Can Chi, escaped haciendas. They hid in the forest and were forced to survive on wild roots and plants, just as they did during severe droughts (Roys 1972). Those who were found were either killed or conscripted into the war. Don Victor explained how his grandfather avoided conscription. "He didn't go to the war. They didn't get him. He escaped. The ones who were caught were captured, but not him.... They weren't found. They hid. That is why they weren't taken." Don Jorge May Cituk's parents and their families hid in caves to escape both the rebels and Mexican soldiers.[10] The eastern territories of the peninsula were left sparsely inhabited as a result of the Caste War. Don José Can Pat described the effects of the war on the region. "War was made. They gathered everyone, they killed them, only the monte remained."[11] Towns and villages, along with sugar plantations, refineries, livestock ranches, cornfields, and churches, were destroyed. Thus the region's economic infrastructure and tax base were dismantled by the chaos of war.

## The Time of *Libertad*

For the Maya of southeastern Yucatán, the period after the Caste War was known as the time of *libertad* (freedom) because the destruction of the plantations ended peonage in this region. In northwest Yucatán, however, peonage continued to be practiced on henequén plantations well into the early twentieth century (Joseph 1982/1995). Paul Sullivan (1989) claims that for the Cruzob Maya, this period was distinguished by their ability to move freely throughout southeastern Yucatán without fear of attack, but this mobility was a mixed blessing because it also exposed these communities to outside and foreign influences that altered village life. On the other hand, Lorena Martos Sosa (1994) argues that for contemporary Cruzob Maya, the concept of libertad encompasses both emancipatory and oppressive experiences. Although no longer conscripted into labor, the Cruzob Maya's lack of self-rule fosters talk about a new type of esclavitud perpetuated by their poverty, their participation in state programs such as agrarian reform, and their adoption of the cultural practices (e.g., clothing, music, religion) of the *¢'ùulóob'* (elite or white men). "Thus, the present emerges as an active time of struggle and not just as a hiatus between wars" (Martos Sosa 1994, 17). Both of these understandings are reflected in Kuchmil residents' interpretration of libertad. They see this period as characterized by freedom of movement and by the end of war and slavery, but it has also come to be marked by a new epoch of slavery, that of wage labor (see chapter 3).

In spite of the increased mobility among native people, or perhaps because of it, the frontier zone was not immediately repopulated after the Caste War. The peasants and macehuales who fled during the war had few reasons to return to this area. Fear of the Cruzob Maya deterred settlers. Don Victor Can Pech recalls that the *tatiches* (generals) were "too aggressive when they get upset . . . Over there in Santa Cruz [now known as Felipe Carrillo Puerto], it is said, they fought with the people from over here." Instead, these macehuales established themselves in towns neighboring Valladolid or in the city itself. By the 1880s, landless people such as don Francisco Can Chi, in seeking terrenos baldíos on which to make milpa, repopulated the abandoned towns in this region. The village of Chan Kom, located northwest of Kuchmil and studied by anthropologists Robert Redfield and Alfonso Villa Rojas in the 1930s, was colonized at this time by Maya originating from within a forty-mile radius (1934/1990). Despite the upheavals of war and slavery that had affected the peninsula thus far, Maya peoples did not stray far from their ancestors' places of origin. The patronymic names (e.g., Can, Pat, May) of the ruling lineage (Cochuah) that controlled the southeastern peninsula at the time of the conquest continued to thrive in this region, including in Kuchmil.[12]

Initially, don Francisco treated Kuchmil as a *milperío* (location for corn production). He traveled weekly to Xi'ikah to spend time with his family. After the Mexican Revolution began in 1910, don Francisco feared being forced to join the federal army because indigenous peasants had provided the bulk of the army for Yucatán's early secession attempts and even helped fight the Maya rebels in the Caste War. He fled Xi'ikah with his family. The father of his neighbor was not so lucky; he was conscripted into the Mexican revolutionary army and fought in Veracruz.[13] Don Francisco and his family transformed Kuchmil from a milperío into a *ranchería* (hamlet). The Postclassic ruins located at this site provided accessible, square-cut stone with which to build homes and walls; the ancient *pozo* (well) provided a steady source of water; ancient vessels and jars with which to catch rain water abounded, as did flat, compact platform mounds on which to build houses. By 1929, nineteen households, made up of ninety-two inhabitants, lived in Kuchmil.

Although the people gained the freedom to move and work for themselves, the presence of the nation-state in their lives did not diminish. The postrevolutionary Mexican government continued to intervene in rural life. Land reform and education became the primary institutions through which the nation-state regulated village life.

## Postrevolutionary Agrarian Reform

To legitimate its political power, the postrevolutionary Mexican government relied heavily on the revolutionary mandates of land and liberty in incorporating peasants and laborers into its political base. Land redistribution in the form of ejidos became central to this process, even in Yucatán, where the local oligarchy did not permit revolutionary movements to germinate and thus agrarian reform had to be imposed "from without" (Joseph 1982/1995). The ejido system was initially modeled after colonial collective landholding communities (also called ejidos) that made up the *república de indios* (Nugent and Alonso 1994).[14] Through the *reforma agraria* (agrarian reform), the nation-state delineated and formalized the boundaries of rural communities. Between 1915 and 1933, Yucatán's state government reallocated one-fifth of Yucatán's farmland to campesinos (Brannon 1991). In 1929, Kuchmil joined its neighbors (Chan Sahkay, Ke'eldzonot and Katzim) to petition for an ejido grant to secure government support for the development of local infrastructure.[15] In 1931, Chan Sahkay received an ejido grant of 17,904 hectares, of which 1,739 hectares was allocated to Kuchmil's twenty-seven ejidatarios.

Ejido land was divided into parcels worked individually (e.g., for cattle grazing or horticulture) or collectively. Ejido land could not be sold, rented, or mortgaged to another party.[16] Usufruct rights to land could only be passed down to family members, thereby converting ejido land into family patrimony (Baitenmann 1997). Ejido membership granted ejidatarios land rights and the political standing to make collective claims on the state for infrastructural support (e.g., schools, roads, electric power). But the institutional, infrastructural, and financial support necessary to address ejido demands was not put in place until President Lázaro Cárdenas's administration (1934–40). In 1938, the National Rural

Confederation (Confederación Nacional Campesina or CNC) established the ejido's tripartite political structure, which included a general assembly, *comisariado ejidal,* and supervisory committee.[17] By 1940, Cárdenas had redistributed 20,137,000 hectares (over 49 million acres and one-half of Mexico's arable land base) to 776,000 ejidatarios.

In spite of its magnitude, the ejido system's implementation occurred unevenly throughout Mexico's diverse ecological regions, varied in the speed of its execution, and was met with resistance (de Janvry et al. 1997; Nugent and Alonso 1994; Stavenhagen 1986). The amount of individual land plots varied, from four up to twenty-four hectares, as did the manner in which collective ejidos were organized (as collective farms or as a rotating system based on swidden agriculture) depending on the region and time period.[18] Yucatán was no exception. Northwestern ejidos were configured primarily as collective henequén farms (carved out of large haciendas), whereas southeastern ejidos were organized collectively on the rotation system and around corn production. Given these geographic distinctions, the outcomes of agrarian reform differed within Yucatán.[19] However, Yucatán experienced one of the largest land reforms in the country under the Cárdenas administration. In 1937, Cárdenas decreed that all haciendas in this state be carved into ejidos and handed over to the peasantry (Joseph 1982/1995). Within two weeks, 272 ejidos were formed. Nonetheless, the lack of technical support and limited financial support provided by the government limited agrarian reform's impact (Stavenhagen 1986).

Although agrarian laws dictated the organization of ejidos, who controlled ejido affairs and resources varied locally and regionally (Baitenmann 1998; Nugent and Alonso 1994; Nuijten 2003). In the state of Yucatán, state control of ejido distribution proved disastrous for particular ejido grants (Fallaw 1995; Joseph 1982/1995). The state carved up numerous haciendas without any concern for production requirements. For example, some ejidos were made up of unproductive land, while others never received land at all (ibid.). Of the 272 ejidos decreed by President Cárdenas, 125 received less land than the legal allotment (Fallaw 1995). Many *hacendados* (landowners), with the help of bureaucratic mismanagement, impeded the distribution of the machinery necessary for processing the henequén being cultivated on these ejidos (ibid.).

The imposition of the ejido system on the countryside homogenized the social and political structures of rural and indigenous communities, but this homogenization did not translate into a shared sense of campesino identity across Mexico's diverse regions. Yet Christopher Boyer (2003) shows that as the campesino identity became radicalized through a class-based discourse in Michoacán during the Cárdenas administration, it evolved into a cultural identity widely adopted throughout the countryside. This process of negotiation between the state and the peasantry transformed campesinos into a political class. This radicalization is evident in Kuchmil, where residents identify themselves first as campesinos. In some cases, peasants appropriated state-imposed institutions like the ejido to resist domination by the state (Boyer 2003; Roseberry 1994).

## The Ejido as Community

The ejido system served as more than a political project. It also generated new ways of organizing economic and social relations. Participation in the ejido required members to establish residency within its boundaries and thus emphasized fixity over mobility as a survival strategy. Before Kuchmil became incorporated into the ejido system, the majority of its farmers lived with their families in the town of Xi'ikah, located near the city of Valladolid. By becoming an ejido, Kuchmil was transformed from a temporary shelter for farmers into a federally recognized village.

The colonial-era Maya notion of community, based on kinship networks, was reconceptualized under the ejido system. Although the ejido system reinforced the division of households into nuclear units—each male resident was granted the right to his own plot of land, including the right to a house plot large enough to build a house, corral, and a garden—it also imposed a structure for governing. To create a balance of power and promote an ethos of cooperation, the ejido system instituted *faenas* (mandatory work requirements) and mandated that all decisions regarding land, politics, and public funds be discussed during general assemblies.[20] General assemblies were called to elect the comisariado, solve conflicts between the ejidatarios, approve new ejido members, distribute resources and subsidies provided by the state through the municipal office, and determine land use and ejido boundaries. In practice, however, caciques dominated these meetings through physical coercion and voting fraud, and abused the faena system (see Fallaw 2001; Friedrich 1986; Re Cruz 1996). In Kuchmil, nonetheless, power was not concentrated in the hands of one person. The extended Maya family provided an alternative social framework for community management (Anderson 2005). Local politics were controlled by the *abuelitos* (grandfathers) and *tíos* (uncles) who represented the three extended kin families and rotated control of political offices. Coercion and fraud existed in Kuchmil, but these tactics were strategically deployed by all three families.

In a small pueblo where everyone is kin, residents who did not fulfill these social expectations strained community relations. The case of don Teo May Balam illustrates how the general assembly regulated social behavior and enforced normative practices within the community.[21] The ejidatarios accused don Teo of failing to complete his faenas and of social conduct unbefitting an ejidatario. They claimed that don Teo had a history of disregarding the community's needs by charging too much for the use of his corn mill, failing to keep it clean, operating it while inebriated, and sexually harassing his female clients. The general assembly ruled that don Teo's presence, due to his irresponsibility, dishonesty, and alcohol abuse, compromised the community's social and economic welfare. He was given six months to leave. This case study demonstrates how the community was able to exert control over a member considered problematic. Residents who refused to adhere to local norms were pressured to leave or migrated out. As such, the ejido system reflected Kuchmil's moral economy.[22] Community was now rooted in the collection of household units organized to maintain a moral, social, and political order for a paternal state.

In regions where swidden agriculture is common, the ejido serves as the steward of the local ecology by supporting field rotation and creating a buffer zone of uncultivated forest. The amount of ejido land each member can cultivate and its location are firmly restricted. The ejido grant of Chan Sahkay accorded each ejidatario with access to forty-eight hectares of land, of which only twelve hectares can be cultivated annually, to permit reforestation. Ejidatarios are allowed to farm four hectares of *monte alto* (tall growth forest) and up to eight hectares of *monte bajo* (shrub forest). Cultivated land must be left fallow for twelve years to allow the forest to regenerate. Each ejidatario is allocated a solar located in the town center and given access to the buffer zone of forest surrounding the town center for the collection of firewood and other forest plants. By and large, ejidatarios abide by these regulations because if they failed to do so they could be fined or expelled.

In practice, land rights in Kuchmil were far more flexible than the ejido structure's prescriptions because participation and access to land were influenced by labor inputs and local settlement practices. The ejido conceived of land ownership as collective, even when land was divided into individual parcels. "What a man owns, and feels he owns, therefore, is the temporary results of his labor: the clearing, the planting, and the harvesting, not the land itself" (Redfield and Villa Rojas 1990, 64). In spite of this emphasis on communal land rights, individual rights were recognized and protected within Kuchmil's ejido. Members retained individual control over cultivated land and their solares. Seizure of this property required compensation. For example, in 1975, when the community decided to amplify the size of the central plaza, the community paid an ejidatario seventy-five pesos for a parcel of his solar located on the periphery of the plaza. In addition, not all of the members who cultivated ejido land lived in Kuchmil; several ejidatarios moved to neighboring cities. As long as the cornfields of these ejidatarios were worked, even if it was by hired hands, ejido membership was retained.

Local conceptions of gender also influenced ejido practices. Communal land tenure does not guarantee gender equity. Prior to 1971, only heads of households and single men qualified for ejido rights. Women were eligible for ejido land only if they were heads of households (as single mothers or widows) and could lose these rights once their children became adults or if they married another ejidatario (Baitenmann 1997). Not surprisingly, ejidatarios in Kuchmil have historically been men, with the exception of a single widow. Article 200 of the 1971 Federal Law of Agrarian Reform expanded ejido rights to any man or woman older than sixteen years of age (Stephen 1997). Regardless, eligible unmarried women in Kuchmil did not claim these rights because local custom forbade these women from working outside the home, working like men, and representing the household (see Deere and León 2002). Ejido membership has thus been influenced not only by residence and legal access, but also by labor inputs, household position, and the local patriarchal system. In light of these multiple significations, this property regime quickly became an economic, political, and cultural institution.

## The Agrarian Crisis

The ejido system provided communities with state recognition of the lands they worked and a system by which to request financial support, albeit limited, from the state, but it did not effectively address demographic and ecological changes. In 1946, changes to Article 27 increased the number of hectares allotted to each ejidatario to twenty. Regardless, many ejidos did not encompass sufficient land to increase allotments. During the first phase of land distribution, ejidatarios were given access to approximately ten hectares of land, which was sufficient to stabilize the ejido's productivity during the first decade of the reforms. Most families cultivated one hectare each year, which produced enough food to feed a nuclear family and permitted them to let cultivated land lie fallow (Warman 1985). However, as more land was redistributed, reducing the virgin forest available, and ejido lands became deforested, production yields began to decline, forcing ejidatarios to cultivate at least two hectares of land each year to produce the same amount of corn. In the 1950s, ejidos could petition to expand their land grants to allow for an increase of up to twenty-four hectares per person through the process known as *ampliación* (expansion). In Yucatán, however, ampliación only generated fifteen hectares per person (ibid.). During the two decades following the Cárdenas administration, land redistribution decreased substantially, while land ownership became increasingly concentrated in private hands and government investment in commercial agriculture grew (Artiz 1986). The decline of governmental support of small-scale agriculture enterprises further exacerbated the ability of subsistence farmers to live off their land (see Montes de Aca 1977). By the late 1960s, the mode of life on ejido land had become sub-subsistence.[23]

The village of Ke'eldzonot illustrates these problems. In 1929, Ke'eldzonot included five ejidatarios, but by 1941, there were fifty-seven. Due to its rapid population growth, Ke'eldzonot was eventually transformed from a town into a municipality, garnering it greater economic resources from the state. But this growth also consumed all the available farmland, forcing ejidatarios to reduce the number of years land lay fallow and thereby face reduced yields. Currently, over two thousand people live in Ke'eldzonot, many of whom do not have access to farm plots. As farmland was reallocated toward cattle ranching, this shift negatively impacted this ejido's productivity rates. Cattle ranching is a more lucrative business, but it requires extensive clearing of forestland for grazing, which results in a reduction of land for corn production, hunting, and gathering natural resources.

In addition to ecological degradation, the Yucatán Peninsula's subsistence economy has been negatively impacted by natural disasters, decreasing prices of agricultural products, excessive logging of hardwoods, and the imposition of modern technologies and farming techniques (e.g., fertilizers, insecticides, hybrid seeds, monocropping) that ignore or destroy local ecologies (Faust 1998; Juárez 2002; Re Cruz 1996a). Kuchmil has kept some of these problems at bay by limiting cattle ranching and by developing a mixed subsistence economy. Like many Maya communities, Kuchmil's residents combined milpa production with hunting, horticulture, and petty entrepreneurship (see Juárez 2002; Villa Rojas 1978). However, since annual rainfall levels fluctuate and as forests and wild animals become scarce, living off the land becomes more difficult. On average, ejidatarios cultivate three hectares annually. With the aid of fertilizer, this produces enough corn to feed a family of six. To create greater yields, households increasingly rely on fertilizer, hybrid seeds, and additional labor. The sustainability of the ejido continues to be compromised by the overcultivation of the existing land, the rising costs of fertilizer, the declining market price of corn and beans, and the increasing price of goods. To limit the impact of these changes, Kuchmil, Katzim, Chan Sahkay and Ke'eldzonot decided to divide their ejido grant.[24] Although each village controlled a parcel of Chan Sahkay's ejido grant, they could not independently request government subsidies; such requests had to be collaborative efforts between all four communities. Dividing the ejido would grant each village an ejido title and the right to independent claims. By the 1960s, this campaign remained unsuccessful, so the inhabitants relied on other means to attain economic stability.

Residents of rural communities who were unable to control their population growth and increase their fields' production were forced to migrate to neighboring cities in search of wage work. Kuchmil relied on out-migration as a way to address these issues. Children were sent away to government boarding schools, which provided food and clothing (see chapter 3). Two families moved to the new and sparsely populated state of Quintana Roo because the federal government advertised the availability of ejido lands with monte alto.[25] Three families moved to the bustling city of Valladolid and the municipal town of Chukab, where they could find jobs and their children could attend secundaria. As a result of out-migration, Kuchmil reduced the stress on its land below the levels experienced by other ejidos.

By the 1970s, large sectors of the residents of the countryside had moved to cities in response to the agricultural crisis, oil boom, and growth in industrial production. In the Yucatán Peninsula, many ejidatarios searched for wage work in Mérida and Cancún. The rise of migration pointed to the limitations of modernization projects in the countryside. To address these problems, the Mexican government chose to reform the agrarian sector, a decision with profound implications for how indigenous communities are organized.

## The New Agrarian Law of 1992

In the 1990s, in an effort to restructure the economy and restore the confidence of foreign investors and the International Monetary Fund, the Salinas administration (1988–94) promoted neoliberal policies dominated by increased export production, reduced tariffs, and the deregulation and privatization of state-owned enterprises.[26] Although communal lands did not fit within this free market approach and treaty, the high social costs that would result from their eradication made it difficult for the government to dismantle the ejido system. Ejidos constituted more than half of Mexico's arable land and sustained more than 3.1 million ejidatarios and their families. But the Salinas administration argued that the lack of development in the countryside was due to the inefficiency and corruption of the ejido system (Diego Quintana 1995). Privatization, the government argued, would protect individual rights to ejido plots, limit the power of the comisariado ejidal in order to permit greater democratization of agrarian communities, and stimulate private capital investment in the countryside (Cornelius and Myhre 1998). Privatization would also ease foreign corporations' fears of land expropriation and pave the way for the ratification of NAFTA by Canada and the United States. The ejido came to represent the outdated property regime of the paternal socialist state, whereas privatization evoked a property regime dominated by free enterprise and individual responsibility. The new Agrarian Law of 1992 ended land redistribution policies and thus proclaimed that the ejido was no longer an inalienable right of the peasantry.

Many bureaucrats, intellectuals, and peasants supported the new Agrarian Law, but other groups, such as the Zapatista National Liberation Army, did not (Collier 1994/1999).[27] These groups criticized the neoliberal policies for withdrawing credits and price supports for ejido agricultural products; transforming the ejido from family patrimony to individual property, thereby restricting thousands of women's and children's rights to land; and ending land redistribution, a move that allowed the government to disregard outstanding and future land claims by the landless and indigenous groups. Further, critics argued that the government's limited technical, infrastructural, and financial support had severely compromised the ejido system's effectiveness (Baños Ramírez 1996; Stavenhagen 1986) and that using claims of ejido corruption was a thinly veiled attempt to dispense with the government's social contract and collective forms of organization (see Chase 2002). Similar neoliberal reforms throughout Latin America have been criticized for placing too much faith in competitive individualism and market efficiency and rationality to solve the economic problems left unresolved or exacerbated by state-led development (Crabtree 2003; McDonald 1999).

Despite its neoliberal rhetoric, the Salinas administration retained aspects of the old modernization project that continued to benefit the ruling party. Although it reduced agrarian subsidies significantly (Appendini 1992), the Mexican government continued providing small subsidies for the poor because the ejidatarios composed a significant voting constituency (Appendini 1998; Myhre 1998). The Programa de Apoyo Directo al Campo (PROCAMPO), established in 1993 and managed by the Secretaría de Agricultura y Recursos Hidraúlicos (SARH; Ministry of Agriculture and Hydraulic Resources), provided acreage-based subsidies for farmers cultivating basic crops. Since the implementation of NAFTA exposed Mexican farmers to direct competition with U.S. and Canadian growers, PROCAMPO subsidies were intended to help farmers compete successfully in the global marketplace. The state agricultural bank (Banco Nacional de Crédito Rural, also known as BANRURAL) distributed the monies. In 1999, the ejidatarios of Kuchmil received approximately 700 pesos ($76) per hectare. The Programa Nacional de Solidaridad (PRONASOL) extended credit to subsistence farmers (Appendini 1998). Crédito a la Palabra, a subprogram of PRONASOL, was created to replace the subsidies previously provided by BANRURAL (Myhre 1998). The Programa de Educación, Salud y Alimentación (PROGRESA; Education, Health, and Nutrition Program) supplemented subsistence farmers' incomes by providing monetary and food subsidies to poor women and children. These "institutions for transition" were meant to gradually wean ejidatarios, like those belonging to Kuchmil's ejido, off government subsidies (Appendini 1998, 31). For example, PROCAMPO subsidies were scheduled to expire in 2008.[28] With the help of these subsidy programs and the money earned from wage work, subsistence farmers and their families eked out a living in the countryside. Yet the funds provided by these programs did not significantly improve the living conditions and economic opportunities of subsistence farmers.

The new Agrarian Law also promoted, but did not require, the privatization of ejido land. In March 1992, to regulate ejido land titles, the Procuraduría Agraria, the federal ministry that manages ejido reform, established the Programa de Certificación de Derechos Ejidales y Titulación de Solares (PROCEDE; Program for the Certification of Ejido Land Rights and the Titling of Urban House Plots). This titling process gave individual ejidatarios private ownership of house plots, and, if agreed upon by two-thirds of the general assembly (the ejido's governing body), private ownership of farmland. As a result, ejidatarios could gain legal control of the land they worked and lived on, making it possible to lawfully mortgage, sharecrop, rent, or sell their plots and solicit domestic and foreign investment or partnerships. The government urged ejido communities to recertify the boundaries of their ejido lands through PROCEDE. Many ejidatarios viewed these changes with suspicion (Mummert 2000; Stephen 1998). Although the new titling process formally recognizes the general assembly as the highest authoritative body within the ejido, in practice, formal government recognition of authority does not guarantee power or control beyond local politics or protection from federal and state government machinations or interference.

In Kuchmil, the residents were excited by the possibility of finally becoming an independent ejido. In spite of their resistance to privatization, Kuchmil's residents joined PROCEDE because they believed that access to government programs was contingent on their participation. They viewed their involvement, however, not as a process by which they could enter the free market as individual landowners or via partnerships with corporations, but as a process by which they could reaffirm the ejido's values and autonomy and secure a *carpeta básica,* a title of full usufruct rights and a definitive map of their ejido's land endowment. Residents did not plan to carve up their ejido into individual land plots because this would result in economic, social, and political suicide. Plus, ejidatarios were unclear on how the dismantling and privatization of the ejido system would impact the request and disbursement of agrarian subsidies. Residents relied heavily on the agrarian subsidies disbursed by PROCAMPO and other, smaller programs that distributed aid annually. Residents feared that government subsidies would decline if individuals, instead of a community, made claims for economic support from the government. They concluded that the power of a collective demand was superior to an individual claim. In January 2004, 66 percent of the nation's ejido land remained communal, but in Yucatán, that number was 78 percent.[29]

In 1997, through PROCEDE, Kuchmil received its *certificado parcelario,* which affirmed the ejido's status as a *parcela* of the larger ejido of Chan Sahkay, but it did not grant them autonomy from Chan Sahkay. The ejido hoped that this documentation would bring it one step closer to becoming an independent ejido under the current property regime. Finally, in May 2006, the Procuraduría Agraria formally recognized Kuchmil as an independent ejido. Due to its shift in legal status and a discrepancy in land measurements, Kuchmil had to begin the titling process all over again, despite having begun this process in 1996. Once again, at their general assembly meeting on June 6, 2006, the ejidatarios affirmed their desire to maintain communal ownership of their land.

For the residents of Kuchmil, privatization was viewed as a regression to a dark past. Don Jorge May Cituk explained that the community kept ejido land as *uso comunal* (communal use) to prevent esclavitud. If people sold their land, some folks would acquire large plots and others would be forced to work for them. This scenario represented a return to slavery.[30] Uso comunal prevents this by prohibiting individual ownership. As Joanne Rappaport (1990) has shown for the Paéz in Peru, indigenous communities rely on the mythical and factual events of the past to preserve a moral continuity and legitimacy carried into the present. Indeed, as farming has become sub-subsistence, rumors of the return of slavery and forced labor—for example, in the form of service jobs for transnational corporations and a reliance on cash to purchase commodities from an unregulated market—have prompted Maya communities to talk about an impending class and race war (Sullivan 1989). "The rich are the ones to benefit [from privatization]," explains don Patricio Kauil Balam. "By not dividing the ejido, we can leave it to our children. It's their patrimony." For communities like Kuchmil, privatization, in spite of its rhetoric of liberating individuals from cacique domination, represented the future loss of individual and collective rights to property and labor.

The new Agrarian Law of 1992 was intended to dismantle the very system used by the Mexican government to legitimize its power after the Revolution. The government argued that inefficiency, low productivity, and corruption of the *campo* were indicators that this system was obsolete and out of sync with global market trends (Cornelius and Myhre 1998). Privatization was proclaimed the most efficient means by which to stimulate increased production, diversification, and investment in the countryside. Yet rural communities like Kuchmil, who have chosen to remain corporate entities, are illustrative of how entrenched the ejido system has become in the campo and of its continued social, political, and economic viability.[31]

## Nation Building through the Cultural Missions

Education also served as a key tool through which to further the post-revolutionary Mexican government's project of modernizing the masses. The high illiteracy rates among the working class and the primitive conditions in which they lived were considered barriers to the development of the nation-state. Although the Mexican government used images of the peasant and indigenous peoples to promote its programs in support of a cultural revolution, the government did not intend to preserve the traditions and values these symbols represented (Vaughan 1982). Rather, it relied on social scientists, primarily anthropologists who came to be known as *indígenistas,* in its effort to assimilate indigenous communities into the mestizo nation. Social science, through its production of knowledge, categories, and racial hierarchies, became a tool for government control of indigenous communities (Lomnitz 2001; Vaughan 2006).

In 1921, the Mexican government established the Secretaría de Educación Pública (SEP; Ministry of Education) and placed intellectual José Vasconcelos in charge of "civilizing" the masses. The SEP created the Department of Indigenous Cultures to administer the programs established to educate indigenous rural communities. These schools and programs, which included the Cultural Missions program, the Casa del Pueblo school system, and the Literacy Campaign, were intended to transform the indigenous peasants into modern citizens. Vasconcelos viewed education as a way to impart "culture"—an urban–middle-class understanding of the term, in which the market economy, not the community, regulated economic relations, and in which modern conceptions of the autonomous, educated self thrived—to the peasantry (Vaughan 1982). Initially, the SEP's approach emphasized the middle-class values of individual land ownership, entrepreneurship, increasing productivity by means of capitalist structures, national unity, and political democracy. This vision excluded communal landholding practices; alternative religious, health, and healing practices; and cultural and linguistic diversity. What was being imposed on the countryside was a European version of high culture (ibid.) and a new form of political subjectivity (Dawson 2004).

To complicate matters, Vasconcelos's education model was based on the early Christian missionaries. Vasconcelos conceptualized teachers as "noble heroes filled with evangelical fervor which had animated the race in the days of the Conquest" who would enlighten the natives with their "work, virtue, and knowledge" (quoted in Vaughan 1982, 141). Vasconcelos imported the zeal, structure, and paternalism of the Christian missionaries into educational programs targeting indigenous communities because he believed these communities could not become literate citizens without guidance from the state—as degenerate subjects, they were incapable of accomplishing this conversion on their own (Dawson 2004; Vaughan 1982). For Vasconcelos, these missions were

> like a religious mission that takes off and travels to every corner of the country, carrying the good news that Mexico awakens from its lethargy and straightens up and walks. . . . Only then did it feel in the bosom and the heart of every Mexican that our educational action was urgent and very Christian, like giving drink to one that is thirsty or food to one that is starving. (quoted in Sierra 1973, 11; my translation)

The cultural mission, like earlier Christian missions, was intent on full conversion, only in this case, the conversion entailed turning the peasantry into literate, productive, and politically active citizens.

The objectives of the Cultural Missions program reflected the pedagogy of the SEP. The Cultural Missions were established after the 1920 First Congress of Teachers, where participants declared the education of the masses to be a social problem requiring a shift in pedagogy (Sierra 1973). The SEP opted for experiential learning as the best way to transform the work and hygiene habits of the peasantry. Following John Dewey, teachers were expected to teach by doing, rather than by lecturing (Vaughan 2006). Thus the original focus of the Cultural Missions was on preparing teachers for rural education programs and schools (Puig Casauranc 1928). Its secondary objective was to assimilate the peasantry by imparting culture and hygiene. Although the missions primarily employed bilingual mestizos, bilingualism was not promoted (Lewis 2006). The first cultural mission began on October 20, 1923, and provided instruction to the teachers of Zacualtipán, Hidalgo, on the following subjects: rural education, *jabonería y perfumería* (hygiene), tannery, agriculture, popular songs and chorus, physical education, and vaccinations. At the end of each mission, the work produced by the residents was put on display. Children, however, were not the only ones targeted for socialization by the first cultural mission. The majority of rural adults had never received a basic education. At the request of local residents and in order to combat what the indígenistas of the early nineteenth century perceived as degenerative behavior (e.g., alcoholism, religious devotion, and teenage pregnancy), teachers offered courses, such as puericulture (the rearing of young children) to the community (Dawson 2004). Due to its success, future missions incorporated an adult education component.

The Cultural Missions of 1923 and 1924 lasted three weeks each and took place in communities with fewer than three thousand inhabitants. By the end of 1924, six additional missions took place within the central western states of Mexico. By 1926, the SEP had established the Department of Cultural Missions to administer the program. This department named 150 *misioneros ambulantes* (traveling instructors) to study and periodically visit communities after the cultural mission departed. In 1928, to improve results, the duration of the Cultural Missions was expanded to a month. These missions continued to provide professional development for local teachers, but they also provided classes for adults and adolescents, which eventually replaced teacher instruction as the primary objective of the Cultural Missions. The classes continued to focus on hygiene, health, and agricultural techniques, but courses were eventually expanded to include business training, music education, home economics, dance, *artesanías* (arts and crafts), and nutrition. These subjects reflected the new objectives of the Cultural Missions: to provide a rudimentary education, promote personal hygiene, improve health, increase the productive capacity of the campo, and teach new skills and "culture" to the peasantry. Later, the missions relied on theater productions to promote literacy and nationalism and to educate rural residents about hygiene and agriculture (Underiner 2004). To this end, between 1942 and 1948, the Cultural Missions constructed two hundred theaters and put on five hundred productions. Thus the education of the entire village had become the principal goal of the cultural mission.

The impact of the Cultural Missions on community development was limited for a number of reasons. First, the missions never addressed the structural problems facing the peasantry, especially indigenous communities (Vaughan 1982). The economic and health needs of rural communities were ignored. Second, the objective of the Cultural Missions was to improve the skills of the teachers working in the countryside, but the short duration of the courses made it impossible for them to adequately improve the knowledge base of rural teachers. Finally, the Cultural Missions did not receive the funds necessary to adequately staff, train, and equip the mission teachers. Many teachers were ignorant of local conditions and returned to the city without fulfilling their responsibilities (Dawson 2004). Some became embroiled in political struggles in which rural communities became pawns (Vaughan 1982). As a result, community participation began to decline.

The problems evident in the early missions continued to plague later missions. When the Cultural Missions arrived in Chan Sahkay around 1958,[32] the mission offered its courses to nearby villages. The missionary teachers traveled to Kuchmil to offer classes on music, sewing, and baking. The residents of Kuchmil held fond memories of the missionary teachers because they were kind and imparted new skills. The music teacher organized a trio: don Dani played the guitar, don Hector played the violin, and don Armando played the bass guitar. Women learned new sewing techniques, while a few men learned how to tailor men's clothing. Both men and women learned to bake cakes on the *k'ooben-k'áak'* (three-stone cooking pit) without a temperature gauge.

While the memories of the mission in Kuchmil were positive, they were also vague, particularly since not all residents took part in the courses. When I asked residents about their recollections, those who participated remembered the skills they learned and the teachers they met, but they could not recall why the Cultural Missions arrived in their region. This lack of understanding can be attributed to the duration of the mission. The program lasted one month, insufficient time to make a deep impression and fundamentally change people's customs, habits, and knowledge. After this mission departed, the community of Kuchmil lost contact with the program for nearly three decades. More important, the skills the cultural mission taught did not result in fundamental structural changes to the local economy or cultural practices. Few could make a living from the skills they learned and even fewer incorporated the nutritional and hygienic values taught by the mission teachers into their lives.

## The Cultural Missions Return

The Cultural Missions sent a mission to the municipality of Ke'eldzonot in 1986 and 1999. Kuchmil did not fall under the jurisdiction of this municipality, but due to its proximity, Kuchmil residents were encouraged to participate in these campaigns by attending courses in Ke'eldzonot. In response, Kuchmil invited the mission teachers to give classes in Kuchmil. Renamed the Misiones Culturales Rurales (Rural Cultural Missions), this program remains under the auspices of the SEP, but it is administered by the Unidad de Educación Básica Para Adultos (Department of Basic Education for Adults). Although it is now framed within a development discourse, the program has retained its missionary zeal and nation-building orientation. According to mission director Rafael Osorio Hurtado, the purpose of the contemporary Rural Cultural Missions is "to promote the economic, social, and cultural improvement of the clusters of peasant communities who for different reasons remain at the margins of the country's development."[33] Adults, not children, are now the primary targets of this program. By providing "pre-capitalist" rural communities with the tools and "culture" necessary to function productively in Mexican society (Palma López 1998), missions intend for these populations to resolve their problems of poverty, underproduction, and so on, on their own.

To accomplish this, the missions' duration has been extended and more staff has been added. Missions now offer courses over a period of one or two years and include a mission coordinator, a social worker, a nurse, agricultural extension agents, a physical education teacher, a music teacher, a carpenter, a masonry teacher, an elementary school teacher, and a teacher of petty rural industries. The lengthier period allows mission workers to get to know a community, to earn the respect of the locals, and to better implement the mission projects. Contemporary mission projects continue to include Vasconcelos's emphasis on "learning by doing." Like the earlier missions, the 1986 and 1999 missions offered local residents courses on sewing, nutrition, agriculture, music, and dance. The Rural Cultural Missions promoted a gendered division of labor through their courses. Women were taught skills to improve the domestic sphere (e.g., sewing, home gardening, baking, nutritious cooking, artesanías), while men were taught skills relevant to the campo. The residents of Kuchmil did not recall participating in the 1986 mission, but archival records from Kuchmil's comisaría municipal show that they solicited the Rural Cultural Missions attention and requested that this mission be extended an additional year.

The 1999 mission in Ke'eldzonot aimed to ameliorate the high rates of poverty, malnutrition, and low educational attainment levels that plagued this municipality. Participants were taught how to raise animals, improve farming techniques, enhance domestic skills, improve hygiene and nutrition, and create arts and crafts for local and global consumption. However, while local residents enjoyed taking these classes, few of the skills they acquired were lucrative or useful. The agriculture, sewing, and nutrition classes offer clear examples. Many of the agricultural projects developed in class were difficult to replicate outside of the classroom because participants did not have the money with which to purchase the raw materials, had a difficult time finding the raw materials, or could not find a market for the items produced. The sewing skills class, on the other hand, was offered to all residents in the area. Almost all the women in Kuchmil took this course. As a result, the local market for tailored clothes never gained momentum because there was too much competition and because ready-to-wear clothing was more accessible and cheaper than tailored clothing. Similarly, in the nutrition class, women learned how to expand their repertoire of recipes and to prepare healthier meals. Kuchmil women enjoyed tasting and making different meals, but the price of goods, time constraints, and the seasonality of fruits, herbs, and vegetables limited the frequency with which they could make these meals at home. The Cultural Missions did not offer start-up funds for participants who wished to establish their own businesses. Instead, the region was flooded with people who knew how to make the same items for sale, bake the same goods, and cultivate the same plants.

The Cultural Missions taught "culture" but within a limited conception: a culture intimately linked with civic order, nationalism, and an essentialized Mexican culture that can be sold abroad. For example, the youth who participated in this program were relegated to classes that taught them an idealized version of Mexican and Maya culture through dance, music, theater, and the arts. These youth learned to dance traditional folk dances like the *jarana* and sew traditional clothing like the huipil. Such an approach fosters knowledge of and pride in essentialized Mexican and Maya cultures and promotes Mexican nationalism, but it excludes these youth from learning the skills and acquiring the knowledge necessary to remain and make a living in the countryside.

The Rural Cultural Missions did not substantially improve the economic and social lives of rural communities. In spite of its aim to develop and expand the skill base of rural residents over an extended period, this program did not teach the language skills or provide the technology necessary to compete in a global labor market, like Cancún's international tourist economy. More important, this program failed to address the structural problems campesinos face in the countryside: the lack of technology that limits their ability to establish a multi-crop production system; the demands of a free market system that undercuts local prices by flooding Mexico with cheap imported produce; declining government subsidies; and the campesinos' lack of collateral with which to secure loans from banks and other sources. In Kuchmil, participants acknowledged the limitations of the Cultural Missions program, but they did not blame it for not resolving the challenges facing rural communities (e.g., migration, agricultural decline, health problems), nor did they demand that it change its curriculum.

In the past, teachers were considered spies for the government, but as education was increasingly perceived as a vehicle for social mobility, teachers began to be treated with respect. Since the majority of the Rural Cultural Missions teachers were Yucatecans, many of whom were Maya and spoke Maya, the residents did not publicly acknowledge the "civilizing" aspect of the Cultural Missions. They considered the mission to be an *ayuda* (help), another subsidy program offered by the government of which they planned to take full advantage. But whether this mission will make a lasting impression has yet to be determined.

## Begging the State

Superficially, life in Kuchmil has not deviated from the descriptions of Maya life captured in early ethnographies by Robert Redfield and Alfonso Villa Rojas. Much of the housing construction remains the same. Farmers continue to grow corn, beans, and squash. Yucatec Maya persists as the primary language. This continuity, however, masks the distinct changes Maya communities have endured as a result of their conflictive relationship with colonial and postrevolutionary governments. These institutions and changes in the global and regional economies have profoundly influenced Maya communties' cultural and social practices and the physical layout and administrative organization of Maya villages. Kuchmil's experience with the Cultural Missions and its participation in agrarian reform illustrate some of these changes. In spite of the Mexican government's assimilation efforts, Maya communities have been just as active in defining the social, cultural, and political contours of their communities. Kuchmil residents participated in the Cultural Missions because they thought its classes would expand their skills and thereby improve their household incomes. In addition, the Cultural Mission provided a new space in which individuals could socialize. By participating in classes together, local residents increased community solidarity. Similarly, participation in agrarian reform provided the framework through which Kuchmil could define itself as a political community. Kuchmil residents embraced the ejido because it provided the structure by which to develop a relationship with the state.

As the sustainability of agricultural production has declined, Kuchmil has actively sought access to both government and nongovernment programs and courted the anthropologists and archaeologists visiting the region. Indigenous communities have learned that they get access to more subsidies and international support if they play the role of poor campesinos trapped in a "culture of poverty" (Lewis 1959). Not surprisingly, they rely on 'óoȼil-t'àan (poor talk or begging) as a way to "sell their poverty."[34] Although this emphasis on rural poverty does not reflect the increasing social stratification evident in the campo (Goldkind 1965; Re Cruz 1996a), this discourse is strategically deployed by rural communities like Kuchmil to demand that the government fulfill the obligations and promises it made during and after the Mexican Revolution. As a proud people, Maya residents of Kuchmil did not consider poor talk to be demeaning. Rather, since it stems from a history of slavery and repression, poor talk represents one of the ways that indigenous peoples engage power under oppressive conditions. In the process, poor talk evokes memories of past abuses that the nation would prefer to forget.

Likewise, Paul Sullivan points out that 'óoȼil-t'àan is a strategic discourse used to solicit money from foreigners and indexes the increasing commoditization of the local economy (1989, 195–9). In their effort to engage my help for the community's benefit, Kuchmil residents sprinkled our conversations with 'óoȼil-t'àan. For Kuchmil, cultivating relationships with institutions of power and with foreigners provides an alternative source of resources. Currently, Kuchmil is working with Manos sobre la Tierra, a nongovernmental organization funded by the Mexican and Italian governments, to increase and diversify agricultural production through organic farming techniques that respect indigenous knowledge and skills. The community is hopeful that this environmentally friendly and inexpensive approach will expand their production and sales of commercial crops. In the meantime, wage work in Cancún provides an important source of revenue to supplement agricultural production. In the following chapter, I examine the factors that inspired the local exodus to Cancún, Mexico's premiere modernization project.

# 3

# Indigenous Education, Adolescent Migration, and Wage Labor

Jesús May Pat does not know how to make milpa. He left Kuchmil at ten years of age to attend a *casa escuela* (boarding school) in the town of Maxcanú, located at least a full day's travel from Kuchmil. Initially, his parents, don Jorge and doña Berta, refused Jesús's request to attend this school because, as the eldest son, his labor was needed in the milpa. Jesús asked his uncle, who planned to send his two eldest sons to the casa escuela, to convince his parents to let him go. A scholarship from the Ministry of Education paid for boarding school expenses, but Jesús's parents were responsible for his transportation to Maxcanú. As a subsistence farmer, his father did not earn a wage, which meant that Jesús could not return home too often. At first, Jesús missed home, but his cousins' presence helped him to adjust until he learned to enjoy boarding school life. The students raised animals, grew vegetables, and tailored their own clothes. Since Jesús was a good student, his teachers encouraged him to continue with his education. With their support, Jesús was awarded a scholarship to attend a *secundaria técnica* (a three-year vocational agriculture school) in the town of Tekax.

Given that he did not know how to make milpa and did not much like working in the milpa, Jesús did not plan to return to Kuchmil after he completed the secundaria. During his final year in Tekax, he volunteered to work as a rural teacher with the Consejo Nacional de Fomento Educativo (CONAFE; National Council of Education Promotion), which assigned him to teach fifth and sixth grades in a small rural community near Tekax. One year of service with CONAFE guaranteed Jesús a three-year scholarship to study the *bachillerato* (three-year college preparatory or vocational degree program). His parents agreed to provide him with a modest sum of money for his daily expenses and arranged for Jesús to live with his cousins, who had moved to Felipe Carrillo Puerto, Quintana Roo, a town large enough to support a COBAY. After earning his vocational degree as an electrician in 1990, Jesús found work in a hotel in Cancún, where he lives to this day.

During the 1970s and early 1980s, it was quite common for families to send their adolescent sons to study at internados scattered throughout the peninsula. Twenty-eight students from Kuchmil attended boarding schools. Although these schools were coeducational, only four girls from Kuchmil were enrolled. These youth studied in places as far east as Maxcanú, near the Campeche state border, and as far west as Bacalar in the state of Quintana Roo, near the national border with Belize. This youthful mobility marked a new turning point for the future of Kuchmil. The first migrants from Kuchmil to settle in Cancún were alumni of boarding schools.

Indigenous boarding schools in Mexico, like Indian boarding schools in the United States, were considered key institutions through which the state could transform indigenous peoples into modern citizens (Dawson 2004; Eiss 2004; Fallaw 2004; Vaughan 1997). By establishing rural boarding schools, the Mexican government aimed to incorporate indigenous populations into national life through a process of assimilation and de-racialization. As a result, boarding schools recruited children as young as five years of age with the objective of training them to become leaders of rural communities. In this chapter, I examine how this nationalist project transformed local constructions of Maya childhood and adolescence. I suggest that Kuchmil adolescents' participation in indigenous boarding schools and later as wage laborers in a global tourist economy resulted in "capitalist contradictions" in their daily lives that offer a critique of modernity (Stephens 1995, 26).

In contrast to the state's efforts at assimilation, Kuchmil families did not send their children to boarding schools to become less Maya nor to become the future leaders of Kuchmil. As Ben Fallaw (2004) has shown during the Cárdenas period, the success of federal schools involved a process of accommodation and resistance by Maya families. In the case of Kuchmil, by improving and expanding their children's educational opportunities, Maya parents positioned their children as wage laborers rather than as subsistence farmers. Through these efforts, Kuchmil families improved their future access to a cash economy via the wage labor of their children and supported their children's emerging roles as active consumers. As a result, youth migration was not solely spurred by the attraction of global markets, but was also directed by the state and promoted by indigenous families. Nevertheless, the boarding school experience did not adequately prepare these children to succeed in the new tourist economy.

## Rural Education in Early Twentieth-Century Yucatán

Before and after the Mexican revolution, education was considered a key institution through which to civilize and govern indigenous populations, especially children (Acevedo Rodrigo 2004; Gill 2001; Vaughan 1982). During the Porfiriato (1876 to 1910, the years Porfirio Díaz ruled Mexico), teachers were sent to the southeastern peninsula to pacify the rebel Maya by exposing their children to educational programs that would "civilize" and assimilate them into the nation-state. This venture proved unsuccessful due to the harsh living conditions the teachers encountered in the tropics, parental resistance, and a lack of communication between Spanish-speaking teachers and Maya-speaking children (Ramos Díaz 2001). Toward the end of the Porfiriato, the Liga de Acción Social, founded in 1909 by a group of "progressive" hacendados who advocated modernizing social and labor conditions on haciendas, promoted education as a way to spiritually enlighten Maya workers and to prevent them from joining popular insurgencies (Wells and Joseph 1996, 92).[1] By 1910, twenty-seven *escuelas rurales* (rural schools) were established on Yucatecan haciendas. These schools emphasized Spanish language acquisition, patriotism, and labor discipline, but their main objective was the moral, spiritual, and racial uplift of Maya workers (ibid.; Eiss 2000).

Salvador Alvarado, the governor of Yucatán (1915–18), expanded the Liga's vision of educational reform. Public education, according to Alvarado, was an important vehicle through which revolutionary ideals could be transmitted to the general populace, and served as the key institution by which to transform indigenous peoples into modern citizens of the nation-state (Eiss 2004). His endeavors were bolstered by the passage of a federal law in 1911 authorizing the construction of rural schools to educate indigenous peoples.[2] By the end of his tenure, Alvarado established over one thousand escuelas rurales on haciendas and in villages throughout Yucatán. These schools emphasized literacy, civic duty, labor discipline, and class solidarity. The schools were met with resistance from hacienda owners and parents, both of whom were deprived of control over students' labor. Critics argued that the escuela rural taught literacy but failed to transform the moral character of indigenous children (Eiss 2000). To address these limitations, Alvarado established the Ciudad Escolar de los Mayas (Scholastic City of the Mayas) in 1917. Possibly modeled after the rural and residential schools for Native American and African American children (Eiss 2004), this short-lived residential program educated indigenous youths to become rural teachers and productive agricultural workers (Ramos Díaz 2001). Alvarado envisioned the Ciudad as a commercial center in which the children used their earnings from their labor to establish a profitable business. In 1918, due to economic problems, student flight, and parental opposition to the state's usurpation of their children's labor, the Ciudad was shut down. Critics blamed the Ciudad's failure not on these factors but on the degenerate nature of the indigenous peoples (Eiss 2000). The Ciudad Escolar, regardless of its limitations, may have served as the template for future boarding schools in Mexico.

In 1921, the SEP was established to provide a public education to the three-quarters of the population that had been denied access to one prior to the Mexican Revolution. The SEP considered exposure to schooling as the best way to improve the living conditions, personal hygiene, production strategies, civic activity, and Spanish fluency of indigenous communities (Loyo Bravo 1985; Ramos Díaz 2001, 84). Through public education, the SEP intended to unify, civilize, and modernize the nation. Again the rural teacher formed an important component of this plan. Modeled on the image of the Spanish missionary, rural teachers were supposed to travel from community to community, leaving established schools in their wake (Alvarez Barret 1971). Yet this ideological construction of the rural teacher as nationalist reformer disregarded cases of teacher abuse of political power (Gillingham 2006) and ignored the problems experienced by rural teachers during the Porfiriato and under Alvarado's administration (Loyo Bravo 1985). Since federal schools demanded financial support from municipalities and emphasized knowledge of farming and trades over literacy, many communities protested the added tax burden and the induction of children's labor in agricultural annexes (Acevedo Rodrigo 2004).

In contrast to the SEP's approach, Felipe Carrillo Puerto (1922–24), Alvarado's successor as Yucatán's governor and leader of the Socialist Party, considered the rural school as the vehicle by which to create a class-conscious worker who would take control of her own labor, instead of submitting to the will of her employer as Alvarado preached (Joseph 1995, 214–17). Given that the SEP refused to disburse federal funds for schooling and did not establish schools in Yucatán before 1925, Carrillo Puerto's educational philosophy serves as a counterpoint to the SEP's approach to indigenous education.[3] Deeply influenced by Spanish anarchist Francisco Ferrer Guardia, Carrillo Puerto established the *escuela racionalista* (rationalist school), which adhered to the separation of the church and state and promoted socialism and bilingual education. Children were taught that the collective mattered more than the individual and were exposed to curriculum oriented around their daily experiences in the countryside. Carrillo Puerto's short-lived administration lacked the funds with which to implement many of these educational reforms, but its emphasis on bilingual education, worker's rights, and social justice presaged the shift toward a socialist education in the 1930s (Vaughan 1982).

In 1926, to address the particular needs of indigenous children and the dearth of bilingual teachers, the SEP developed the Casa del Estudiante Indígena (House of the Indigenous Student) program, in which over 200 indigenous children from different ethnic backgrounds were interned in a boarding school in Mexico City (Loyo Bravo 1996).[4] The Casa's main objective was for its pupils to transmit their acquired knowledge of Western civilization to their communities of origin. While this program failed because the students refused to return home, it proved that the intellectual capacity of indigenous peoples was equal to that of Westerners, an issue that had been seriously debated over the previous century.[5]

Following this shift, President Lázaro Cárdenas's administration (1934–40) reformed Article 3 of the Constitution to establish a socialist education in Mexico that exalted indigenous culture and languages. Under this administration, the SEP's educational objective to create modern citizens was fused with the socialist ideology of workers' rights and agrarian reform (Loyo Bravo 1985). The previous administration's efforts to "incorporate" indigenous peoples were replaced with an emphasis on the "integration" of indigenous cultures and Western ideals (Loyo Bravo 1996, 147). In adherence to this ideological shift, the SEP established the Centros de Educación Indígena (CEI; Center for Indigenous Education) to educate indigenous children *within* their communities. By bringing "civilization" to the countryside, it hoped to avoid the failure of urban education models like the Casa del Estudiante Indígena (ibid.). Organized as boarding schools and run by newly established socialist brigades, these centers aimed to educate and train indigenous adolescents to become the future teachers of their communities (Fallaw 2004; Modiano 1973). The curriculum centered on the skills and knowledge necessary for rural life, such as animal husbandry, agricultural production, and domestic duties. In contrast to previous boarding school projects, the students who attended CEIs were allowed to speak Maya. In 1933, such a school was established in Chan Santa Cruz, Quintana Roo.[6] However, this project was short-lived. The socialist brigades came to denounce the oppressive conditions in which indigenous communities lived and thus clashed with local elites (Loyo Bravo 1996). Additionally, problems with recruitment, staffing, and funding brought about the CEI's quick demise (Fallaw 2004).[7]

## Internados

In light of these failures, indigenous education required a new approach. The first Interamerican Indigenist Congress (1940), held in Pátzcuaro, Michoacán, recognized the right of indigenous peoples throughout Latin America to retain their cultures and languages. To ensure this pluralistic vision, it recommended the creation of an indigenous institute with administrative centers throughout the Americas. However, the onset of World War II and U.S. demands for supplies stimulated Mexico's industrialization and its need for educated, disciplined workers. The socialist discourse of the Cárdenas administration was usurped by an emphasis on "national unity" and commercial production (Echeverría V. 1993). To thwart efforts promoting pluralism and indigenous self-determination, President Manuel Avila Camacho (1940–46) established the Instituto Nacional Indígenista (INI; National Indigenous Institute) (Dawson 2004). The INI was dedicated to the educational, physical, and social growth needs of indigenous communities that had been met previously by the state through the SEP's rural education program and Cultural Missions. To gain the confidence of indigenous communities, the INI cultivated patron-client relationships with young progressive indigenous leaders who served as bilingual *promotores* (cultural brokers) between indigenous communities and the state (Rus 1994). Although the INI's first director, Alfonso Caso, attended the first Interamerican Indigenist Congress, the INI's pluralistic vision was limited to the support of indigenous languages. Its main objective was centered on the acculturation of indigenous communities (Modiano 1973).[8]

The SEP's objectives during this time reflected the shift in national discourse. It considered rural education's failure to modernize and integrate indigenous communities into national life to be indicative of a need to reconceptualize its objectives. As part of the national effort to reform rural education, the First National Congress on Indigenous Education was held in 1948. This congress served as a forum by which to address the problems that continued to plague rural education: teacher absenteeism, parental resistance, and student flight. The modernization and integration of the countryside were firmly promoted, along with the need to "improve the material, cultural, and moral conditions of the pueblo" (Aguilar Padilla 1988, 61, my translation). To accomplish this task, the Congress focused on the rural teacher. It proposed that the rural teacher be inculcated with a "social attitude" attentive to the problems of campesinos; be familiar with village life; be proficient in the native language of indigenous villages; and become infused with the "sincere desire to give himself/herself to their service [of the community], as if it were the mission of his/her life" (ibid., 62, my translation). Once again, rural teachers were viewed as missionaries in charge of improving the spiritual, cultural, and material lives of indigenous folk, but this time they would be armed with the linguistic capabilities necessary to succeed at this task. To solve the problem of teacher absenteeism and desertion, the Congress proposed setting up a new training program dedicated to developing the skills of rural teachers and to instilling a sense of social obligation in the rural teacher for the entire village, not just for its students. Unfortunately, these efforts did not significantly increase student participation in rural Yucatán (Echeverría V. 1993).

In the early 1960s, the INI and SEP established internados to provide an elementary and junior high school education to children from isolated rural and indigenous communities. The SEP trained the teachers that staffed these schools (Greaves 1999). Internados took different shapes depending on their location and source of funding. The SEP created the casa escuela, which solely housed students who attended local elementary schools, and the secundaria técnica, a junior high school that housed students on school grounds who lived too far to commute; whereas the INI established *albergues escolares* (elementary boarding schools), which recruited students from towns located within a fifteen-kilometer radius and housed all students on school grounds. Albergues escolares were supervised by the *Centros Coordinadores Indigenistas* (CCI; Coordinating Indigenous Centers), regional administrative centers funded by the INI that coordinated programs and resources directed toward indigenous communities

(INI 1994). Internados also were organized by grade. Albergues escolares recruited students from first through sixth grades. Casa escuelas housed fourth- through sixth-grade students, and secundarias técnicas educated students from seventh through ninth grade.

Boarding schools aimed to improve student attendance through the provision of meals, housing, and medical care (INI 1994). Reminiscent of the Casa del Estudiante Indígena, the internados in the Yucatán Peninsula also helped transition indigenous children into mainstream society by teaching them Spanish, personal hygiene, vocational skills, and citizenship. Hence their purpose was similar to Indian boarding schools in the United States, which isolated Indian children to make them "forget their barbarous practices and acquire the knowledge and benefits of civilization" (Lomawaima 1994; Niezen 2000, 47). To recruit students, radio announcements extolled the benefits of this type of education, as did teachers from the internados who traveled to rural villages. In 1964, when INI schools merged with SEP schools, the presence of bilingual teachers and bilingual books in rural classrooms increased substantially (Berkley 1998; Modiano 1973). Between 1964 and 1973, twenty-nine internados rurales were established throughout the Mexican countryside to provide a continuing education (fourth to sixth grade) to indigenous students who completed the third grade (Aguilar Padilla 1988). By 1976, the SEP administered 591 albergues escolares in Mexico. In the late 1960s and throughout the 1970s, twenty-eight children in Kuchmil attended internados. Of these students, fifteen pursued secondary education at internados located throughout the peninsula.

## Schools in Southeastern Yucatán

Alvarado and Carrillo Puerto established a large number of schools in Yucatán from 1915 to 1923, but few of the schools located in the southeastern region were successful. From 1929 to 1935, the SEP built schools and federalized existing schools in over 200 communities in southeastern Yucatán (Fallaw 2004). The SEP's initial efforts in this region were fraught with difficulties: religious differences, local politics, and linguistic barriers interfered with enrollment and participation; diseases like malaria affected attendance; schools suffered from a high rate of teacher absenteeism and desertion; and the lack of decent school buildings offended parents' sensibilities (Fallaw 2004; Ramos Díaz 2001). Parental resistance to schooling also remained strong in this region. Few parents were willing to go without the help of their children's labor in the milpa and solar, which was essential to a rural household's maintenance. By their teen years, Maya children's labor generates a surplus that helps pay for the reproductive costs of younger siblings (Kramer 2005). In addition, Maya parents rejected the SEP's coeducation policy, preferring to keep their daughters at home rather than expose them to potential physical and sexual abuse from male teachers (Fallaw 2004). Finally, local suspicion of government officials and institutions also contributed to parents' misgivings.

Yet, in Kuchmil, parents were dissatisfied with the village's single-classroom schoolhouse. They believed teacher absenteeism degraded the quality of the education their children received. Prior to the construction of a paved road in 1991, rocky paths served as the only exits and entryways to Kuchmil. SEP teachers assigned to work in rural communities commuted weekly to rural villages via horseback or bicycle. Depending on where the teacher lived, this commute could take a few hours or a couple of days. Until he could afford to buy a motorcycle, Domingo Pat Rodríguez, the elementary school teacher during the decade in which I worked in Kuchmil, commuted via bicycle from Tekax every few days, a journey that took all day, particularly during the hot, dry spring months. Since few teachers were accustomed to life in a small isolated village lacking urban amenities such as electricity, many worked as few days as possible.[9]

Although the community treated teachers with respect, Kuchmil parents complained that the students enrolled in grades four through six did not receive as much instruction as younger children. "[During the 1970s] there wasn't a school," recalled Jesús May Pat. "Well, there was a school but it was limited to a certain grade. Once you pass that grade, you can't study anymore." The older students, who were primarily male, received minimal instruction within such a setting and consequently were at risk of not advancing their literacy and bilingual skills. Reduced instruction was a common problem in rural schools. In Chiapas, for example, teachers taught fewer hours than the mandatory five hours set by the SEP (Modiano 1973). As a result, boarding schools became an attractive alternative for rural households.

Although a CCI was established in Peto, Yucatán, in 1960 to address the needs of Maya communities, the INI (in conjunction with the SEP) did not establish an albergue escolar near Kuchmil until the late 1960s. Located in the neighboring town of Ke'eldzonot, this gratuitous school included first through sixth grade. Its proximity made it possible for families to educate more than one child. The teachers were bilingual, which made it easier for parents to communicate their concerns. The students, however, did not learn much Spanish because all of the students spoke Maya and the bilingual teachers did not enforce Spanish-only rules. "Very little [Spanish] we learned because we were embarrassed to speak in Spanish. We mainly spoke Maya. . . . We did not learn [to read and write] Maya," observed Enrique May Kauil. The primary objectives of the albergue escolar were to promote Spanish literacy and impart vocational skills.[10] Enrique May Kauil recalled, "They [the teachers] did teach us a little bit about how to sow seeds, raise animals, grow radishes and cabbage, water plants." But not all children were exposed to these activities and therefore they did not learn within a school setting to become productive small farmers. From the late 1960s through the 1970s, sixteen children from Kuchmil attended the albergue in Ke'eldzonot.

In the late 1970s, the SEP established a casa escuela in Maxcanú to address the educational needs of students in fourth through sixth grades. The casa escuela provisioned students with food, housing, a hammock, clothing, and a small allowance. But unlike the albergue, the casa escuela in Maxcanú was not a school. The students lived in a large dormitory across town from the public elementary school, in which the casa escuela students were enrolled. Staffed by monolingual Spanish teachers, this public school promoted Spanish instruction. Therefore, the students spoke, read, and wrote in Spanish. The school's emphasis on agricultural technology provided the students with a strong background in horticulture. Due to the school's distance from Kuchmil (one full day's travel), students only visited their parents during vacation periods. As a result, the teachers had more time to nurture the students' physical, mental, and social development. Thirteen boys and two girls, three of whom previously attended the albergue escolar in Ke'eldzonot, were sent to the school in Maxcanú before the casa escuela closed around 1983.[11]

## Men Read and Women Count

In spite of the INI's and SEP's coeducation policy, few girls attended the internados. Traditionally, the eldest son of each Maya household was sent to school to become literate and bilingual (Berkley 1998). Consequently by the 1960s, all male adults except one had attended elementary school as children, but they only studied long enough to learn how to sign their name, to speak rudimentary Spanish, to count, and to acquire enough literacy to read government documents. Girls, in contrast, were rarely sent to school. Only three of the married women in Kuchmil attended elementary school. According to anthropologist Anthony Berkley, this gendered approach to education results in a "familial interdependence" within households in which men read and women count (1998, 107). These expectations continued to shape educational outcomes in Kuchmil up to the 1960s.

Kuchmil parents did not feel comfortable sending their daughters away to school because they would not be able to regulate their sexual behavior as custom required. Although the school was located within walking distance, this trek was quite a distance for a small child to travel alone or with friends. Parents were too busy with household and farm chores to accompany their children. Celia Kauil May walked to the albergue with her older sister Laura. "I was five years old when I went to the internado in Ke'eldzonot, from Monday through Friday. Only on Saturday and Sunday, I was at home. Come Monday very early, at five in the morning, we had to walk to school." In addition, parents were upset that boys and girls slept in same-sex dormitories. Since the teachers did not sleep in the dormitories, most parents believed that the dormitories placed their daughters' sexual innocence at risk. Finally, parents were suspicious of internados because they limited student/parent contact and supervision. Pupils were required to live on school grounds during the week and were only allowed to visit their families on weekends.

In spite of these expectations, four girls were allowed to attend the albergue escolar.[12] These girls came from households with educated mothers or with parents who wished all their children to benefit from schooling. Echoing the explanations offered by the Cruzob Maya for sending their children to school during the 1920s (Ramos Díaz 2001), doña Andrea May Citep allowed her two daughters to attend internados because their "father wanted [them] to learn to write, to learn to read." Nonetheless, of the parents inclined to educate their daughters, few let their daughters finish elementary school once they entered puberty. "When one is a woman, parents don't let you finish studying [complete elementary school]. During this time period, parents thought that the girls like to flirt with the boys," clarified Jeni Moo Chi. When these fears came true, girls experienced severe setbacks in their education. Celia was not allowed to study beyond the sixth grade after her older sister Laura committed such a transgression. She explained, "My older sister was studying the secundaria when she ran away with her boyfriend. After that my father said that now no one would continue studying." Fearing that Celia might succumb to the same temptation, her parents kept her home. But they did not fear the same fate for their sons. Aware of this gender inequality, the boys who attended boarding schools observed that "girls weren't allowed to leave [the village]" and of the few girls who did go to school, "not all of them finished because of their parents."

Of the twenty-eight children who completed elementary school at internados, thirteen boys and two girls proceeded to study the secundaria. Four went to the internado in Nohbec in Quintana Roo, whose tuition was free to children who scored a "B" average in elementary school. Two of these young men, Nícolas Can Tun and Enrique May Kauil, did not complete their studies due to economic hardship. Since they were not awarded a scholarship to cover room and board, their families attempted to cover these expenses, but fell short most months. After facing near starvation, Nícolas and Enrique dropped out. Another boy attended an internado in Balantún, near Valladolid, on scholarship. Three boys earned full scholarships (tuition, room, and board) to study in the *secundaria técnica,* which was also an internado, located in the town of Tekax. One of these young men was Jesús May Pat. The families of the remaining seven students (five boys, all of whom were brothers, and two girls) paid for their children to attend a public secundaria in Tihosuco. Celia's older sister was one of these girls, but she did not finish the secundaria because she eloped. The youngest boy of the five brothers transferred to the Balantún internado after he was awarded a scholarship.

Of these fifteen children, nine (eight boys and one girl) went on to study the bachillerato. To pay for this degree, three joined CONAFE and completed their degree with the scholarship CONAFE gives in exchange for one to two years of service. The girl became a teacher, but this was possible because her parents moved with her to Carrillo Puerto where she studied this profession. Another student became a promotor for INI with the help of his uncle, but he moved to Cancún before completing his training. Four of the boys decided to end their studies early and try their luck in the new international tourist center of Cancún.

## The Hardships of Schooling

Like Native American families who used boarding schools to resolve economic problems (Child 1998; Lomawaima 1994), Maya families also turned to internados to ease their poverty and to improve their children's physical and nutritional well-being. Hunger and sickness plague rural families. In 1991 during my first to Kuchmil, the majority of the infants in Kuchmil were malnourished and underweight.[13] Children followed me, begging for food and snacks. Over 60 percent of the indigenous children who attended albergues escolares in Yucatán suffered from chronic malnutrition (Hernández Murrillo and Thacker 1992). In the 1960s, the hunger may have been worse. The internados, proclaimed the radio commercials and recruiters, provided access not only to better schools, but also to food and clothing. According to Enrique May Kauil, a student at the albergue escolar in Ke'eldzonot, the internados relieved parental stress.

> The government sent food. They built a large house, like a dormitory. They gave us a hammock once, a blanket. Everyone has their little locker with their key. [The school] helps with all of your expenses, with the food. It behooves the parents [to send their children to boarding schools] because sometimes at home with difficulty [their children] eat. They don't even drink milk. During that time period, they get a small scholarship, a bit of money. It helps.

By sending them to boarding schools, Kuchmil parents also improved their children's nutritional intake.

Agrarian crises were at the root of the hunger facing these families. As the economic sustainability of the ejido diminished and mass-produced goods flooded markets in the 1960s, Maya families turned to wage labor to supplement or replace farm work and gain access to cash. Wage work, however, was more difficult to obtain. Due to their poor educational backgrounds, adult males seeking wage labor faced limited options. They could only find work in construction.[14] As a result of these experiences with the labor market, parents did not want their children to be restricted to manual labor or farm work. Roberto Can Kauil explained his own parents' frustration with farm work and manual labor.

> So that I won't follow the same path he took, that of being a campesino, because he doesn't want me to work in the campo [fields]. My mother agreed. . . . We heard from others that a school was going to be built, that food would be given. No one would have to pay anything, not one cent. My father told me that I had to go. I didn't want to go. "Too bad," replied my father. "We have to get ahead."

According to him, his father had a bit [of money] so they could go to school but they never sent him. My father was happy that I agreed to study there. His idea was for me not to return to the pueblo. During that time period, the milpa did produce but not 100 percent. How are you going to produce 100 percent when there is always a loss. . . . [Parents] knew that when their sons go there [the internado], they will learn more and maybe will acquire a better job so that they won't have to work in the milpa. That was how each father thought.

As one father put it, "One cannot get ahead by working in the milpa." Encouraged by the teachers sent to recruit students, Kuchmil parents turned toward education as one solution to the agricultural crisis.

Maya families knew that enrolling their children in boarding schools would transform their lives. Doña Berta, Jesús's mother, acknowledged that an education would alter her son's life course. "I think that he isn't going to return to make his milpa. I know that he will live there [far away] always, to work with a profession." Ironically, even as internados trained pupils to be rural leaders, they curbed children's exposure to village life and agricultural production techniques used in the village. The boys and girls who attended internados located far from home spent only two months of the year in residence in Kuchmil. Their absence prevented them from learning or practicing the skills necessary to effectively run and support an agrarian household: to plant and harvest corn; to prepare the *nixtamal* (tortilla dough) and make tortillas; to cook; to develop the endurance to pull and carry water from the wells; to learn the names and use of healing herbs and plants; to hunt; and to perform rituals, such as the *čáah-čáak* (rain ceremony), to the necessary gods. Instead, they were taught to speak Spanish fluently; to read and write; to design and construct engineering and art projects; to plant fruits and vegetables not grown at home; and to develop their leadership, teaching, and oratory skills. These students became accustomed to life in busy commercial towns or cities and were trained to be small commercial farmers or for a vocation in such a setting. Their parents also expected them to migrate to a city where they could use their skills and education and earn an income. Both students and parents pointed out that Kuchmil youths could not find a job for which they were trained in Kuchmil because its size and isolation inhibited the growth of industry and commerce. If they wished to use their education and help their parents financially, they had to migrate.

Although boarding schools were subsidized by the state, few families dependent on subsistence farming could afford to pay the additional expenses incurred by a boarding school education (e.g., transportation, money for personal expenses, and clothes). Although in some cases, like that of Jesús, rural youths received scholarships to attend internados, these scholarships did not cover all expenses. Jesús's mother explained, "The school supplies, clothes, shoes, and food were given there [in the internado]. He [their son Jesús] hardly asked for money. He worked for his own *gastada* (allowance). We only provided additional school supplies [supplies required but not provided by the school]. We sold pigs, we sold chickens [to pay for these]." Yet, not all students excelled in the required exams. In these cases, parents paid for school expenses from personal funds or requested financial help from a relative. Few families in Kuchmil could afford to continue their children's education without financial and social support from relatives. Extended kin networks provided housing, food, or money for tuition and school supplies. In order for children to continue their education beyond the sixth grade, they had to leave their community. This move entailed paying for housing, meals, transportation, tuition, and school supplies. When Rubén Can Kauil's uncle offered to pay for his education, his father (don Dani's brother) sent Rubén to Valladolid, where he completed elementary and junior high school. Rubén remained in Valladolid until the age of sixteen when he migrated to Cancún in search of work. Not all families took advantage of their kin networks because they could not repay such a debt. Nicolás, don Dani's eldest son, provides such an example. "There wasn't a way for me to keep studying [beyond the secundaria]. We were too poor in those days. What little we had was to maintain us [the household]. Until one day, don Jerónimo Kauil Balam offered to take on the expense so that I could continue, but since he wasn't my father, I didn't accept."

By sending their children to internados, Kuchmil parents sacrificed their children's household labor. When the eldest son was sent away to school, campesino households lost the additional farm labor provided by the eldest and strongest son. The absent child's chores were divided up among the parents or the remaining children, increasing the workload for each individual. For those families who educated more than one child, maintaining a rural household economy was difficult. In addition to the loss of labor, boarding schools extracted emotional costs from Maya families and their children and, in the process, altered local conceptions of childhood.

## Rethinking Childhood

Given that childhood is a social construction and that modern childhood is culturally and historically specific (Stephens 1995), it is not surprising that Maya conceptions of childhood did not align with the pedagogy of boarding schools. The state's modern conceptualization of childhood is based on a Western ideal, in which children's innocence must be protected (Ariès 1962). For the state, boarding schools disciplined Mexico's future workforce and transformed indigenous children into modern Spanish-speaking Mexican citizens. But children also played games and watched movies. Therefore, play, along with discipline, formed an integral part of a boarding school education.

In contrast, in the 1960s, Maya parents did not consider education to be central to a child's development. Given their limited experience with schools, these parents perceived schools to be institutions for Spanish language acquisition and literacy. They considered discipline to be their domain, not the schools', and did not consider play to be an integral part of formal education. Rather, children were allowed to play and were given few responsibilities in their early years. In many ways, this stage corresponds with the contemporary Western concept of childhood as a separate life stage requiring care and nurturance in order to develop the physical, emotional, and social needs of the child (see Ariès 1962). During these years, children were introduced into social and religious life through baptism and the *héec̣-méek'*, the straddle-hip ceremony conducted during the early months of life with the purpose of developing the intellectual, physical, and social capacities of the child. Maya children were given few responsibilities because they were not yet mature and strong enough to handle them. By the age of three, parents typically began to teach their children how to do small chores, but children were not expected to obey parental demands until around age six, at which point they were entrusted with errands. Among certain families who needed the labor, children were expected to participate fully in the household at this early age, which significantly reduced the early years of play.

Although children are recognized as individuals early on, usually after six months of age, they do not become involved in the household decision-making process until they contribute to its upkeep, beginning at ten years of age.[15] As sentient beings with individual personalities, young children were expected to perform acts of *ko'* (mischievousness) and disobedience.[16]

These antics entertained adults. As one family member amusingly noted when a young toddler threw a tantrum on the tile floor of her grandfather's store, "She has a *chan mal genio* (bad temperament)." However, by the age of ten, children are expected to have learned how to properly respond to adult authority and complete their chores but without losing their sense of self. As children mature, their opinions are held in higher esteem within the household. For most students, attending school gave them the opportunity to extend their early childhood years of play and no chores.

Similar to Native Americans whose boarding school experience was traumatic for some and enjoyable for others (Lomawaima 1994), Maya students recalled their internado experiences with mixed feelings. Some children, like Roberto Can Kauil, dreaded the idea of leaving home, while others were anxious to attend school away from home. Alberto emphasized that he was not given a choice. Jesús also claimed that he left because his parents made him attend the internado, but doña Berta recalled, "[Jesús] cried to leave because he liked school. He wanted to go. He wouldn't eat, wouldn't do anything that I told him to do. He was upset all day. That's why we let him go." Only two of the boys left the boarding school in Maxcanú before finishing their first year. Like Native American students who relied on flight to escape a boarding school education (Child 1998), one boy escaped late at night. The other never returned after coming home from Christmas vacation. Sebastián, one of those two boys, explained, "I didn't like to study much." Enrique, who studied at the secundaria near Chetumal, suffered emotionally and physically while away at school.

> I began the secundaria but I went too far away to study it. It was harder because I couldn't come home every week [like before when he studied in Ke'eldzonot]. It was too far which is why I couldn't stick it out. . . . Also the food, they gave so little: two tortillas with a soda, fried beans. One can't stand the hunger pangs. Four months I stayed. . . . I wanted to study, but I couldn't handle it. I returned, began to work in the milpa. I was fifteen years old.

Enrique did not want to experience another year of the financial hardship involved in studying away from home. Unfortunately, Enrique could not study closer to home because his family did not have any social networks in Valladolid and Felipe Carrillo Puerto. To the rigid schedule and to the long separations from their families, these children felt *má' u sùuktali'*

(Yucatec Maya phrase commonly used to describe discomfort and nostalgia created by being away from one's accustomed surroundings).

In contrast, Abel Kauil Tun suggested that attendance "was our choice." Children who attended the albergue in Ke'eldzonot experienced less homesickness because they could go home every weekend due to the school's proximity to Kuchmil. Some students, such as Enrique, were even allowed to go home during the week. "The school was close to my home. There was a path behind my house. At first they told us that those who attend enter on Monday and leave on Friday. But they gave us breakfast [and before the first session of classes began in the morning] we could go home if we liked." However, not all children lived as close as Enrique. In many cases, the children's acquiescence to attend school was spurred by the threat of milpa work and by their parents' desire to relieve them from the harsh physical labor involved in subsistence agriculture. According to Abel, "During that time, it was said by parents, 'You don't want to go to school? Then grab your machete and head out to the milpa.' I'd rather go to school than go to the milpa. I never liked it because it was extremely hard. We worked hard. It's better to say 'school' because I know that I won't be working in the campo." Similarly, Gustavo Kauil Tun stressed the difficulty of making milpa.

> I don't like working in the campo. . . . It's far more difficult. You spend the entire day in the sun, you have to carry water with you, you have to carry your food with you . . . and you have to walk through the forest. . . . It's *matado* [loosely translated: wears you out], they say, because you cannot not work in order to have something.

During the early years of settlement, even the girls were sent to work in the milpa. "We worked like men," complained Carla Be' Can, who eagerly accepted work as a domestic servant for a local schoolteacher in order to avoid being "treated like a man."

Kuchmil parents described their children's departures with a sense of pragmatism rooted in the local conception of childhood. When I asked doña Andrea if she had had any qualms about sending her young daughter to boarding school, she explained, "She wasn't little, she was ten years old, she washed her own clothes." Being capable of washing clothes, an arduous task, demonstrated to doña Andrea that her daughter was not only responsible but also mature enough to live away from home. Visiting the

*A young boy carries wood with a tumpline.*

casa escuela also alleviated parents' fears, as is evident by doña Andrea's remarks. "We couldn't afford her books which is why we sent her to Maxcanú. I never cried for her because the girl was fine where she studied. I saw it [the school]. There was a bed, there was a hammock." Doña Berta also spoke pragmatically about her son's departure, but she recalled the pain of letting him go as well. "When one thinks of him not returning to live with us . . . When I would sleep every night, *lo estoy soñando* [I would dream of him]." In Maya culture, dreaming about someone is associated with nostalgia, yearning, and grief. According to Allan Burns (1983), dreams also serve as a way to communicate these feelings to others. Doña Berta's melancholy was exacerbated by her fears of what might happen to Jesús in a city that "is full of bad men."

Once at school, the majority of the children truly enjoyed their boarding school experience because of the respite from work and the opportunity to partake in activities difficult to come by in their isolated community (see Child 1998).[17] The boys recalled meeting boys from *todos lados* (all over). Abel, who attended the internado in Ke'eldzonot, pointed out the attractive proposition the schools presented for poor rural schoolboys. "We liked [the internados] because of the scholarship. Since we lived close to home, we didn't spend the money, except on soda pop. They gave you three meals per day." With a wide smile and a far-off look, Celia reminisced over the activities she enjoyed in the internado in Maxcanú.

> I really liked it. There we ate. They gave us everything. . . . We had physical education, carpentry, sewing, and even dance classes. Saturdays and Sundays they showed movies in one of the classrooms, of the old kind like *Cinderella.* Vendors would sell cookies. Every fifteen days they gave us an allowance, fifteen pesos. . . . I liked it. Sometimes you think about your mother and your father, like during the time of the new corn [in the month of October].

After the casa escuela shut down in Maxcanú, Celia returned to Kuchmil to complete the sixth grade. "I didn't like it [the single schoolhouse in Kuchmil] because I wasn't used to being there." As Maya parents became more exposed to rural education through the presence of bilingual teachers and as education became more accessible, school attendance increasingly became part of the stages of growth for children and adolescents.

## Investing in an Education

The cost of educating more than one child through boarding schools, even with scholarship support, and especially beyond sixth grade, was prohibitive for rural families. By the mid-1980s, migrant remittances helped defray some of these costs, but only a quarter of Kuchmil households received remittances. Consequently, the community petitioned the government to build a federally subsidized secundaria nearby. This pressure—along with local population growth and the government's increasing interest in developing the southeastern region's infrastructure to facilitate the exploitation of its coasts, hardwoods, and archaeological sites—increased the construction of schools in southeastern Yucatán. In 1986, the government built a secundaria in the neighboring town of Ke'eldzonot. A decade later, a COBAY was established in Ke'eldzonot. These schools, in conjunction with migrant remittances, improved the educational opportunities of boys and girls in Kuchmil.

The proximity of the secundaria allowed the youths of Kuchmil to study near home. Since the secundaria was located a few kilometers outside of town, students walked or rode their bicycles daily. The construction of a gravel road through Kuchmil was conducive to cycling, which decreased the time traveled between Kuchmil and Ke'eldzonot. In 1991, during my first trip to Kuchmil, every household owned at least one bicycle, which adolescent boys maintained and repaired with extreme care.[18] The secundaria's split-day schedule also made it possible for children to continue to help their parents with farm work. The morning session excused students at one o'clock and the afternoon classes began at two. The students from Kuchmil enrolled in the morning session in order to dedicate their afternoons to household chores.

The construction of the secundaria in Ke'eldzonot, however, did not guarantee the attendance of both sexes. In spite of the secundaria's proximity, its location at the far side of town was not ideal. Parents feared their daughters would be harassed on their way to school by drunks from Ke'eldzonot. These fears were not unfounded. During my visits to Ke'eldzonot, it was common to encounter inebriated men wandering around town and along the road leading to town, even in the early morning hours. In 1989, after a cluster of girls graduated from the sixth grade, their families relented and allowed them to attend the secundaria because they thought there would be safety in numbers. To decrease the risks associated with walking to school, however, many families gave their daughters bicycles. By 1992, ten

*A young girl rides her new bike.*

of the twenty-two girls living in Kuchmil were enrolled in the secundaria.[19] Of those remaining, three attended elementary school, while nine dropped out after completing the sixth grade.

As more young women attend secundaria, gender differences in schooling attendance have decreased. By 2001, of the twenty-six students who graduated from the local secundaria, six were female. Today all children commute via bicycle to attend school in Ke'eldzonot. By the time the COBAY was established in Ke'eldzonot in 1997, girls were just as likely as boys to enroll. Its first cohort included thirty-five students. Of this cohort, only one student, Selena Kauil May, came from Kuchmil. Selena was the youngest sister of two of the girls (Celia and Laura) who attended the internados. Selena was the first Kuchmil graduate of the COBAY. After graduation, she studied business administration at the university in Valladolid.[20] Selena's presence at the COBAY and the university attests to the shift in gender relations experienced in Kuchmil within the past decade. In 2001, one of the three students who completed the bachillerato was female, as were three of the six students studying at the university.

These changes in gender relations did not happen over night but were the result of an ongoing negotiation between students and their parents. Ramona May Pat's experience illustrates this negotiation process. Raised by don Jorge and doña Berta to believe that education should be available to both boys and girls, Ramona was surprised to encounter her father's resistance to her interest in obtaining a vocational degree. Her mother related the story to me.

> He didn't want her to go away to school. . . . When she went to request applications for the adult education program in the *palacio* of Zací, she went to investigate [the school]. Immediately she registered. I didn't know. After she came home, she told me, "I am going to study." She wanted to study accounting. She says, "Mamá, if you don't let me go away to study, we are never going to get ahead. What if you get sick [doña Berta suffers from diabetes] and Papá doesn't have any money. If I go away to study, I will have money to take you to the doctor. If you won't let me study, we are both going to cry a lot because we don't have anything." I told her, "If you take care of yourself [to not get pregnant], if you want to study, well it's all right. We'll see how we are going to see about it [pay for it]." And that's why I began to sell huipiles in Cancún so that we would

have something with which to help her. That career is costly, the texts. . . . He [don Jorge] was upset after she registered. . . . Even if he was a bit upset, he calmed down.

In this case, Ramona took the initiative without consulting her parents. Once her mother realized the extent of her interest and commitment, she agreed to support her daughter financially. To earn a scholarship to help pay for her studies, Ramona, like her brother Jesús, signed up for one year of teaching service with CONAFE. Ramona's decisions had repercussions for her younger sister. Doña Berta made it clear to Nora, her youngest daughter, that she would have the same opportunity as Ramona.

With the construction of a secundaria and COBAY, Kuchmil youth no longer need to leave their homes to continue their postsecondary education. However, for those students who seek a university degree, few options exist. Most students enroll in CONAFE to pay for these studies. But this scholarship only pays for three years of university work and does not cover all of the costs associated with a university degree. Therefore, these students spend their summers working in Cancún to supplement their scholarship or rely on the financial support of their siblings in Cancún. Based on their experiences in low-entry service jobs, these migrants eagerly supported their younger siblings' endeavors to earn a university or vocational degree.

## Learning to Labor

When Cancún was first established in 1974, a labor shortage made jobs plentiful, regardless of one's educational background. However, as Cancún has evolved from a small fishing village to a prime international tourist destination with a population of over half a million people, this labor shortage was transformed into a labor surplus. In response, the hotel industry began to carefully screen their employees, preferring educated applicants to applicants with only a few years of schooling, particularly for positions that offered an opportunity for social mobility. Hotels soon required applicants to submit proof of their educational background, such as a copy of their diploma or a letter confirming attendance from the school principal. Migrants informed their younger brothers, sisters, and cousins of the shifting employment trends in Cancún's service industry. They counseled them to complete the secundaria and helped finance this endeavor.

Additionally, Kuchmil migrants prepared their siblings and cousins for the job market by inviting them to experience urban life and wage work prior to graduation. As a result, youths as young as eleven years of age spent their summer vacations in Cancún. Their siblings and relatives took them shopping and on family outings to the beach, movies, and dances. But a significant part of the migration experience involves becoming accustomed to proletarian schedules and an urban spatial habitus (Rouse 1995). This vacation also served as a time to expose these youths to the alienating aspects of city life. Kuchmil youths learned to maneuver the city's downtown, Zona Hotelera, and regiones via foot and public and private transportation systems. Family, friends, and neighbors shared crime stories that prepared them for possible situations of aggression and violence. They explained how the job market worked. By the time these young people graduated from high school, Cancún had become a familiar place.

Work also formed an integral part of this summer experience. Maya youths spent their summers working to earn money to pay for school supplies for the upcoming school year. Young boys worked for older relatives or neighbors in commercial settings. One young boy helped his brother in his store, while another worked as an apprentice to his uncle in the construction industry. Jesús May Pat invited Tómas to spend his school holidays helping him in his corner grocery store. After completing his studies, Tómas was unable to procure a teaching post. While he waited for an opening, he worked full-time in Jesús's store. In contrast, young girls were employed as part-time domestic servants for a neighboring family. Minerva Can Uc's experience is representative of this experience. Minerva spent her summer washing other people's laundry and adapting to urban life in Cancún. She allocated her wages toward school supplies and a bicycle to transport her to school. Based on these visits, Minerva decided that she liked living in Cancún and could tolerate the workload and claustrophobic living quarters. Thus these preliminary visits allowed youths to earn a wage prior to graduation, to become accustomed to urban life, and to explore where they wanted to work and live.

## The Obligation to Give in a Changing Economy

As children spent more time at school and outside of Kuchmil, their productive roles in the household decreased. But their family's expectations of these youths' participation in the households' maintenance did not disappear. Maya parents who oriented their children's future toward full-time wage labor expected to receive a portion of these wages. This obligation to give is not something new, but is rooted in reciprocal relations among rural Maya households.

The nuclear family serves as the primary unit of social organization for Maya society. Robert Redfield (1941, 1950) and Mary Elmendorf (1976) have documented that rural Maya households were organized around a gendered division of labor and there were clear ideas about how gender roles were performed.[21] This was typical of rural communities in the Mexican countryside (D'Aubeterre Buznego 2000; Mummert 1994). In spite of the changes incurred by migration, the rural household continued to emphasize this division of labor. Men worked in the cornfields, while women took care of domestic chores and kitchen gardens. Children worked to support the household. The economic independence of nuclear households continued to be stressed, even though the ejido community, migrant remittances, and extended kin networks played a critical role in sustaining nuclear households during times of economic hardship.

However, Kuchmil's gendered division of labor entailed more than a distinction of gender roles. This division formed part of the stages of the life course (Tuirán 1996).[22] Lynn Morgan suggests that "the process through which young lives come to be valued is derived in part from these factors [e.g., women's status, social stratification, etc.], but personhood is also a function of cultural divisions of the life cycle . . . and social systems of achievement" (1992, 24). Indeed, Maya children were taught at an early age about the activities essential to becoming full, mature persons who are socially valued. I suggest that adolescent boys and girls performed personhood through this gendered division of labor. As Judith Butler's work (1990), among others, suggests, gender is not an essence or a fact but a cultural construction that is made possible through a set of stylized acts of repetition that constitute a performance of gender. By learning to repeat the activities of the gendered division of labor, boys and girls learned to perform gender in a particular way. These gendered practices formed the foundation of Maya personhood. Children were taught that becoming full persons in their community entailed learning how to perform these activities and stages of the life course.

Consequently, adolescence came with responsibilities. I define "adolescence" as the period in which children, both boys and girls, are taught the activities and counseled in the behaviors necessary for marriage, the next step in the life course. During the initial stages of fieldwork, I considered adolescence to begin with menstruation and end with marriage. But after more time in the field, I revised these markers to reflect children's actual responsibilities.[23] The age at which children bear partial responsibility for the household's maintenance has become my new marker for the beginning of adolescence. From the age of ten, sometimes earlier, girls were taught how to efficiently pull water from the well, wash clothes, make the nixtamal, and care for younger siblings. Likewise, boys were taught the medicinal properties of forest plants, to weed the milpa, to collect firewood, and to care for animals. Given these practices, I mark adolescence as beginning around the age of ten—from the moment young boys and girls begin to take on the responsibilities and activities that prepare them for marriage and the effective management of a rural household—and ending with marriage (see Kramer 2005).

Upon marrying, adolescents became "persons" but did not achieve full personhood, which requires the possession of knowledge acquired by participating in other stages of the life course (e.g., parenthood, ritual coparenthood, positions of authority, etc.) that entail their own sets of activities. After parents began investing in their children's education, many children could no longer perform personhood through the gendered division of labor because they were absent from their communities. Once they became full-time wage laborers, they relied on mass-produced goods instead of rural activities with which to perform personhood. Therefore, adolescent boys and girls who migrated to Cancún or attended boarding school remained under the authority of their parents, regardless of the distance between the village and the city in which they lived, and continued to remain so until they married. Heedless of their age, migrants who postponed marriage due to their social and financial obligations to their immediate household continued to defer to their parents' counsel. Not surprisingly, the rise in youth migration has resulted in an expansion of the adolescent stage in the life course in Kuchmil.

Maya parents expect their unmarried children (male and female), even the ones who were sent to study a profession far from home, to contribute economically to the household. On average, unmarried migrants give one-fourth to one-third of their salaries to their families in Kuchmil.[24] Berenice May Can's work experiences illustrate this practice. When Berenice was sixteen years old, she began working in a textile factory in Valladolid that subcontracted to a clothing company from the United States. Berenice earned between $30 and $40 per week, depending on product demand by the U.S. company. Each week, she gave one-third of her salary to her mother to cover household expenses. Unmarried migrants working in Cancún remitted more money than those working in Valladolid, an average of $50 per month every few months. Doña Berta explained the importance of these remittances. "[Jesús] helps us. It's not a lot but he gives us 300 pesos when I go there [to Cancún]. The same with my other children [who live in Cancún]." Of her three children, only Ramona was married at the time.

In contrast, married children may continue to contribute to their parents' household, but they are not obligated to give because their primary responsibility is to take care of their own nuclear family. At an average of $20 every few months, married migrants' remittances were significantly less than those provided by their unmarried siblings. Horacio May Kauil explained why married children contributed less than unmarried migrants. "I rarely give [money to my family] because I have a small child and we spend too much. . . . Now that we are married we have responsibilities." He pointed out that his younger brother was in a better economic position to bear this responsibility. "Right now . . . the one I think should help [my parents] more is my younger brother because he is single." Horacio's older brother, Reynaldo, further explained the relay nature of this obligation:

> Yes, because when I wasn't married, I gave constantly. Since I married, this responsibility fell into my younger brother's hands. Now [that he is married], it is now my youngest brother's [responsibility]. We still send [help], but not like before . . . [Once my youngest brother marries], well, between all of us, we will have to put together [money] to send home. We have already discussed it.

Notwithstanding these contributions, Maya youths keep a substantial portion, about two-thirds, of their income, to cover their own expenses, a practice promoted and supported by their parents.[25] For example, while Berenice contributed a third of her salary to her parents, she spent the remaining wages on her own *gustos* (tastes). She bought clothing and shoes, spent it on entertainment, and contributed to her younger sister's school expenses. Parents did not interfere with how their children spent their money because they recognized that the transformation from adolescence to adulthood generates costs. "Young people," stated doña Jimena

Can Kauil (Berenice's mother), "work all day in the factory. She gives me enough to help me out. What's left over, she keeps. She has expenses, too." As children enter adolescence, this maturity comes with expenses. Young women need clothes and makeup to mark their transition into adulthood and to attract a suitable suitor. In the past, these expenses were paid by the girls' parents or by the boys' family, but the practice of providing gift contributions prior to an engagement has declined with time, and parents do not have the money to purchase the ready-to-wear clothing that has replaced homemade clothes and the traditional huipil. Among Maya families, then, recognition of children's individuality reinforces children's rights to wages earned through their own labor, money they can spend as they wish (see Gaskins 2003). At the same time, Kuchmil's communal ethos assures that children contribute a portion of their earnings to their household and, in specific instances, that they provide the household with access to their entire income.

## Living Contradictions

If we consider class to be a "learned position," not static, one that children are exposed to as they go through life (Steedman 1997, 13), then it is important to clarify the class transformations experienced by Kuchmil migrants. Richard Scase considers class to be a "structuring of *control* relations" (1992, 15), which means that how much control one has over one's labor determines one's class position. Yet, control of one's labor does not automatically translate into social and economic capital and social mobility, particularly for subsistence farmers. Kuchmil farmers control their labor, but since they do not have control over the markets that price their goods, it is difficult for them to accumulate social and economic capital within the systems of power in which they are situated. Class status is marked not just by control of labor power but also by one's position within a broader system of structural relations.

For Kuchmil farmers, wage work offers a tempting proposition because it gives workers access to a steady income, which can be used to generate and accumulate social and economic capital. Kuchmil families consider wage work a vehicle for social mobility, in which social mobility is conceptualized as the ability to move from a position of powerlessness and poverty (the position in which many Maya find themselves) to one of being an educated and knowledgeable person with financial stability. Yet,

Kuchmil migrants who worked in service positions realized that this work was not all they and their parents had dreamed about. As short-term contract employees, they lacked job security. Entry-level positions as busboys, stewards, and assistant bartenders did not provide a living wage. These jobs failed to provide the freedom and respect they were seeking. To illustrate the work experience and social mobility of migrant workers, I narrate Jesús May Pat's experiences after he moved to Cancún.

After obtaining certification as an electrician in the late 1980s, Jesús's job search led him to Cancún. His friends and neighbors informed him that this city offered the best employment opportunities and the highest wages in the peninsula. Jesús was fortunate that his aunt and uncle, who were his hosts while he studied in Carrillo Puerto, also owned a home in Cancún. They offered to house him during his job search. As a skilled laborer, Jesús quickly found work in the maintenance department of an international hotel. A model worker, Jesús steadily moved up the labor hierarchy within the hotel industry.

Yet, even as Jesús acquired new titles, moving from an "electrician's assistant" to "maintenance supervisor," increasing his wages accordingly, he still struggled to earn the respect of the managerial staff, and eventually hit the wage ceiling for his trade.[26] Jesús describes this growing disenchantment by relating his experiences working as maintenance supervisor in a chain of five-star hotels.

Well, I was sent over there [to another hotel] and I knew that it wouldn't be worth my while. He [the boss] didn't pay attention to me; he put me in charge of the rooms and then would disappear. . . . And since there were a ton of problems, [the job] was no longer the same. His support wasn't the same. Even though the rest [of the employees] sat down, he didn't say anything to them. And I observed and said no. I went directly to [the person in charge of] maintenance [for the entire hotel] and told him, "Here you have my radio. Here you have everything. I am leaving." I turned in everything and about two days later, I began working as a bellboy at the Horizon.

In other words, his occupational mobility did not translate into a shift in class status, from a subordinate position to a position of confianza in which employees have more control of their labor and are treated with respect (see Sennett and Cobb 1972).

Jesús's occupational shift from an electrician, which requires a bachillerato and certification, to a bellboy, which requires at most completion of the secundaria, may appear to be a case of downward social and economic mobility. As a bellboy, however, Jesús increased his wages via his monthly tips, which exceeded his wages as an electrician. More important, he had more control of his wages because he could augment his salary with what he earned in tips. By acquiring a job that required public demonstrations of congeniality, respect, and a willingness to help, Jesús felt that his ability to offer these qualities in abundance earned him more respect and esteem from his colleagues, the administration, and the tourists.[27] It is these qualities, after all, that garner an employee big tips. By making his labor visible to the clients of the tourist industry, Jesús reaped more rewards than through his previous highly skilled but "invisible" position.

Jesús was able to make the transition from electrician to bellboy because he spoke fluent English, the lingua franca of the leisure industry in Mexico. In Cancún's tourist industry, fluency in English is a requirement for most professional and upper-level service positions. To work as a waiter, bellboy, and bartender, positions that depend on customer-client interaction, hotels require up to 80 percent English fluency.[28] Recognizing the importance and necessity of this language in the service industry, and that his mobility within the hotel industry depended on his language skills, Jesús studied English at a language school for three years. When I asked Jesús why he studied English, he responded, "Well, practically speaking, you could remain [in your job], but if you want to improve yourself, you have to look for other options." Jesús spent ten years working as an electrician before he switched careers. In the meantime, he prepared himself for this transition by learning English, talking to other service employees about their employment experiences, and experiencing the corporate culture of different hotel chains. Like his parents, who associated education with class mobility, Jesús identified the study of the English language as his ticket to a higher salary.

Although his parents' investment in his education helped Jesús acquire a skilled job, these skills and background failed to significantly improve Jesús's class status. In spite of his skills and his position as a supervisor, Jesús worked in a blue-collar job with minimal job security. Electricians earned a maximum salary of $500 a month, excluding the food and transportation subsidies provided to hotel employees. Jesús reached this ceiling a few years before he became a bellboy. Job stability did not come with the bellboy position, but as Jesús explained, "There is more money than where I was [as an electrician], the wages are higher. . . . That is enough." But Jesús acknowledged that earning high wages was not enough because he lacked the power to influence his work environment. As a bellboy, although he earned more, Jesús encountered similar power struggles between the management and the staff, and between tourists and service employees, and now he was more dependent on fostering smoother working relations than in his previous career because bellboys were easily replaced.

As a result of his disillusionment, Jesús and a partner prepared a business plan. A few months into his new job, Jesús and his partner opened up a corner grocery store in a developing región. What began as a few cartons of Coke turned into a thriving business within a few months. Jesús quit working for others to work full-time for himself. Although he continues earning much of his income as a bellboy, this employment is seasonal. The rest of his time is spent as a small-business owner, a position that allows Jesús to control his labor and to be treated respectfully by his employees and neighbors. In many ways, this position is similar to that of his parents who as subsistence farmers control their time and are respected by their neighbors, with the exception that Jesús does not perform manual labor and earns a profit from his business.

## Slavery versus Freedom

Although the majority of the youths chose to migrate to Cancún after graduation, not all migrants remained in Cancún. A few chose to remain in or return to Kuchmil because they preferred life in the countryside. Ignacio Be' Can was one of these return migrants. Ignacio spent a few months working as a cook in Cancún. By living with his elder sister, he saved money and enjoyed the benefits of family ties in a new city. The ten-hour day schedules, frequently punctuated by double shifts, physically wore him out, while the everyday threat of violence as he walked home at night psychologically frustrated him. After he was injured on the job—he burned himself while cooking—and was never compensated by his employers for his medical bills and lost wages, Ignacio claimed that life in Cancún was like living in the epoch of slavery, during which Maya workers were forced to work in peonage on haciendas. Like these hacienda workers, service workers worked long hours, did not control their work schedule, were sleep deprived from working double shifts, were paid meager wages, were given very little time off, and in some instances worked under hazardous conditions. In places like Cancún where everything must be purchased, workers are obligated to work in order to live. For Ignacio, these constraints on his time, his body, and his sense of freedom were similar to those experienced by his ancestors. In contrast to the urban city and wage work, Ignacio considered village life and milpa work to represent libertad—freedom from the yolk of wage work—because the energy and hours spent in the milpa were not regulated by an employer. Ignacio concluded that he was willing to sacrifice a wage to keep his soul.

Ironically, while young men linked urban life to slavery, girls and young women associated it with libertad. In Kuchmil, like in many places in Mexico, adolescent females and young women must be chaperoned in public spaces.[29] Girls constantly regulated their behavior, dress, language, and sexuality to protect their reputations as *mujeres decentes* (morally upstanding women) (Castellanos 2007). While these regulatory practices persisted in Cancún, the daily realities of urban living made them more difficult to enforce (see Greene 2001b). Invited by older siblings and relatives to work, study, or visit Cancún, Kuchmil girls discovered that their chaperones' role was constricted by rigid work schedules and childcare duties. After the initial tour of Cancún in the presence of family, the girls learned to navigate the regiones, commercial centers, and beaches of Cancún on their own or with friends. They learned to overcome their fear of the city as they traveled on several different bus lines to get from home to work. This freedom, in combination with wages and the anonymity made possible by urban sprawl, transformed Cancún into an attractive living space for girls and young women.

Although some migrants returned to Kuchmil because they disliked urban life and yearned for the libertad of rural life, others returned to care for their parents or to provide them with companionship. These returns were gendered. For example, migrant men typically returned to Kuchmil to attend to an ailing parent. However, returns motivated by health crises were rarely permanent. These men spent a few days to a few weeks with their parents before returning to Cancún. In contrast, migrant women returned to Kuchmil to provide their mothers with companionship, returns that spanned months to years. I call this type of migration "stand-in migration" because it is based on a system of rotating presence and affection (Castellanos 2009a). To provide their mother with a constant companion and to help with domestic work, sisters took turns migrating. Mariela

Can Tun's experiences illustrate this process of caretaking and emotional support. Mariela spent several years working as a domestic servant in Tízimin, while her younger sister Jovana fulfilled the role of companion and domestic assistant to her ailing mother. As soon as Jovana married, Mariela returned home to take over these responsibilities. After a few years, her youngest sister was mature enough to take over for Mariela, which allowed Mariela to go back to work in the city. These return migrations demonstrate that in spite of the household's dependence on cash, not all Maya youths were expected to leave Kuchmil.

## Adolescent Migration in a Global Era

As Mexico's rural population continues to flock to urban areas, poverty rates in cities increase correspondingly (Bartell 2001). Although more than 50 percent of working children in Mexico are concentrated in rural areas, particularly in export agriculture (Cos-Montiel 2001), a significant number of children and juveniles work in the informal sector in urban areas, a sector characterized by a lack of job security, health insurance, regulated working conditions, and a living wage. As a result, we cannot ignore the plight of working children in Latin America. Doing so, Ernest Bartell (2001) suggests, will produce a generation of exploited individuals who lack knowledge of their rights and of alternative models for economic development in a global economy.

The case of Kuchmil demonstrates how modernization projects and a global economy transform social constructions of childhood. Prior to the declining prices for agricultural products, rural communities were somewhat self-sufficient (Collier 1994/1999; Warman 1976). Maya children were valued for the warmth and joy they brought as infants, and the work they performed during adolescence. However, campesinos' increasing dependence on global markets, along with expanded telecommunications and transportation networks, shifted children's roles in the countryside. Children accrued another role: that of potential wageworker. To accomplish this transformation, Maya children were enrolled in boarding schools, postponing their work contributions to the household. By becoming wageworkers during their adolescent years, Kuchmil's youths experience an early departure from their nurturing households and become important economic contributors to their natal families, earning an important decision-making role in the household. Yet, these shifts in the social construction of childhood are not all beneficial. Jason Pribilsky demonstrates that in Ecuador "young children who increasingly find themselves socialized outside the household lack the same opportunities of reciprocity that children once enjoyed with their parents," resulting in the affliction of *nervios* (anxiety attacks) in children, a physiological way for them to deal with this role shift (2001, 268). Children in Kuchmil were not afflicted by nervios, but migration is transforming the productive role of childhood into an increasingly unproductive one, particularly for Kuchmil families in Cancún, while at the same time postponing this productivity for later years, which increases household dependence on older children and forces them to postpone marriage to fulfill this obligation.

Even as Maya families consider education to be one solution to their marginalization within a market-driven economy, the experiences of their educated sons and daughters demonstrate the limitations of this approach. On the one hand, the education their children receive is not sufficient to meet the demands of a technologically oriented and increasingly English-dominated economy. On the other hand, the abundance of jobs made available as a result of NAFTA and free-market economics are low-skilled, low-wage jobs that lack job security, as is evidenced by Jesús's experiences in Cancún's labor market. Kuchmil parents fail to recognize that providing their children with an education will not immediately translate into job security, a living wage, and middle-class status. Regardless of their educational background, whether they earned vocational degrees or not, Kuchmil migrants must enter the labor market at the bottom of the labor hierarchy. They work long hours cleaning floors and tables, making beds, washing dishes, and picking up garbage without job security or an effective and truly representative labor union. Maya migrants who considered these working conditions to be degrading preferred working their own milpa. The lack of alternatives and the declining productivity rates and market value of milpa cultivation force the majority of Kuchmil migrants to ignore the downward mobility of the urban labor market in an effort to work diligently toward improving their future prospects. In the following chapters, I examine the experiences of migrants who remained in Cancún and their endeavors to provide cash and goods to their natal families and to acquire a stable economic position for themselves.

# 4

## Civilizing Bodies: Learning to Labor in Cancún

On an intensely humid and sunny afternoon in August 2001, I followed César Can Poot (don Dani's nephew) along a dusty unpaved road. At my request, César showed me the way to Reynaldo May Kauil's house, all the while indicating physical markers that I could later use as guideposts. César's work schedule for this month prohibited us from taking our *šíimbʼal* (walk) during a cooler time of day.[1] He worked nights as a bartender in a five-star hotel in Cancún, which meant that he spent the morning hours catching up on his sleep. I found César still sleeping when I knocked on his door that afternoon. Although working nights left him exhausted, this schedule did allow him to spend his afternoons visiting friends and family, and to serve as my guide to his neighborhood. Reynaldo lived four blocks south of César's home. The proximity of their homes made it easy for them to get together on a frequent basis.

During our walk, we passed undistinguishable concrete-block and wood houses. As we walked, the heat blurred the surroundings, transforming the thick wall of tropical jungle visible at the end of the sandy road into an oasis, a mirage. Without the shelter of the dense tangle of trees and bush that previously covered this area, the wind blew away the red clay earth, leaving in its place white sand that coated shoes and the interior of homes with a fine layer of dust. The fruit trees and potted plants decorating homes provided the only shade from the sun's unforgiving rays. As we neared the jungle wall that marked the beginning of ejido lands and the city's limits, César pointed to a tree that would later serve as my beacon for Reynaldo's house. "There it is, the banana tree." Contrary to the image I had in mind of a tall tree with wide waxy green leaves and a thick smooth trunk leaning slightly from the weight of its fruit, like banana trees in Kuchmil, this tree, no taller than four feet, had wilted yellow-green leaves and lacked fruit. I took one look at it and realized that I would never have found Reynaldo without help.

Reynaldo, unfortunately, was not home. He had left for work shortly before we arrived and would not be home until 11:00 p.m., or if he worked a double shift, the early hours of the morning. Work schedules in the hotel industry change every month and usually entail overtime, making it difficult to predict when a service worker will get home. Since Reynaldo had switched shifts just a few days ago, there had not been enough time to inform César of his new work schedule. Long and conflicting work schedules made it difficult for Kuchmil migrants to spend time with each other. Rest days, assigned randomly, rarely overlapped among family members. Visits were also constrained by the long distances between migrants' residences. The low vacancy rate in Cancún's housing market forced migrants to rent rooms according to availability, even if that meant living an hour away from siblings and social networks.

The concrete jungle that makes up Cancún, with its constant movement of people and goods, contrasts sharply with village life in Kuchmil. Living in Cancún requires rural residents to acquire an alternative sense of time and space, and a new rhythm of work and social life (as would happen to urban residents if they moved to the countryside) (see Ong 1987; Rouse 1992; Thompson 1967). In the country, people's lives are rooted in a dense textured weave of social relations, but fluid and ephemeral social relations characterize life in Cancún.[2] The haphazard and unregulated infrastructure of this city, in conjunction with the proletarianization experienced in the service industry, reinforced Kuchmil migrants' feelings of loneliness, isolation, and fear, particularly among recent arrivals. The previous chapter discussed the difficulties migrants faced in the transition from village to urban life. This chapter focuses on migrants' experiences as workers in Cancún in order to capture the cultural and class transformations that occur with settlement (see Rouse 1992).[3] In so doing, I examine how rural indigenous people are transformed into modern citizens and urban workers and how they engage with the ideological struggles generated by experiencing work and life within export-processing zones dominated by the production of services.

## Free Trade, Tourism, and Capitalist Discipline

In an effort to attract foreign investment, impoverished countries created free-trade zones (FTZs). FTZs offer incentives, in the form of subsidies and reduced regulations and tariffs, to attract transnational corporations.

The growth of FTZs demonstrates the increasing reliance of poor countries on the support of wealthy industrialized nations for this form of "development." FTZs have contributed to the feminization of the labor force within poor countries, to the transference of industrial production from industrialized countries to underdeveloped countries, and to increased capitalist discipline on the shop floor in order to comply with post-Fordist, just-in-time production systems.[4] These changes, which are felt differently depending on one's position within this new global order, result in the realignment of power relations within families, nations, and global political systems (see Tiano 1994).

Studies of free-trade zones primarily focus on export-processing zones dedicated to assembly of textiles and electronics where goods are manufactured on a piece-rate basis, then assembled en masse for export (Collins 2003; Fernández-Kelly 1983; Klein 2002; Lugo 1990; Mills 1999; Ngai 2005; Ong 1987; Salzinger 2003; Wolf 1992). More recently, the global assembly line has expanded to include the export of information via data call centers (Freeman 2000). In Mexico, as in many other countries, free-trade zones are also made up of tourist sites (Clancy 2001). In the late 1960s and early 1970s, the Mexican government established free-trade zones for assembly work and tourism in its northern and southern states. In 1973, the state of Quintana Roo, where Cancún is located, was designated a free-trade zone. Therefore I situate Cancún within the literature on FTZs to show that workers in the tourism industry experience many of the same problems faced by women and men working in export-processing zones dedicated to assembly work and informatics.

Like the maquiladora industry, the tourist industry is dominated by a handful of Western multinational corporations. Scholar Harvey Perkins suggests that in 1986 thirteen corporations (six of which are U.S. owned) controlled the world's tourism industry (cited in Madeley 1992, 79). In 1989, the Mexican government, which had retained tight control of this industry, relaxed its laws to permit foreign companies to invest in the Mexican tourist industry without the previously mandated Mexican investment partners. By 1997, although the majority of Cancún's hotels continued to be run and owned by Mexican investors, at least one-half of luxury (Gran Turismo) and five-star hotels were regulated by foreign franchise agreements (Torres and Momsen 2005a). National ownership, however, does not preclude the presence of international capital; transnational Mexican corporations controlled the majority of hotels in Cancún, as well as many of the hotel chains throughout Latin America (Clancy 1999; Wilson 2008). Thus the logic of neoliberalism was imposed on Cancún long before NAFTA.

Studies of export-processing zones suggest that just-in-time production strategies of assembly plants require new ways of disciplining workers. Here I rely on Aihwa Ong's definition of "discipline" as "the effect of the exercise of power in the interests of capitalist production" in which "social control can be traced through a variety of cultural forms which enforce compliance and order within and outside economic enterprises" (1987, xiii–xiv). The flexibility required by just-in-time production involves disciplining natives to accept low-wage jobs that offer few benefits, lack job security, limit their physical mobility, and attempt to control their sexuality (Nash and Fernández-Kelly 1983). Donald Lowe points out that these "new production practices consist of varying, differential combinations of structural, discursive, systematic, and semiotic components" (1995, 17). The production of new workers requires a new set of practices within and outside the workplace. This holistic approach aims to produce not only good workers, but also good citizens and consumers (Freeman 2000; Rouse 1992).

Of course, these disciplinary practices target gendered and racialized bodies. As in the maquiladora industry, gender-differentiated labor forms a critical component of the tourist industry. Women occupy the lowest-paid positions within the labor hierarchy (e.g., as domestic servants, laundresses, and chambermaids), while men hold positions with access to social and economic mobility, albeit limited (e.g., as janitors, dishwashers, stewards, assistant bartenders, and construction workers, but with experience a steward can become a head waiter and a dishwasher can become a head chef, etc.). Although women are just as involved as men in hotel and restaurant work in Mexico's major tourist centers, women continue to be relegated to positions with the least public interaction (Wilson 2008). As Leslie Salzinger points out for the maquiladora industry, the ideal female worker continues to serve as a trope by which "workers, potential and actual, are addressed and understood, and around which production is itself designed" (2003, 15). Within the tourist industry, the submissive, exotic, racialized body—which is feminized by virtue of the work being performed, regardless of the fact that both men and women are employed within this industry—serves as the universal trope by which production is organized and worker subjectivities are constituted. In the context of Cancún, the Maya worker represents this ideal body.

Due to its emphasis on care work, hotel work was feminized and racialized (Adler and Adler 2004; Sherman 2005, 2007). Hotel employers actively sought out employees who were of Maya descent because they were considered to be *muy trabajadores* (hard workers) and less antagonistic— that is, less likely to question authority—than workers from other regions of Mexico.[5] Linda Fermín Cantú, the head of housekeeping in a four-star hotel, claimed that hotel management preferred to hire Maya workers because they were "more loyal" and less likely to quit.[6] A similar discourse suffused relationships between domestic servants and their employers. Like hotel work, domestic work in Cancún is deliberately racialized (cf. Hondagneu-Sotelo 2001). Middle-class Mexicans informed me that they intentionally hired Maya maids because they were better workers and more trustworthy than mestiza maids.[7] These gender and ethnic preferences are based on racist and sexist ideas that presume indigenous peoples to be "naturally" docile, servile, and childlike, characteristics sought after in the service industry (Madsen Camacho 2000).

As Mexico's largest service sector, tourism also forms part of the service industry, an industry that is expanding at an accelerated rate and quickly becoming one of the leading commodities traded globally (Adler and Adler 2004; Clancy 2001). In spite of the tourist industry's growth worldwide, few studies examine how production practices discipline workers in this service industry and how service workers resist these disciplinarian practices within translocal spaces.[8]

## Servicing a Translocality

Translocalities like Cancún are marked by a growing disconnection with the region they occupy and a pronounced articulation with a global economy. By catering to a foreign clientele and to the transnational hotel corporations that dominate the Zona Hotelera, Cancún orients its business and public profile toward an international, not national, audience. Yet even as the transnational economy has expanded, an expansion rooted in the industrial growth associated with the presence of FTZs and cheap labor, tourism has spurred national and regional growth. Tourism generates 7 percent of the nation's gross domestic product (Madsen Camacho 1996). At the local level, Cancún's growth has increased the development of local and regional businesses (Hiernaux Nicolas 1999). As one of Mexico's top tourist destinations (it attracts 25 percent of Mexico's international tourists) (Torres and Momsen 2005b), Cancún accounts for a significant portion of foreign exchange earnings and is a leading source of employment. As a consequence, nearly half of Cancún's residents were born elsewhere (Wilson 2008). This city's critical role in the national economy, its orientation toward a "transnational market space," and its urban atmosphere, however, are also correlated with a rise in income inequality (Hiernaux Nicolas 1999; Maldonado Torres 2000; Sassen 1994, xiv; Torres and Momsen 2005b).[9]

In its initial stages, this tourist center generated jobs, but they were primarily low-skilled jobs in construction and services (e.g., hotels, shops, restaurants) that were filled by Maya campesinos. The two villages that occupied the area, Puerto Juárez and Kan Kún (which eventually became known as Cancún), were sparsely populated. In 1969, 117 inhabitants resided in Puerto Juárez, while three people lived in Kan Kún (Martí 1991, 20–21). Due to a labor shortage, developers recruited workers from the surrounding countryside and neighboring state of Yucatán. But they failed to provide adequate housing. The houses being constructed in what would soon become Cancún's commercial district were too expensive for these low-wage workers, forcing them to live in the surrounding forest or in the neighboring town of Puerto Juárez (Bosselman 1978; Re Cruz 1996b). Although the initial development plan included creating housing for ten thousand workers in this "support city," the bulk of this housing was oriented toward the middle class.[10] By 1971, more than six thousand workers had been recruited and lived in camps or squatted in the surrounding forest, many without access to water, electricity, or a sewage system and with limited access to consumer goods (Bosselman 1978; Martí 1991).

Between 1974 and 1977, skilled jobs in services and construction increased (Bosselman 1978). More experienced workers from other parts of Mexico migrated to Cancún to fill these positions. By the early 1980s, as Mexico faced an oil debt crisis and as Cancún gained international fame, hotel construction sped up and focused on large hotels (with over 200 rooms) in an effort to increase foreign exchange earnings. Recruitment of both high-skilled and low-skilled workers increased. According to Gustavo Kauil Tun, who arrived in Cancún in 1980, hotels sent recruiters directly to the regiones to recruit workers by offering high salaries for menial labor. "During that time period, the pressure from the labor union didn't exist. You worked. . . . They didn't hold any meetings. . . . It wasn't a problem to get work. . . . You could leave your job on one day and the next day, you could find another one." By 1984, fifty-seven hotels, including 6,106 rooms, had been constructed (Hiernaux Nicolas 1989). In 1985, 750,000 tourists visited Cancún, and 35,000 residents lived in the "support city," most of whom originated from the neighboring state of Yucatán and the central states of Mexico (Martí 1991).

Since its first hotels opened in 1974, Cancún's population has grown tremendously (see Table 1). By 1980, 37,190 people lived in the county of Benito Juárez, in which the city of Cancún is located (INEGI 1999, 3). By 2000, this number increased exponentially to 419,815 inhabitants (INEGI 2001, 41). Over half a million people live in Cancún today.[11] Most of this growth is due to migration. In 2000, migrants constituted 69 percent of Quintana Roo's residents (INEGI 2001, 85), with 40 percent of these migrants originating from rural Yucatán (INEGI 1999, 27). Maya migrants constitute a significant portion of Cancún's population. The 2005 census estimates that 12 percent of the county's population speaks Yucatec Maya (INEGI 2006). However, by only counting self-identified Yucatec Maya speakers ages five and up as Maya, the census undercounts the Maya population. In fact, Maya migrants make up a third of Cancún's population.[12]

TABLE 1

**Population growth in county of Benito Juárez and city of Cancún, 1969–2005**

| YEAR | BENITO JUÁREZ | CANCÚN |
| --- | --- | --- |
| 1969 | n/a | 3 |
| 1971 | n/a | 6,000 |
| 1980 | 37,190 | 33,273 |
| 1990 | 176,765 | n/a |
| 1995 | 311,696 | 297,183 |
| 2000 | 419,815 | n/a |
| 2005 | 572,973 | 526,701 |

*Note:* The numbers for 1969 refer to households; all other numbers refer to population counts.

*Sources:* For data for 1969 and 1971, Martí (1991); for data for 1980, 1990, and 1995, INEGI (1999); for data for 2000, Cuaderno Estadístico Municipal, *Edición 1999: Benito Juárez, Estado de Quintana Roo* (Mexico); for data for 2005, INEGI (2006).

Nearly 60 percent of all economically active residents in the *municipio* of Benito Juárez are employed in the service sector, an industry dominated by transnational corporations such as the Marriot Hotels, Hard Rock Cafe, Van Cleef and Arpels, and clothing designers Donna Karan, Benetton, and Zarah (INEGI 2000a, 58).[13] In 2001, Cancún comprised 142 hotels with slightly over 26,000 hotel rooms that generated nearly $2 billion (H. Ayuntamiento Benito Juárez 2002, 65).[14] Yet the majority of the residents in this city cannot afford to purchase the commodities sold by the transnational corporations for whom they work. In 2001, nearly 50 percent of the municipio's employed adults earned between one minimum daily wage of 35.85 pesos (approximately $3.90 per day, $117 per month) to three minimum daily wages ($350 per month), while only 17 percent of the population made more than $17 per day (slightly over $400 per month) (INEGI 2000a, 59).[15]

As a labor-intensive industry, tourism manufactures lots of low-wage, seasonal jobs. Through the marketing of leisure, which entails the development of extensive geographic areas, tourism also generates employment opportunities in areas beyond the hotel industry, such as food, transportation, and recreation, thereby developing industries at a regional level (Hiernaux Nicolas and Rodríguez Woog 1991). The emphasis on services (e.g., food, consumer goods) and the increasing participation of women as workers in the formal tourist sector also result in a corresponding growth of the informal sector (e.g., domestic service, street vending, hustling, prostitution, and drug trafficking) (see Cabezas 2008; Chant 1992; Gregory 2007; Padilla 2007; Pattullo 1996/2005). But there are limits to the Mexican tourism model. Social scientists Daniel Hiernaux Nicolas and Manuel Rodríguez Woog point out that "the implications for the social and regional development of areas surrounding tourist centers are clear: few employment opportunities exist for more skilled labor" (1991, 325). Regional development is circumscribed by the emphasis on low-wage, seasonal jobs over well-paid administrative and managerial positions.

Cancún was built along the classic tourism model designed to attract "sun, sand and sea" tourists, primarily from Canada and the United States, who were willing to pay top dollar for exclusive access to its white sandy beaches and turquoise waters and for tours of the Maya ruins in Tulum and Chichén Itzá. Two-thirds of the hotels built by 1981 were classified as five-star luxury resorts (Carr 2008). This type of tourism was premised on a sharp separation between work and leisure, requiring the construction of a tourist city in which workers and clients rarely interacted (Hiernaux Nicolas 1999). Hotels in Cancún were constructed to face outward toward the sea, with their backs to the lagoon and commercial center of Cancún, while service workers and their facilities were hidden out of view from tourists (Map 2). Employees entered the hotel through a separate entrance, where security guards checked their identification cards and occasionally searched through their bags at the end of the workday. The laundry, kitchen, and storage were usually located in the basement, hidden out of view. Hotel workers ate their meals in the dining hall located in the bowels of the hotel, where most of their work took place. Correspondingly, employees, with the exception of those in visible posts like bartenders, receptionists, and bellboys, were trained to limit their interactions with tourists, thereby reinforcing this spatial divide. Daniel Hiernaux Nicolas suggests, "In these ways, Cancún was the most authentic expression of Taylorist principles of efficiency applied to hotel space: it reflected the idealistic, quasi-utopian spatial organization, with a total division between labor and leisure, workers and tourists" (ibid., 131).

By the mid-1980s, however, the rise in mass tourism demanded a shift in these practices, transforming the classic model of tourism through a demand for variety (Urry 1990). Activities oriented around the sun and the sea no longer satisfied tourists. New sites for consumption were established or renovated (e.g., shopping centers, outdoor water activities, lagoon activities, and the commercial center, particularly in the form of outdoor *mercados* [markets]). The increase in charter planes to Cancún also propagated an increase in the construction of large tourist hotels. These charter flights formed part of the "all-inclusive" packages provided by tour companies; tourists paid one fee that covered expenses for airfare, hotel, and food. By 1994, charter planes constituted half of the arrivals in Cancún (Hiernaux Nicolas 1999). This period was also marked by hotel consolidation as transnational hotel companies acquired and merged with independent hotels, resulting in greater homogenization in hotel facilities, services, and prices (Cabezas 2008). The growth in mass tourism resulted in a construction boom and the development of an array of tourist activities (albeit standardized), both of which infused the region with tourist dollars. Thus between 1984 and 1994, the Yucatán Peninsula was one of the fastest growing regions in Mexico.

Unfortunately, these new trends in tourism did not substantially increase foreign exchange earnings. For example, all-inclusive tour packages

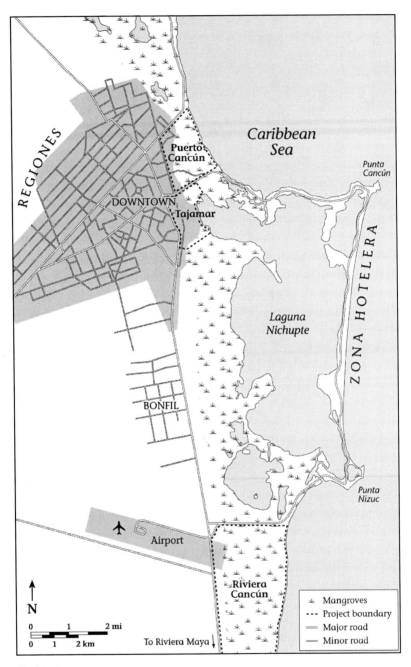

Caribbean
Sea

Punta
Cancún

REGIONES

Puerto
Cancún

DOWNTOWN
Tajamar

ZONA HOTELERA

Laguna
Nichupte

BONFIL

Punta
Nizuc

Airport

N

0          1          2 mi
0      1      2 km

Riviera
Cancún

To Riviera Maya ↓

⊥ Mangroves
- - - Project boundary
═══ Major road
─── Minor road

*City of Cancún.*

decreased the amount of money tourists spent on local businesses because many budget-oriented tourists ate in their hotels or purchased food and drink at the downtown Wal-Mart instead of eating out and shopping at mercados and malls. In addition, activities not sanctioned by the state, such as prostitution, drug trafficking, and money laundering, increased substantially.[16] Tourists' demands for new leisure sites stimulated the development of the coast all the way to the Belizean border, the area known as the Riviera Maya, which detracted from tourism to Cancún. As a result of these changes, FONATUR shifted its approach toward "adventure tourism" or "eco-tourism" in which sun and beach activities are complemented by, and in many instances replaced with, cultural activities in an ecologically friendly environment.[17] FONATUR's new Costa Maya project, located along Mexico's border with Belize and projected to be completed by the year 2020, is oriented toward ecotourism along the Ruta Maya.[18] Through such efforts, FONATUR aimed to increase the foreign exchange earnings of local businesses.

## Labor Segmentation

The characteristics of this shifting tourism model are extremely relevant to the lives of Kuchmil migrants who formed part of this gender-segmented and predominantly low-wage workforce. From the 1980s to the early 1990s, the tourist industry offered a degree of social mobility (also see Re Cruz 1996b). Due to a labor shortage, hotel corporations were willing to train and educate their employees. Kuchmil male migrants who arrived in Cancún during this period moved up the labor hierarchy from low-skilled positions to skilled and professional jobs. By 2001, this cohort worked as head chefs, accountants, bilingual receptionists, topographers, and electricians. However, only six of the twenty-seven male migrants from Kuchmil working in Cancún at this time form part of this cohort because most migrants arrived in Cancún after this period of social mobility. As Cancún expanded, it attracted workers, both skilled and unskilled, from across the country, leading to a pool of surplus labor by the late 1990s. As a result workers lost the bargaining power afforded them by labor shortages. Hotel companies curtailed offering incentives, like English-language schooling and high wages, previously made available to low-skilled employees.

Male migrants who recently arrived in Cancún have been stuck working in low-wage and short-term contract positions. Many worked as "apprentices" in hotels and in construction in the hopes of eventually getting promoted. Apprenticeships in hotels (e.g., stewards, assistant waiters, assistant cooks), however, benefited the employer, not the employee, because these employees often performed the work of higher-ranking jobs without receiving the corresponding benefits, monetary and otherwise. Unless apprentices found a better job elsewhere, few were promoted. Many of the Kuchmil migrants who moved to Cancún within the last fifteen years have found themselves in these positions. Of the twenty-seven male migrants working in Cancún, seven held low-wage, entry-level posts (e.g., stewards, busboys, janitors), and eleven were concentrated in posts that required more skill but did not offer a significant increase in salary (e.g., waiter, bartender, assistant cook). Three worked as entrepreneurs in the informal economy, eschewing the hotel industry altogether. Thus Kuchmil migrants found themselves relegated to low-wage work in the formal sector, regardless of their educational background.

Likewise, female migrants remained concentrated in low-wage and low-skilled jobs, but in the informal sector. In Mexico's major tourist centers, women engaged in restaurant and hotel work at a higher rate than men (Wilson 2008), but in Cancún, men have a higher participation rate than women. In 2001, of the eighteen female migrants from Kuchmil residing in Cancún, eleven were employed, but few worked in hotels and restaurants. Of those employed, six worked as domestic servants for the middle and upper classes, and two worked in white-collar jobs (e.g., receptionist and accountant).[19] Three worked as chambermaids and janitors in hotels; these positions were considered culturally inappropriate for unmarried Maya women. For women, hotel positions offer little occupational mobility because they form part of a truncated hierarchical ranking structure in which an entire department is overseen by one supervisor (Chant 1992).

According to Cynthia Enloe, "The very structure of international tourism *needs* patriarchy to survive" (1989, 41). In the case of Cancún, tourism also needs migration to survive. Yet patriarchy can inhibit women's mobility. Beginning in the 1960s in central Mexico and throughout Latin America, women migrated to cities more often than men (Jelin 1977). In Kuchmil, however, few women participated in migration prior to 1992. Feminist scholars suggest that Maya women are considered to be the "guardians of tradition" and thus there is a serious investment in keeping daughters and wives in rural villages (Kintz 1998; Re Cruz 1998). Girls were not allowed to travel outside of Kuchmil without a chaperone. For years, due to my status as a young, single woman, a child accompanied me whenever I visited a neighboring town. As the guardians of tradition, girls were expected to leave Kuchmil upon marriage, but not before. The community approved of young girls who traveled to help relatives with household duties because their behavior conformed to expected gender roles. But they did not consider it appropriate for young women to work outside the household because they could not be protected from harm—sexual and physical. Nevertheless, some women did leave Kuchmil. One fled to Cancún after a painful divorce, while two others left as young girls to work as live-in maids and nannies for local teachers. These girls were allowed to work because their families trusted the teachers and needed the money. In 1991, during my interviews with young women in Kuchmil, they expressed a desire to work, but they were not permitted to do so. To my surprise, when I returned the following summer, seven of the twenty-two young females (ages twelve to twenty-four) living in Kuchmil left their community to find work in neighboring cities of Valladolid, Tízimin, and Cancún. Unlike their brothers who migrated after completing their schooling, the majority of these women had not studied past the sixth grade.

Female migration from Kuchmil was made possible by the nation-state's emphasis on tourism development, an improved transportation system, and the expansion of kin networks in neighboring cities, particularly Cancún. In 1991, the road leading into the village was paved, and a regional bus route was established that made travel cheaper, faster, and more secure. The road reduced travel to Cancún from two days to five hours. The presence of the bus route made it possible for kin residing in Cancún to invite their family members to Cancún. Male migrants who were educated in the internados and their wives invited their mothers, siblings, and cousins to visit. More important, they persuaded their unmarried female relatives to find jobs working for Cancún's middle class. Even though jobs were readily available in the newly built assembly plants around Valladolid, Kuchmil migrants convinced their siblings that jobs in Cancún paid better and that there were more opportunities for social mobility. Although families in Kuchmil had extended kin networks in Valladolid and Mérida, their closest kin relations were in Cancún. These consolidated kin networks facilitated female migration. Through these visits, the young women of Kuchmil became acquainted with urban life in Cancún and became integrated into the informal labor market through domestic wage work and in the formal labor market as chambermaids and store clerks. These events, in conjunction with the ongoing agrarian crisis, made it possible for women who migrated from Kuchmil in the 1990s to face minimal community sanctions and criticism for their actions.

## Performing Gender, Race, and Class

Sylvia Chant suggests that within the tourist industry employers place men in visible positions that involve direct contact with employers and tourists, and relegate women to behind-the-scenes positions as maids and kitchen assistants that provide support to male employees (1991, 82, 102). When hotels did recruit women to occupy visible posts, it was because their sex, race, and age mattered. Beauty and youth improved one's economic opportunities in the hotel industry.[20] In Cancún, women's sexual and racial appeal to consumers relegated them into visible posts such as store clerks, hotel receptionists, and beach waitresses. In addition, physical characteristics such as blonde hair and fair skin that marked racial difference guaranteed women visible hotel posts that were less labor intensive as receptionists, clerks, and hotel animators (social organizers). Hotel supervisor Luis Escada Roman suggested that if I was interested in working in a hotel, my language skills, my youthful age, and my pleasing *presentación* (appearance) would guarantee me a position as a hostess or receptionist.[21] According to Escada Roman, women were relegated to work as waitresses on the beach and in the pool area because they provided the guests with a "visual attraction" that enabled them to sell more liquor than male waiters. Miniskirts that "show[ed] off their legs," makeup, and a "flirtatious" attitude constituted the uniform and persona waitresses were required to don as they wandered the beach selling refreshments and liquor. Women who filled visible posts were exceptions to the standard sexual division of labor. Furthermore, Escada Roman explained that the presence of female employees formed an integral part of a hotel's "special touch" and "attention to detail," like chocolates left on pillows. Such details differentiate ordinary hotels from luxury hotels.

The five-star Hotel Arena (a pseudonym) provides a clear example of this gender segmentation. Of the 600 employees working for this hotel, which was a subsidiary of a large international hotel chain owned by an American company, only 30 percent were women. Of these women, 30 percent were employed as *camaristas* (chambermaids), 8 percent as *cajeras* (clerks), 6 percent as waitresses, 6 percent as cooks (including assistants), 5 percent as supervisors, 4 percent in public area maintenance, 4 percent as hostesses, and 2 percent as managers. The remaining female employees (35 percent) were employed individually or clustered in groups of two or three as assistants, receptionists, stewards, hotel animators, tailors, dancers, and so forth. Jobs that were visible posts (e.g., hostesses, waitresses, and clerks) required women to be young. The age range for the women who occupied these positions fell between eighteen and thirty. The age of the hotel animators was younger. They were all in their early twenties. Three of these employees were the only foreigners employed by the hotel. The majority of the supervisors and managers were from Mexico's central states (e.g., Distrito Federal, San Luis Potosí) and a few southern states (e.g., Oaxaca, Veracruz, Chiapas). In contrast, the average age for camaristas was thirty-three years of age; their ages ranged from eighteen to forty-eight years. Thirty-eight percent of the camaristas were from the states of Yucatán and Quintana Roo. Of these women, the majority had Maya surnames, but only about a third spoke Yucatec Maya. Maya women were older than the majority of the female employees, and a significant number were divorced or separated from their husbands. Therefore, through the imposition of uniforms, specific ideas about gender and race, and standards of hygiene, beauty, and disposition, the service industry commodified workers' bodies (Madsen Camacho 2000).

For migrants, the transition from farm work to service work did not simply entail a reworking of attitudes and approaches to work, but was also a reconfiguration of the gender of work itself and perceptions of class. This shift in class status becomes marked by migrants' skin color. Since most migrants worked indoors and were no longer exposed to the harsh sun, the color of their skin lightened. According to Alicia Re Cruz, this whitening of the skin—"*dzu sut sac* (she/he has returned white)"—marked the cultural and social transformation of migrant workers, of their shift from subsistence farmers to proletariats (1996a, 150). White skin physically marked migrants as wage laborers, as part of a different class of higher status. This transition, however, did not automatically grant migrants a position of respectability. Although white skin was praised by some Maya families, white skin was also associated with the Spanish conquistadors and Mexican elites, who were called *¢'ùulóob'* due to their white skin. Thus service work becomes a contested site for the performance of gender, race, and class (Karjanen 2008).

## The Civilizing Process

As Cancún grew, finding workers was relatively easy. Finding "good" workers, and transforming them into "modern" citizens, was a different matter altogether. Most jobs, even unskilled positions, required a certain set of behaviors from employees, be it submissiveness, cleanliness, timeliness, specific knowledge, beauty, and so forth. The majority of the people who migrated to Cancún originated from the surrounding countryside, which meant they brought with them ideas about time, work, and social relations rooted in the rhythms of agricultural production that contrasted with the time-thrift mentality of global capitalism (see Thompson 1967). To form their employees into the kind of workers who generate profits and are representative of their business ethos, corporations relied on intensive training programs, discursive strategies, and new technology. As Michel Foucault suggests, this process is a "question not of treating the body, en masse, 'wholesale', as if it were an indissociable unity, but of working it 'retail', individually; of exercising upon it a subtle coercion, of obtaining holds upon it at the level of the mechanism itself—movements, gestures, attitudes, rapidity: an infinitesimal power over the active body" (1995, 137). This "civilizing process" was intended to change human nature and behavior and impose self-restraint on the human body (Elias 1978/2000).

Migrants who were previously engaged in farm labor and now engaged in service work underwent this process. They learned to adhere to a time clock, acquired new skills, and adopted new behaviors and attitudes (e.g., submissiveness and attentiveness). Migrants who participated in Mexico's public education system previously encountered the concepts of individualism, timeliness, submissiveness, and conformity before moving to Cancún. These ideas were further reinforced at work as they learned the intricacies of service: setting a table, greeting a client, adopting a hotel's standards of cleanliness, and so forth. Linda Fermín Cantú explained that management hired inexperienced workers because they preferred to "mold" and "shape" their employees. A standard job application asks applicants to rate their personality, appearance, expressiveness, emotional stability, treatment of others, experience, comprehension skills, ability to be supervised, and levels of responsibility, cooperation, and technical knowledge. Regardless of one's assessment, all new hotel employees were required to participate in a training program, giving management the opportunity to inculcate new employees with the hotel's particular ideology of service and exorcise "bad" habits learned at prior work sites or derived from what managers perceived to be degenerate cultural practices. According to Linda Fermín Cantú, hotel management regarded this training as an "investment" in their workforce and, by extension, their brand.

The service industry's concern with hygiene illustrates these disciplinary tactics. Hotel maids, stewards, and janitors are "retrained" in how to clean a room, a table, or hotel grounds.[22] In discussing the chambermaid training she received in a luxury hotel, Ramona May Pat described her experience fulfilling a hotel's standards of cleanliness. After she cleaned the first room on her own, her supervisor checked for dust by running her index finger along the wood furniture and inspecting the room's corners. If she found dust, Ramona was required to clean the entire room again. Ramona frustratingly observed, "You have to clean even if there aren't any guests. The hotel is very strict, very hygienic." Cleanliness standards, however, must be maintained with the utmost efficiency. Before being hired, potential employees were tested on how quickly they could set a table, wash dishes, and so forth. Once hired, Ramona was taught the most efficient way to clean a room and make a bed using a minimum number of arm movements, while stewards were taught the most efficient way to clear a table and carry dishes. As a result, hotels end up with a facade of cleanliness in which the *appearance* of clean is the ultimate goal, given the time constraints under which employees work (see Ehrenreich 2001). Like in assembly work, these disciplinary tactics were intended to produce greater efficiency and increase productivity and profits.

This concern with hygiene also extends to migrants' bodies. Tourism is made up of a "sensuous geography" in which the eye plays a central role (Urry 1999).[23] An employee in the tourist industry must be pleasing to the senses, in terms of physical beauty, tastes, and smell (Madsen Camacho 2000). Consequently, hygiene in all aspects of work becomes a cornerstone of the disciplined modern worker. During the job application process, potential employees are asked to evaluate their own appearance, on a scale ranging from *sin presentación* (lacking a pleasing physical presence) to impeccable presence. Employees are urged to keep their hair trimmed and neat, to wash and iron their uniforms, and to bathe before coming to work (see Freeman 2000). The head of housekeeping at a four-star hotel spoke of this process as a form of "indoctrination." This approach underscores the disciplinary tactics driving corporate interests in the tourist industry.

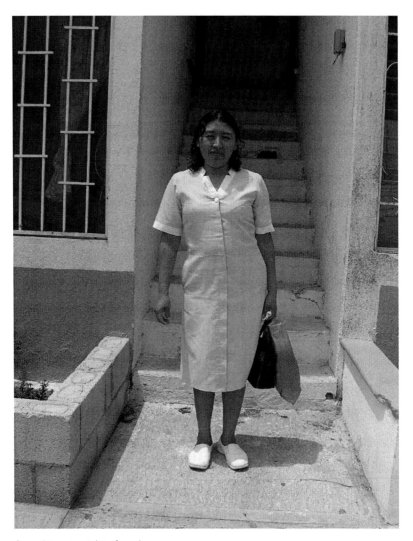

*A camarista prepares to leave for work.*

Within Cancún's service industry, a good worker must not only be responsible, productive, knowledgeable, and hygienic, but also should be internally motivated and have a gregarious personality. Hotel manager Luis Escada Roman informed me that management looks for "a person who is active, who is on top of it." Applicants are asked to rate their personality, emotional stability, and ability to express themselves. Roman further suggested, "all people have the possibility to improve themselves. It's a question of initiative, of being *muy vivo* [very proactive]." Based on this ideology of individual responsibility, the head of human resources urged Ramona, upon seeing her hesitation, to take the job of camarista. "You have opportunities. The people who put in the energy, who work very well, who have lots of personality, move up." She promised Ramona that with effort on her part, Ramona could eventually acquire a post as an accountant, the career in which Ramona was professionally trained. Even though employees work in teams or in pairs, very little is said about collaboration. Rather, what is being produced by this emphasis on personal responsibility and self-interest is the neoliberal individual.

In spite of this emphasis on charisma and temperament, most hotel employees are restricted, if not banned, from interacting with tourists. Some jobs, like the kitchen and event organizing staff, do not involve any interaction with guests. Other positions, like camaristas, busboys, and janitors, involve limited interaction. These employees are taught to smile politely at tourists, but they are censured if they are caught engaging in conversation. Eva, Miguel Can Poot's wife, worked as a camarista for a brief time. She recalled management's instructions regarding camaristas' interactions with guests. "They [supervisors] instruct you not to speak to the tourists. They were upset if they saw you speak to them [tourists], even if they are only asking for towels. Sometimes the hotel guests ask you for recommendations of places to visit, but we are told to inform the guests to speak to the concierge. If the tourists are men, it's even less likely [that you will be allowed to speak to them]." Male camaristas were given similar instructions.[24]

During my stay at a four-star hotel in the Zona Hotelera, approximately half of the camaristas were men. Since camaristas cleaned guests' rooms when they were not in it, I rarely interacted with them. One afternoon, I remained in my room, so I could speak with the camarista assigned to my room. I tried to engage him in conversation, but he informed me that he was not supposed to speak to hotel guests. Throughout our brief conversation, he looked frequently toward the doorway. As they cleaned, camaristas were required to keep the guest room door open, which allowed supervisors to observe them at work. The hotel's circular shape and open hallways—reminiscent of Foucault's Panopticon—gave supervisors and security guards, who communicated with each other via walkie-talkies, the perfect vantage point to monitor the movements of employees and guests. Interactions can happen outside the work site, although this was rarely the case among Maya migrants due to their tight work schedules.[25]

Gender differences not withstanding, only specific employees are allowed to interact with tourists. For example, bartenders and waitresses are required to speak with and be friendly toward tourists. Yet due to the short duration of most tourists' vacations, which range from three to ten days (but rarely much longer), employees have very little time to cultivate lasting friendships. A few Maya migrants, like Jesús and Horacio, attempt to do so. But for most Maya migrants, the work itself gets in the way of making lasting friendships. Miguel's experience working at a nightclub serves as an example. As an assistant bartender, Miguel was required to be friendly to the customers. The loud dance music and the brisk pace of orders needing to be filled, however, limited the depth and scope of these encounters. "I didn't have time to speak to the tourists. You have too much work. Every now and then you have time to flirt and joke, but most of the time you are working." Therefore, these displays of friendship are just that, displays. For these reasons, few tourist encounters are included in this book.

In addition, service workers are expected to shelve their feelings upon arriving at work. Workers are taught to "come to work 'clean', without any [emotional baggage]." Yet feelings are central to their work. Service workers are expected to perform "emotional labor" by presenting a charming, smiling exterior to tourists (Hochschild 1983, 7). As Horacio May Kauil explained, work requires "delicacy and patience," especially for bartenders whose primary objective is to persuade tourists to drink and yet ensure that they do not get too drunk. Horacio clarified, "You give them [the guests] more than your service. You surprise them with your attitude, your drinks, or the food you prepare." In her study of luxury hotels in the United States, Rachel Sherman (2007) points out that the personalization of service is what distinguishes luxury hotels from nonluxury hotels. To this end, Horacio, who works in one of the most luxurious hotels in the Riviera Maya, memorizes guests' names and their personal histories so that he can enthusiastically welcome them by name upon their return. This personalized attention and care is delivered with the intention of persuading guests to return. In exchange, hotel workers who are recognized by guests for their "excellent" service are granted a one-day pass to enjoy the hotel grounds. Through this emphasis on attitude and behavior, the service industry disciplined the bodies of Maya migrants.

## Becoming a Good Worker

According to hotel corporations' prevailing ideology of subordination, care, and personality (Sherman 2007), success or failure in the service industry depends on individual personalities and motivation, not on the financial and physical constraints imposed on employees via transnational corporations. Yet hotel companies rely on external forces to produce docile workers. In Cancún, hotel corporations used kin and social networks to control workers. Hotels preferred to hire the relatives or friends of "model" employees. Migrants would inform their relatives and friends in Cancún or recruit a relative or friend from Kuchmil to fill a vacancy. As a result, Kuchmil migrants relied less and less on job-seeking strategies typical of recent migrants, such as visiting hotels to ask for employment and searching the newspaper for openings. This recruitment process resulted in the clustering of Kuchmil migrants in specific trades and within the same corporations. For example, the men in one Kuchmil household all worked as bartenders in the same hotel chain, or family members held different positions (stewards, busboys, waiters, and bartenders) in one of Cancún's popular nightclubs. Kuchmil women's employment experiences demonstrate a similar practice. Kuchmil women employed as domestic servants worked either in the same neighborhoods or for one extended family. Due to the informal nature of the domestic service industry, these positions were highly dependent on personal references. This recruitment process resulted in a concentration of fictive and biological kin networks within particular hotel chains and employer social networks.

Employees regarded the success or failure of new recruits as a reflection of their own work ethic. Therefore, they pressured these recruits to become good workers. Hotel management took advantage of this fear and pressure to produce docile workers. Néstor Canul Canche's employment history provides a clear example of ethnic clustering within the hotel industry and of the psychological costs involved in modernization. Before moving to Cancún, Néstor spent three years studying computer science at a vocational school in Valladolid. He and his wife Ramona moved in with her brother, Francisco. As a well-educated, soft-spoken young man, Néstor immediately found a job that required computer skills in a law office, but this job was part-time and did not include health benefits, which Néstor needed because Ramona was pregnant. To make ends meet, Néstor took a second job working as a busboy at a restaurant that was part of a national chain. After a year of working two jobs, Néstor quit the computer job to work full-time as a busboy because his tips exceeded his salary as a computer programmer. A few months later, during the summer season, Néstor requested time off from his job so he and his family could spend some time with their parents in Kuchmil and Ke'eldzonot. The restaurant refused to give him time off, so Néstor quit his job.

For Néstor, working in low-wage jobs was a means to an end. He planned to save up enough money to buy a computer so he could improve his knowledge of computer programming. Upon returning to Cancún in September, Néstor decided that he could fulfill his dream of working as a computer technician by slowly moving up the labor hierarchy of the hotel industry. With the help of Ramona's family, Néstor got a job as an assistant bartender in a five-star hotel in the Zona Hotelera. His new work colleagues, who drank socially most evenings, convinced Néstor to accompany them for drinks after work. Eventually, these social drinks turned into drinking binges. In late November, the hotel refused to renew Néstor's three-month contract. Néstor told his family that the hotel was overstaffed. Although it was quite common for employees to lose their jobs during the low tourist season from September to early November, it was quite uncommon for employees to be let go this late in the season, because December, the start of the high tourist season, was right around the corner. While it was unclear if the termination of the contract was related to excessive alcohol consumption on the job, Ramona and her family accepted Néstor's explanation with reservations. Concerned about his brother-in-law's spotty employment record, Francisco quickly found Néstor a job in the hotel where he worked. "That's why I put him to work with me, to see how he works. He never stays more than a few months in one job. That's not right."

The presence of Francisco at his work site set up expectations for Néstor to become a model worker. Any other behavior would reflect poorly on Francisco, who placed his reputation on the line to find Néstor a job. Néstor did make an attempt to do a good job at work, but his attitude at home began to deteriorate as he continued his drinking binges. As soon as he was paid, he went drinking with his new colleagues from work. Unfortunately, Néstor was not able to save enough money to purchase the computer he wanted or to help Ramona save money for a down payment on a plot of land.

Néstor's experience illustrates how wage work can curtail a person's spirit. Both Néstor and Ramona believed that their educational background would serve as a vehicle for social mobility. Francisco pointed out that their middle-class aspirations would not be realized just because they had the proper qualifications. Instead, he suggested, "Here in Cancún, it is difficult to find a job if you don't know anyone. I have told her [Ramona] to take classes. To show her face so they can give her an opportunity. But she won't do it." After Ramona threatened to leave him and as a result of his brother-in-law's counsel, Néstor decreased his alcohol consumption and increased his contributions to the household. He gave up his dream of becoming a computer programmer and replaced it with the occasional numbing effect of liquor.

Before Néstor settled down his addiction quickly consumed most of his income, forcing his wife to search for work. Ramona read in the newspaper that Laguna Hotel (a pseudonym), a newly constructed five-star hotel, was hiring *camaristas sin experiencia* (chambermaids without experience). The wording of the advertisement motivated Ramona to consider work in the hotel industry. While Kuchmil men preferred working in the hotels, few Kuchmil women chose hotel work because these posts were considered to leave women open to the risk of being raped, seduced, or abused by tourists or by male coworkers. Kuchmil women preferred to work as domestic servants for a middle-class family because this work was perceived to be less demanding than hotel work and more dignified. Unfortunately, Ramona did not have social networks to find a job as a maid. But as a result of the three years she spent living and studying in Valladolid, she was not afraid to venture forth to seek work in the hotel industry. More important, as a married woman, Ramona did not face the same sanctions as unmarried women who sought work in this industry.

Ramona told Néstor, "I'm going to see about it." She made arrangements for her neighbor to babysit her son. Since she had never traveled alone to the Zona Hotelera, Néstor agreed to accompany her to solicit the job. A long line of interested candidates awaited them when they arrived at the Laguna's hotel employee entrance. Tourists and employees were differentiated from each other not only by uniforms and ethnicity, but also by separate entrances and the brightly colored bands tourists wore on their wrists. The wristbands are used predominantly in all-inclusive hotels to distinguish a guest from a visitor and an employee.[26] The presence of so many people made Ramona nervous. She thought she did not stand a chance among so many applicants. Néstor, however, knew the drill; he convinced Ramona to stay for the interview. New hotels did not necessarily have established social networks from which to cull future employees, and if they did, these networks were relatively small and consisted of highly skilled and professional referrals that only filled a few positions out of the large number of employees needed to run a five-star hotel. Obtaining a position within a new hotel depended more on a positive physical appearance, age, and disposition, than on whom you knew. The corporation was also interested in hiring inexperienced people because this quality made it easier for employees to absorb the corporation's approach to leisure and its expectations of its workers. "They told us [that all the hired women] lack experience because [the hotel] trains you, their strategy, their standards," Ramona explained.

Ramona was hired for a twenty-four-day trial period, during which she was trained and did not receive health benefits. During the first four days, Ramona observed her more experienced colleagues. As she cleaned the four rooms assigned to her, she practiced the techniques they taught her, techniques intended to increase efficiency. For example, Ramona learned how to make a bed with one quick toss and a few tugs of the sheet. The efficiency and cleanliness mandates, however, were difficult to achieve without placing severe stress on the body. "I saw that it was easy but when they made me perform the tasks, I couldn't. . . . My legs hurt and I had only cleaned four rooms. . . . I felt that I couldn't hold my son [because my arms hurt]," exclaimed Ramona. The company policy required chambermaids to work as many hours as it took them to finish cleaning the twelve rooms assigned daily to them. "You leave when you finish," she was informed at the interview. The idea of working more than eight hours a day discouraged Ramona. "The second day, I didn't want to go. My entire body hurt. I couldn't do it. I couldn't learn it." On the fifth day, Ramona was assigned twelve rooms to clean, and now had access to tips. She managed to finish her contract, but decided not to renew it because the long work hours and the time away from her son were not worth the $3 in tips she earned per day. Her decision was also influenced by Néstor's improved behavior.

These work histories illustrate the production practices, both discursive and structural, that corporations used to transform Kuchmil migrants into modern workers. They also reveal the capitalist contradictions Maya workers face as they transition into wage labor. Néstor and Ramona were both educated beyond the rudimentary education their parents received. While their experiences in school prepared them for wage work by inculcating the concepts of individualism, time efficiency, and conformity, these experiences also set up expectations of social mobility. Kuchmil migrants like Jesús May Pat and Gustavo Kauil Tun, who arrived prior to 1991, were able to achieve this dream because they began working during the courtship phase of the multinational hotel industry and the economic boom stimulated by mass tourism. Néstor and Ramona moved to Cancún in 1999 and thus experienced a different reality, in which their educational backgrounds did not improve their economic opportunities. They were stuck working in low-wage jobs that required a significant amount of work and sacrifice without necessarily guaranteeing social mobility.

## Discipline, Technology, and the State

The nation-state also works in conjunction with global capitalism to transform migrants into "modern" citizens, into individuals who adopt the notion of time as money, participate politically, consume goods, own land, produce few children, and speak Spanish. The rise of new technologies makes possible new disciplinarian techniques. Satellite technology that promotes transnational banking systems provides a clear example of this process. When I first visited Cancún in 1991, few working-class employees used bank accounts to manage their money because hotel corporations paid their employees with checks; workers lacked knowledge of the banking system; and few workers trusted the economic stability of Mexico's banks, with good reason. As Mexico's banking system has become more technologically sophisticated, hotels have switched from paying their employees by check to directly depositing their salary into a bank account. Employees access their salary through bank cards deployed at automatic teller machines (ATMs).

What role do ATMs play in disciplining workers? Direct-deposit bank accounts make it easier for the government to tax employees and "count" its citizens, because as part of formal institutions, bank accounts can be regulated by the Mexican government.[27] In the past, when hotel employees were paid by check, employees did not necessarily cash their checks at banks. For a fee, checks could be cashed at stores, pawn shops, and other businesses. Given the hike in interest rates and peso devaluations after the 1982 oil debt crisis that caused many families to lose their homes and bank savings, few migrants opened and deposited their wages into bank accounts. As a result, a significant portion of Mexico's population was not investing in Mexico's banks and thereby into the Mexican nation. By incorporating their employees into Mexico's banking system, multinational companies captured the revenues of a large portion of the population that previously did not participate in this economic sector.

Many employers that I spoke with critiqued the conspicuous consumption of their low-skilled employees. They complained that "they don't know how to save." This constant refrain is rooted in racist and classist stereotypes of campesinos, indios, and the urban poor as not capable of sustaining themselves and managing their money effectively and thereby straining national subsidy programs and hindering Mexico's transition from underdeveloped to modern nation. Transnational corporations relied on direct-deposit bank accounts as a way to train their employees not only how to use an ATM, but also how to save their money and refrain from conspicuous consumption. To do so, multinational hotels offered their employees the option of opening a savings account. An authorized amount of money was automatically deducted from employees' wages. Through such a system, employees' disposable income was reduced, thereby limiting their conspicuous consumption, and Mexican banks were infused with capital reserves. New technologies—such as satellite systems that allowed for the use of ATMs, cable television, and scanning equipment, in conjunction with production strategies such as identification bracelets and cards on hotel grounds, training programs, electrical gates, and separate entryways for employees and tourists—regulated worker behavior and reinforced modes of production that increased capital accumulation and the "appropriate" consumption of particular goods by service workers (see Freeman 2000).

## Weakening Strong Ties

E. P. Thompson (1967) claimed that capitalism requires a division between work and social life, whereas in agricultural societies, work is social. Given the seasonal demands of the tourism industry and the nature of service work in an era of late capitalism, this distinction has blurred. Service work requires employees to be social, to establish friendships with tourists. At the same time, employees are expected to prioritize work above family and social commitments. Cancún's hotel workers were often asked without notice to work double shifts or work on their days off. Since employees can be easily replaced, few turned down these requests. Under such circumstances, it was difficult for Maya migrants to give of themselves to their families and friends. For Maya migrants, this capitalist work ideol-

ogy strained social relations and made service work, in spite of its emphasis on flexibility, appear to be inflexible.

The majority of the workers I spoke to adhered to the ideology of the
responsible yet internally motivated worker, an ideology that was rooted
in Puritanism and the Horatio Alger myth of pulling oneself up by one's
bootstraps (see Fernández-Kelly 1983). Horacio May Kauil, a hotel bartender and Kuchmil migrant, explained this ideology:

> Those who spend their time with a broom cleaning, washing bath-
> rooms, stuff like that. They don't want to be there, they want to move
> upstairs, but those who move upstairs are those who put much more
> effort into their work, who behave accordingly or who get along well
> with the boss. . . . I know lots of people who have worked for years
> and years [as janitors or stewards] and never think of improving
> their situation. I should have improved my situation long ago, but
> I didn't want to. Later I regretted it because if I had improved my
> situation long ago, I would have been earning a good salary by now.

Within such a system, social mobility depends on individual motivation,
erasing the tactics multinational hotels use to keep their employees from
improving their wages and (literally) moving up the job hierarchy.

Adhering to the philosophy of the good modern worker was challenging for Kuchmil migrants, because this mantra of individualism negated
the collectivist orientation that formed an important part of rural life.
Maya society recognizes the individual as a social actor within a web of
dense social relations, but being a good moral person also requires *active*
participation in systems of mutual reciprocity. The tension generated by
the recognition and salience of the self within a collectivist society was
heightened with migration and made evident through migration narratives. Adherence to a capitalist ideology can truncate family ties and relationships. The ambition, energy, and devotion required for success in the
service industry did not leave room for one to spend time with family in
Cancún and Kuchmil.

This absence negatively impacted the positions of authority men held
within their household. As sub chef (sous-chef, assistant to the head chef)
at a five-star hotel, Gustavo Kauil Tun was an employee de confianza, which
meant that his income was based on a fixed salary rather than on the
number of hours he worked. Employees de confianza are usually highly

skilled or professionals and do not participate in the "total reward system" in which basic pay is supplemented by perks such as tips, transportation costs, and so forth.[28] The total reward system is the norm for low-wage, low-skill hotel employees. To mark their class status and social position within the corporation and manufacture their consent, highly skilled and professional hotel employees are treated differently (Chivers 1973; Urry 1990). Their salary is not fixed but must be negotiated individually. They do not have access to tips but are given access to other perks, such as the ability to socialize with the clientele and a flexible schedule so that they may visit other restaurants and improve their training (but not necessarily to spend more time with their families). As an employee de confianza, Gustavo spent long hours at work. During special events, he was required to work all day and all night, even if this meant forfeiting his day off. His schedule was so erratic that his wife Mónica Can Uc never knew when he would be home, and his visits to Kuchmil became more and more infrequent. Mónica understood the importance of Gustavo's job and the sacrifices it entailed, such as limiting his visits to Kuchmil to once or twice a year. Since Gustavo gave her a generous allowance, Mónica was able to run the household without his physical presence. As their children got older, though, Mónica found it more difficult to guide their educational success and to limit how much time they spent hanging out on the street, a place considered dangerous. To reinforce his authority while absent from the household, Gustavo bought cell phones for himself, his wife, and his teenage daughter. Reducing his work hours was not an option for Gustavo because with each promotion, he bought further into the capitalist ideology. Gustavo explained why he had curtailed his visits and responsibilities in Kuchmil:

> I can't leave my job. It's a great responsibility that I have in this job. I can't commit myself [to carry out religious cargos] because in reality I don't know that I have the time. To carry out a cargo you need to take a few days off, not just one or two. You need to return constantly to make all the preparations. . . . Sometimes when the festival in the village occurs, I have to work. I can't abandon it to attend.

Dedication to work can also result in the abuse of authority by the head of the household. The story of Gustavo's brother, Macario, illustrates this process. Macario presented the picture of the modern worker. He was charming, handsome, well dressed, and spoke Spanish flawlessly. Gustavo invited Macario to Cancún after he finished the secundaria, at which point he began to work immediately as an assistant cook. He liked it so much that he decided to stay. In his search for "excellency," a concept he adopted from his hotel training, he sought out posts that would allow him to improve his talents. He quickly became head chef at one of the most internationally renowned luxury hotels in the world. With this promotion, Macario felt that he had finally acquired the prestige to which he had been aspiring, particularly now that the corporation had offered to transfer him, a self-trained chef, to one of their European hotels. His wife Paula Chan Yah, however, refused to go with him, based on past experience. When Macario had been transferred for a time to a franchise on the island of Cozumel, Paula suffered greatly from the isolation she experienced. Loneliness was not the only concern Paula had with respect to her husband's occupational mobility. She feared that in moving farther away, she would lose access to the social networks on which she depended for food and money. In spite of Macario's high salary, he contributed a very small portion toward household expenses, which forced Paula to cover the remaining expenses by working longer hours in the informal economy.

## Resisting the Civilizing Process

Even as tourist work and urban life undermine the dense Maya social relations nurtured during village life, Maya migrants make concerted efforts to combat these fragmenting forces and new power relations. Lila Abu-Lughod (1990) cautions us that acts of resistance do not always result in altering relations of power, but rather may cement the systems of power in which people are already enmeshed or locate them within new systems of domination. Yet, it is important to reflect on the significance of these acts in developing and solidifying particular types of social relationships that migrants perceive as less constraining or less domineering.

The high concentration of Maya women in domestic service constitutes a form of resistance against global capitalism. While service work can be extremely exploitative (Bunster and Chaney 1989; Chaney and García Castro 1989; Hondagneu-Sotelo 1994, 2001; Romero 1992), Kuchmil women described it as more flexible than hotel work because of the patron-client relationships they established with their employers. Domestic work required employees to develop an intimate relationship with an employer and their employer's family. Servants became privy to family feuds and secrets. By not choosing to perform live-in domestic service work, and by working for multiple employers, Kuchmil women also avoided many of the exploitative situations domestic servants faced. Once employers learned to trust them, Kuchmil women were able to request time off to visit family and secure funds and goods during times of need. Domestic work was well paid in Cancún because of the high turnover rate. In addition, middle- and upper-class women preferred to employ rural Maya women because they considered them to be more reliable and trustworthy. Kuchmil women earned $60 per week on average as domestic servants, a salary twice as high as that of a chambermaid. By selecting domestic service work over hotel work, Kuchmil women opted for an occupation that blurred the capitalist division between work and social life. Their ability to meet their obligations to their families in Kuchmil and Cancún depended on working in an environment that recognized these women as humans and acknowledged the value of their kin ties and the responsibilities that came along with these ties.

In contrast, hotel work was viewed by Kuchmil migrants, both men and women, as a transgressive occupation for both married and unmarried women because such work put women's sexuality on display and at risk. Although few unmarried women worked in hotels, married women often did so on a short-term basis: to ride out a rough economic period, as was the case with Ramona, or to help save up money to purchase a plot of land, fund a business, or build a home. Hotel work was only considered a long-term job under particular circumstances such as those experienced by Nereida Kauil Tun. After divorcing an abusive husband, Nereida fled to Cancún where she worked, at first, as a domestic servant. After Nereida had a child out of wedlock, she needed a job with health insurance, so she became a camarista. She did not worry about putting her sexuality at risk, because she was already stigmatized for having a child out of wedlock. Additionally, Nereida was attracted to hotel work because it lacked the intimacy involved in domestic work. Since guests are constantly changing, Nereida considered camarista work to be impersonal. In addition, employees' interactions with each other were also limited because they cleaned rooms at a fast pace and worked alone or with another person, although always under constant supervision. Due to this lack of social interaction, work was completely detached from Nereida's home life and lacked many of the social attachments involved in domestic service (see García Castro

1989; Katzman 1981). Nereida preferred this detachment because it allowed her to focus on sustaining her kin ties. Under these circumstances, hotel work was perceived as less constraining than domestic work.

To subvert the civilizing process, workers also relied on the new production practices used by transnational corporations and the nation-state to transform rural workers into modern urban individuals. Migrants used the money they saved in the hotel savings accounts to consume luxury goods, such as flat-screen Sony televisions, stereo systems, and video cameras; and to pay for rituals, like the Virgen de Guadalupe festival, which cements kin and social relations among migrants and their natal community. Migrants also consumed new technologies like ATM cards and cellular phones to curtail feelings of isolation and to challenge the individualization promoted at work.

With the increasing use of automatic teller machines in the region, ATM cards became portable bank accounts for Kuchmil migrants that increased communal and reciprocal ties across the region. ATMs were installed in Valladolid, the closest city to Kuchmil, in the late 1990s. Since then, migrants have taken advantage of ATM cards to give their rural families in Kuchmil access to their wages without traveling to Cancún. Hotel corporations facilitated this practice by providing workers with two debit cards. Leonardo May Kauil described how this system worked. "I get paid through the bank, but through the automatic teller. When I first started [the job], I was given two debit cards. I left one card in Valladolid. My parents go there to recover the money. I call them by telephone and I tell them that I have so much money, for them to take it. They go and pull it out." While only a few migrants left their debit cards in Kuchmil, this system is becoming more popular, especially since a cellular phone was installed in Kuchmil that allowed migrants to inform their families about pending deposits. ATM cards made it easier for migrants to fulfill their economic obligations in Kuchmil and to participate in new reciprocal relationships.

As migrants worked longer hours and committed to more demanding jobs, they looked for alternative ways to maintain contact with family members, without having to spend the money and time involved in traveling to Kuchmil. Cellular phones provide another example of technology that has allowed migrants to maintain a sense of community across time and space. When I first visited Kuchmil in 1991, telephone communication with Kuchmil via a call box in the neighboring town was difficult due to faulty electrical wiring. If migrants wished to contact their relatives in

Kuchmil, they had to return to the village. In 1998, however, an entrepreneur in a neighboring village installed a cellular phone with an ample service area provided by a satellite connection.[29] Migrants contacted family members at this number. To reduce the travel required to use this service, Kuchmil demanded a similar service from its municipal president. In 2001, Telcel, Mexico's largest telecommunications company, installed a cellular pay phone in Kuchmil, providing rural families with direct access to their migrant children in Cancún. Yet, in Cancún, the majority of the apartments available in the shantytowns did not include access to telephone land lines, which were expensive to contract in Mexico.

By 2001, cell phones with prepaid phone cards had become readily available for the urban poor. Cell phones, nonetheless, were expensive. In 2001, migrants paid at least $100 for a new cell phone (not including the prepaid phone card of $10), but this amount was cheaper than installing a land line, which entailed installment and monthly rental fees. At least a third of the Kuchmil migrants purchased cell phones for the primary purpose of maintaining contact with their natal families. Presently, all migrants in Cancún own or have access to a cell phone or land line. Migrants kept abreast via telephone of the political rallies taking place in Kuchmil, and invited rural family members to birthday parties and other events in Cancún. In addition, cell phones facilitated increased communication among Kuchmil migrants residing in Cancún, making social gatherings and emergency crises easier to organize and manage. Cell phones also decreased the isolation migrants experienced while living in Cancún's shantytowns. Consequently, as new production technologies are adopted by transnational corporations and the nation-state to discipline workers, they also provide migrants with the opportunity to further their own social and political agendas.

## Manufacturing Consent

The service industry is dominated by a low-wage, unskilled workforce. Given the need to keep wages low within this industry, manufacturing consent is of central importance to hotel corporations. By analyzing the role new production practices played in disciplining the bodies of service workers, I demonstrate that consent was manufactured not only through such tactics as time tests and productivity rates, but also through a process of sociocultural transformation. As they maneuvered bureaucratic institutions (e.g., hotels, banks, and hospitals) and navigated a translocality segregated by class and race, Maya migrants faced discursive, ideological, structural, systematic, and semiotic technologies intended to teach them how to become good workers and citizens of Mexico.

However, just as workers historically employed foot-dragging strategies to resist capitalism's efficiency mandate (see Scott 1985), service workers also used emergent technologies, such as ATMs and cell phones, and other strategies to challenge the individualization of the workforce and to maintain and strengthen community and kin ties across time and space. For Kuchmil women, the informal sector, with its emphasis on emotional attachments and trust, constituted a better alternative to formal service work. Through these practices, migrants offset the isolation experienced as workers in the service industry and as residents of an urban shantytown. Considering the increasing shift to a service economy worldwide, understanding the role new production practices play in controlling this workforce, and the strategies of resistance service workers employ, is critical to future studies of global capitalism.

# 5

# *Gustos,* Goods, and Gender:
# Reproducing Maya Social Relations

Dining room table = $223
Dining room chair = $95
14-inch television = $167
Monthly rent for a room measuring 4 meters by 4 meters = $89
Daily minimum wage = $3.90[1]

In Cancún, migrants informed me, "todo es comprado" (everything must be purchased), such as water, food, housing, furniture, and so forth (see Re Cruz 2003); unlike in Kuchmil, where residents grow their own food, do not pay rent, use natural resources to build their homes, and receive government subsidies to pay for water usage, school supplies, and corn production. Lacking similar resources in Cancún, working-class migrants find it difficult to survive on minimum-wage salaries. Daily expenses such as food and transportation, monthly housing and utility bills, and costs associated with unexpected health crises consume migrant wages. To feed and clothe their families and themselves, they rely on tips from the service-based economy and income from services rendered within the informal economy. In 2001, migrants were restricted to paying cash for clothing and durable goods from commercial stores and *tianguis* (flea markets) because credit targeting the working class was scarce.[2] Given the cost of goods, saving money in Cancún's dollar-based economy to send to families in Kuchmil posed a challenge to many migrants.

In light of these economic constraints, how do migrants manage to do so? Money spent on daily expenses in Cancún cannot be allocated to rural households. Migrant consumption, then, in addition to wages, affects remittance practices. By remittance practices, I am referring to the money and goods migrants send to their communities of origin. Thus what is given needs to be understood within the context of what is consumed. Néstor

García Canclini suggests that "when we select goods and appropriate them, we define what we consider publicly valuable, the ways we integrate and distinguish ourselves in society, and the ways to combine pragmatism with pleasure" (2001, 20). As such, consumption practices serve as acts of self-expression and as statements of values. Correspondingly, what we give says as much about ourselves and our values as the items that we consume. What we give also says a great deal about how we value others. Since goods—not just cash—form part and parcel of migrant remittances and if we consider "any thing intended for exchange" as a commodity (Appadurai 1986, 9), I conceptualize remittance practices as a form of consumption.

While the consumption and promotion of electronic goods is a common phenomenon of the global economy, I suggest that Maya migrants used consumption and remittance practices to mediate the contradictory roles they experienced as they participated in Mexico's modernization projects, such as the contradiction of fulfilling social obligations to their families and community of origin when migrants lived far away from this community. Providing remittances allowed both male and female migrants to maintain their standing within Kuchmil's moral economy despite the distance. Thus the consumption and circulation of goods and money reproduced Maya social relations and notions of personhood across the de-territorialized social space of the migrant circuit. Consumption practices, then, become key spaces for understanding the interplay between social obligations and individual self-expression among migrant workers.

## Consumption as a Social Process

The study of mass consumption as a social process has emerged as a focus in the social sciences within the last three decades. Although earlier studies discussed consumption practices, particularly as part of systems of exchange and production, these studies paid scant attention to mass consumption as a site for the production of meaning (e.g., Malinowski 1922/1961; Mauss 1954/1990; Wolf 1966). Instead, the consumption of Western goods was considered either to erode culture or to highlight culture's flexibility to incorporate new elements (e.g., Kroeber 1939; Redfield 1941). Current studies "no longer view [mass consumption] as part continuity of cultural difference and part loss," but as embedded in the process of cultural meaning-making (Miller 1995, 268).[3]

Anthropological studies of consumption suggest that social values define each object consumed, in contrast to economic analyses that consider consumption to be solely an individual choice (Douglas and Isherwood 1979/1996). Goods are laden with meanings imposed not just by corporations and their advertisements, but by people themselves; meanings that are socially constructed and, thereby, context and culture dependent (Appadurai 1986; Chin 2001; Miller 1998; Park 2005). For example, a television, an item found in most Mexican households, represents different social values in Kuchmil than it does in Cancún. In Kuchmil, a television provides entertainment and information and marks class status, social mobility, and economic success. In Cancún, while migrants attribute similar social values to a television, they also ascribe new meanings derived from urban living. A television represents a security system because the noise keeps thieves at bay; a babysitter for children who are not allowed to play outside without supervision; a representation of one's consumer tastes; and a visible marker of one's labor, equivalent to harvested corn in Kuchmil. A Kuchmil migrant's purchase of a television is motivated by most, if not all, of these social values. As Mary Douglas and Baron Isherwood point out, goods "assembled together in ownership make physical, visible statements about the hierarchy of values to which their chooser subscribes" (1996, ix).

Understanding consumption as a social process challenges economic approaches to consumption based on rational choice and maximal utility theory. The rational individual who attempts to maximize the utility of his/her money forms the basis for many economic models of consumption. Yet, these models ignore cultural differences and historical contexts, and thereby ahistoricize consumption practices (ibid.). For example, drinking Coke in Kuchmil today differs qualitatively from drinking Coke fifteen years ago because the meanings involved in the consumption of Coke have changed over time; they are not constant (see Nash 2007). In the past, Coke was a luxury item to be consumed as an occasional treat or during special events such as weddings and festivals. Today, Pepsi (owned by PepsiCo, Inc.) has made significant inroads into Coca-Cola Company's monopoly of the Mexican countryside. Competitive pricing, and the increased access to cash by Kuchmil households, has converted these beverages from a luxury drink consumed on special occasions to the beverage that accompanies the midday meal.[4]

In addition, economic approaches to consumption based on rational choice theory assume that the concept of rationality itself is objective, neutral, and cross-cultural. This presumption ignores the ideological and cultural dimensions implicit in this usage (Lave 1988; Sahlins 1976). Whose rationality or cultural logic is being used to define consumer tastes and practices? Few models account for taste in economic theories of consumption. As such, tastes or preferences are assumed to be a given in rational choice and maximal utility theories (Douglas and Isherwood 1979/1996).[5] Pierre Bourdieu (1984) argues that taste is learned, that it is socially derived. For Bourdieu, taste is defined by social status and education; that is, the upper and middle class set up the boundaries of taste for the working class (Miller 1995). In contrast, I consider tastes to be multiple, overlapping, and context-dependent. The working class sets up its own standards for taste, while at the same time incorporating or rejecting standards set by the upper class and within the context of a global economy, by other cultures (see Chin 2001). Therefore purely utilitarian models of consumption, which fail to account for taste, cannot fully explain the distinct social meanings attributed to objects—meanings that transform goods from objects into values and values into consumption practices—or the tastes that inspired their consumption. Why would a young man, like Francisco May Pat, who makes a little over $200 per month, consider spending $600 on a Sony 27″ WEGA stereo television with a flat picture tube, when he already owns a functioning 14″ television? Doesn't this purchase undercut the utility of the previous one? Is this a "rational" purchase? How do we explain his decision? How do we account for taste? Following recent works that address taste in relation to identity construction, class formation, and production (Dávila 2001; Freeman 2000; García Canclini 2001; O'Dougherty 2002; Park 2005; Rothstein 2005), this chapter discusses the cultural production of taste among indigenous migrant workers who recently joined the urban working class. It examines why migrants consume particular goods, the rationality behind this conspicuous consumption, and the relationship between conspicuous consumption, remittances, and social obligations.

## Gustos as Personhood

Horacio May Kauil and his wife Mari live with their daughter in a small room, measuring about three meters by six meters, in one of the more established regiones, close to the busy commercial center of Cancún. In 1996, Horacio left Kuchmil to find work in Mexico's most popular tourist city. While the exterior of his house was simple, with its wooden frame, glassless window, and black corrugated cardboard roof, the interior was not. The entire space was crammed with goods. Stored inside were two televisions, a stereo system, a VCR, a gas stove, a microwave, a glass dining room table with four chairs, two adult bicycles, a child's bicycle, a full-size bed, a refrigerator, an armoire, and the latest purchase, a china cabinet. I came across similar scenes to this one during my time in Cancún. Certainly during the sixteen years I have worked with the community of Kuchmil, I have seen how the circulation of mass-produced goods in the peninsula has grown as a result of migration. In Horacio's parental home, the color television Horacio sent home was placed on the altar next to the *Virgen de Guadalupe*. The presence of these goods led me to ask: Considering Cancún's emphasis on the modern consumer, does the conspicuous consumption of expensive, durable goods represent a transformation from peasant to proletariat, from rural to modern, as modernization theories would have us believe? More important, what social values and cultural logics were attached to these goods? What do these goods tell us about Maya social relations and their historical transformations?

Daniel Miller (1995) argues that consumption is not an act of free choice because it is shaped by factors beyond an individual's control, such as the consumer taste index, the interests of major corporations, and advertisements. Indeed, migrants are drawn to the sexy, innovative ads and commercials that represent the kind of lifestyle they would like to live. Yet, advertisements and commercials are not the only forms of communication that teach migrants that one is defined by what one owns. At the same time, we must bear in mind, as Jonathan Parry and Maurice Bloch (1989) propose, that commodities do not always have to be the carriers of modernity or serve as indicators of the transformative processes of modernity. Advertisements and commercials are not the only forms of communication that teach migrants that one is defined by what one owns and, I would add, by what one gives. That is, we cannot assume that the goods filling Horacio's home represent his transformation into an autonomous neoliberal individual. Nor can we assume that the consumption of these goods represents something else altogether because migrants were bombarded with similar pressures to consume as the rest of us. Understanding Kuchmil migrants' consumption of mass-produced goods, then, requires that we tease out the multiple and often contradictory meanings attributed to these goods and the cultural logics that regulate these practices. As

Marilyn Strathern notes for migrants in Melanesia, commodities that are exchanged represent "parts of persons" and in the process "create *mediated* relations" (1988, 178). Commodities, then, can become imbued with the attributes of the consumer and the giver. Strathern's insight is a useful way of understanding the meaning and value of the goods consumed and circulated by Maya migrants. I suggest that goods consumed through Maya wage labor and sent to Kuchmil also created mediated relations between individuals, households, and the global economy.

Maya migrants are taught at an early age to state their *gustos* (tastes and desires), in terms of food, clothing, activities, television programs, and so forth. These gustos serve to distinguish individuals throughout the life cycle (cf. Alonso 1992). It is through these choices—these desires and tastes—that Maya children express their individual personality. As one mother stated of her one-year-old son, "How will my son know what he likes if I don't make him tell me?" Children were prodded by their parents to "decir cual es su gusto" (state their tastes), because these outbursts of opinions not only marked individuality, but more important, represented the normal development of the child, who should be inquisitive, stubborn, and playful. Shy and quiet children were considered abnormal; their mental development was believed to be occurring at a slower rate, in some cases due to exposure to trauma from residing in an abusive household. It was through these choices, these statements of tastes—even nonverbal ones—that Maya children and adults expressed their individual personality and marked their development into responsible and intelligent persons. As children grew older and began to earn money, they purchased goods that helped to visibly distinguish them from others. Certainly, adolescents make statements about who they are and want to become through their dress and hairstyles (see Greene 2001a; Mills 1997; Pancake 1991). Likewise, for adults, purchasing items that one desires is considered a normal expression of taste, regardless of whether the item is a necklace, clothes, or a stereo. Through her study of rural women in northern Mexico, Ana María Alonso suggests that "public displays of 'good taste' *(buen gusto)* and beauty are sources of social value for women, enhancing their prestige vis-à-vis both women and men" (1992, 177). Gustos are also gendered practices because men and women display and perform their gustos in distinct ways (cf. Butler 1990). In Maya society, gustos marked the boundaries of the self and distinguished the self from a collective identity. Gustos, then, serve as a lens through which we can understand Maya personhood.[6] In contrast to studies that depict indigenous communities as primarily rooted in strong collective identities, this understanding of Maya personhood emphasizes the important role the self also plays in constructing the social world inhabited by Maya migrants.[7]

The recognition of the individual within a collectively oriented society did result in tensions, especially as more youths migrated to Cancún. In Kuchmil, the physical embellishment and decoration of the body has only recently become associated with conformity to Western standards of physical beauty, made more visible by access to satellite television and beauty magazines. Youths appropriated behaviors, images, and styles they observed in the media. Young men and women concerned themselves with hairstyles, trendy clothing, and owning goods. As young men and women became increasingly exposed to this ideal via television and big-city life, the qualities appreciated in both sexes became more aligned with this ideal. As in the United States, accessories and brand names of shoes and clothes matter. Visiting or returning migrants brought home goods, such as stereos, bicycles, clothing, jewelry, and perfumes; goods that are advertised on television and whet the consumer appetites of Kuchmil's youths. Cancún, like most cities, becomes marked as the place that has everything—for a steep price, of course. The presence of these luxury goods amid the poverty of the Mexican countryside (here I am referring to a dearth of goods, not necessarily a dearth of wealth, because not all campesinos are cash-poor or land-poor) creates what Steedman calls the "politics of envy"; that is, "the desire of people for the things of this earth" (1997, 7). These desires also spur migrations to the places where these yearnings can be fulfilled, regardless of the economic instability migrants encounter there. These desires, these gustos, also create yearnings among rural residents who remain in the countryside, but who must devise alternative methods by which to acquire these goods. To do so, they manipulate local power struggles and state conceptualizations of the rural poor, and rely on temporary wage labor. As Steedman eloquently suggests, "the other side of waiting [for political and economic inclusion] is wanting" (22).

Instead of demanding these goods from their parents, migrant youths purchase them with their own income. This presentation of self was one of the primary motivators for the exodus of young women and girls from Kuchmil in 1992. The families of these young women did not have the money necessary to purchase school supplies, or the clothes and makeup desired for fiestas. Kuchmil families explained that they earned just enough money to get by, which was not enough to spend on the items desired by image-conscious adolescents and aspiring students. Enrique May Kauil, Berenice's father, who moved his family to Valladolid but continues to farm in Kuchmil, expressed the strain of supporting a family on a minimum-wage job, the relief experienced after his daughters contributed toward household expenses, and the motivation behind his children's entry into the labor market:

> [Our money] barely suffices. Sometimes it doesn't, but our two little daughters are working. Well, they help us complete the payment for the gas. Because if it's left up to me to support all of them, I can't. It doesn't suffice. Only because they are working. Well, with what they earn, they purchase their clothes, their shoes. Whatever they want they buy because I don't make enough so that I can purchase these items for them. That's why they didn't continue studying, that's why they say, "I want to use pretty clothes. I want to buy my pretty shoes." They had to go to work to accomplish this. Because if I [had to do it] alone, I can't. I can't make enough— the money doesn't suffice. Four hundred pesos is a little bit, just enough to cover food.

By allowing adolescents to enter the labor force, parents reduced the economic strain placed on households by their children's demands for consumer goods.

The story of Mario Can Tun illustrates the complex relationship between the right to self-expression, consumption, and parental demands. Mario's family migrated to Cancún when he was thirteen years old. During weekends, he performed for tourists with his father (don Dani Can Balam), brother, and cousin in an itinerant mariachi band.[8] Due to his age, Mario attracted a crowd. In spite of Mario's young age, he received an equal share of the earnings (on average $40 daily). Regardless of age and status, the four members split their wages evenly every day. Mario gave a third of his wages to his mother and kept the rest to spend on his own gustos (i.e., a bicycle, music tapes, and clothes). When Mario turned fifteen, his family moved back to Kuchmil. After living in Cancún, Mario was very selective of the clothes he wore and his musical tastes. In spite of his dream of becoming a professional mariachi singer like Vicente Fernández, he preferred techno music to cumbias (the most popular dance form in the

*A mariachi group in Cancún.*

area), tennis shoes to boots, khaki pants to jeans, and torn faded baseball hats (what he called "Enrique Iglesias style") to sombreros.[9] Mario's tastes in music and dress derived from his urban experience, from the images and music he absorbed while working and living in Cancún. By adopting an urban rock dress style, Mario clearly marked his gustos and set himself apart from his peers, the majority of whom preferred the dress style of the urban *vaquero* (cowboy) and listened to *música tropical* and *ranchera* (tropical and country music). Even though these tastes insinuated a rejection of rural Maya culture, Mario's parents and siblings publicly supported his gustos by catering to his tastes and by discussing how Mario's tastes and activities distinguished him from the other adolescents in Kuchmil. "He is not like other young people around here," they exclaimed. When Mario was crowned King of Carnaval (during the annual festivities celebrated before Lent), his family claimed that his popularity was based on his success at distinguishing himself from other adolescents through the presentation of his gustos. I further elaborate on the tensions created by this self-expression later in the chapter, but first I discuss who is obligated to give in contemporary Maya society, and how these obligations structure the performance of gustos.

## Who Gives?

Marcel Mauss (1954/1990) points out that the obligation to give is a social contract, not just an economic one, regardless of who is obligated to give. In other words, who gives does not occur in isolation from established kin and social networks. Migrant remittances and resources form part of this gift economy because all gifts incur some form of obligation, be it symbolic or material. Given the systems of reciprocity in which migrants and their contributions are embedded (see chapter 3), does migration transform Kuchmil's gift economy?

While migration results in the physical rupture of the nuclear unit, it does not result in a complete financial or social rupture. Maya society recognizes the individual as a social actor within a web of dense social relations regardless of where individuals live. Nonetheless, just as married children in Kuchmil, whose primary allegiance is to their own nuclear unit, are not expected to contribute steady infusions of cash into their parents' households, married migrants are also not expected to remit.[10] In contrast, unmarried children who work in Cancún are expected to continue contributing to the nuclear household because they remain under the authority of their parents, regardless of the distance between the village and city in which they live, and continue to be so until they marry. Out of respect for parental authority, and in response to parental demands for income, migrant children substitute their labor with wages and goods. Studies of transnational migrant remittances demonstrate the inverse relationship between remittances and settlement; the longer migrants remain in the migrant site, the less they remit (Lowell and de la Garza 2000). While this correlation is true among married Maya migrants, it is not the case among unmarried Maya migrants whose remittances remain steady with time.[11] Consequently by becoming wageworkers during their adolescent years, young Maya men and women experience an early departure from their nurturing households and become important economic contributors to their natal families.

For these migrants, remittances mediated the contradictory roles that result from participation in wage labor in Cancún and from being part of the moral economy in Kuchmil. This was evident in three ways. First, remittances fulfilled migrants' social obligation to provide their labor to their household. Second, they served as visible displays of migrants' labor. And third, they served as physical representations of their owners' *gustos.*

## The Financial Life of Remittances

To understand what people give requires knowledge of how people pay for what they give. I trace the "social lives" of remittances by first examining their financial roots (Appadurai 1986, 3). Given that labor-market processes limit the income of the working poor, they must come up with alternative and creative ways to acquire extra income (e.g., Bourgois 1995; Stack 1974). Similarly, Maya migrants, like all of Cancún's working class, creatively manage their minimum-wage salaries to purchase the goods and services that make up life in Cancún. The sources of income available to migrants included wages and tips earned in the formal economy, money generated from the informal economy, and personal loans.

Regardless of the kind of labor they performed, migrants who worked in the formal economy (usually hotel and restaurant work) earned at least the daily minimum wage of $3.90, paid in bimonthly installments. This wage, however, barely covered daily living expenses. Mexico's Ley Federal de Trabajo (Federal Labor Law) stipulates that employers are required to pay a 5 percent payroll tax per employee into the Instituto Nacional del Fondo de la Vivienda para los Trabajadores (INFONAVIT; National Fund for Employee Housing) and to provide workers with health insurance through the Instituto Mexicano del Seguro Social (IMSS; Mexican Institute of Social Security), a retirement account, and an *aguinaldo* (Christmas bonus) equivalent to fifteen days' salary. In Cancún, the hotel industry also supplemented their employees' daily minimum wage with food and transportation coupons. These subsidies helped stretch workers' income. Although the limitations to the national health system guaranteed that most employees sought out a private medical diagnosis and prescription drugs during severe illnesses, medical coverage through the IMSS provided essential preventive care for working-class families.[12] Food vouchers ranged from $100 to $200 per month and could be used at commercial grocery stores like Wal-Mart Supercenters and Comercial Mexicana. Transportation coupons covered 50 to 100 percent of public bus rides, depending on the route accessible to employees. Some hotels contracted private buses to transport their employees. By using vouchers to pay for food and transportation expenses, wages became more flexible.

Nonetheless, the limited purchasing power of the daily minimum wage and work subsidies forced migrants to rely on discretionary sources of income with which to purchase durable goods and provide remittances.

Tips from the service industry formed the primary source of discretionary income for male migrants. While the amount of tips earned varied by employment and position along the service industry labor hierarchy, they consisted, on average, of at least a daily minimum wage per shift. For example, stewards or busboys (low-level entry positions in hotels and nightclubs) earned $1 to $5 in tips per night during the low season (May through November). However, tips increased to $20 to $50 per night during the peak tourist months (February through April). Migrants working as assistant bartenders earned up to $110 per night in nightclubs during the peak season. As a result, male migrants were able to accumulate a significant amount of money from tips. Saúl Chi Be', a steward in a nightclub, saved $600 from his tips.

Although work in the informal economy was not regulated and thus could lead to exploitation, it sometimes paid better. Domestic servants, an unregulated position, earned a significantly higher wage—$8 for four hours of labor—than most entry-level hotel workers, but female migrants who worked as domestic servants in the informal economy did not have access to tips. To generate alternative sources of income, they engaged in additional activities in the informal economy. Mariela, who worked as a domestic servant, sold Jafra makeup, a more expensive cosmetic line than Avon, with items ranging from $15 to $40. By selling Jafra, Mariela gained access to this expensive product; that is, she reinvested her profits into makeup products for herself. Paula sewed clothes for a flat fee of $5 per item, while Ramona earned pocket money by providing at-home health care services to her working-class neighbors. She gave injections of vaccinations, medications, and vitamins. Female migrants used these informal sources of income to purchase inexpensive luxuries and durable goods, to pay bills, and to remit money home. These sources of income, however, did not generate as much revenue as the tips male migrants earned. Consequently, women had a more difficult time saving up large sums of money.

Another strategy to gain access to money was participating in *tandas,* informal rotating credit associations made up of friends and neighbors. Tandas are a common alternative method of savings among Mexican urban households. This cooperative credit system is an effective way of acquiring a large sum of money within a short period of time. Kuchmil migrants participated in tandas that paid out between $110 and $1,000 per investment cycle. Tandas are formed by members of a trusted social network, which ensures that social pressure restricts the possibility of defaulting on the group. After deciding how much they want to contribute and for how long, members deposit money (everyone deposits the same amount) in weekly or bimonthly contributions over a short period of time, usually four months. Each week or every two weeks, members rotate withdrawing the total sum deposited. The order in which the contributors receive the money depends on each person's financial need. Some may need the money more quickly than others, while others prefer to be last because it ensures they will not owe any money once they collect the tanda.[13] The exclusion of migrant women from formal systems of credit transformed tandas into the best opportunity for them to acquire large sums of money. Ramona May Pat joined a tanda that paid out $1,000. Not surprisingly, women relied on tandas more often than men.

Formal credit systems also provided access to goods. Although few formal credit systems exist that target the working poor, Maya migrants relied on the existing systems, even if these systems involved higher interest rates. Elektra, an electronics and furniture store that targets the lower-middle class, offered store credit for its goods. Although Elektra charged a higher price for its goods than stores that did not offer credit, migrants who were eligible for store credit preferred Elektra because they claimed that their goods were better quality.[14] The service industry, likewise, set up its own systems of credit. Hotel companies offered loans to employees, which were deducted from their salary on a monthly basis. Male migrants who were not eligible for store credit relied on employer credit. It is important to note that male migrants were the only ones able to take advantage of this type of credit. Regardless of these options for credit, the majority of migrants preferred to pay cash, rather than buy on credit. Debt was seen as too risky given their already precarious economic situations.

Not all goods were purchased in stores. Many items were purchased through the informal economy. An informal secondhand goods market circulated among friends in Cancún. To sell used goods, migrants circulated the news among friends, relatives, and work colleagues. The transient nature of Cancún's tourist industry assured the constant circulation of goods from household to household. Maya migrants took advantage of these opportunities to purchase used quality goods at reduced prices, like cameras, video cameras, stereos, refrigerators, and cell phones. Before I moved back to the United States, I sold the few durable goods (television, table and chairs, and air conditioner) I had collected during my stay in

Cancún; months before my departure, Kuchmil migrants requested that I reserve these items for them. In some instances, migrants accepted goods in exchange for money owed by friends and relatives. Maya migrants also purchased secondhand goods from the hotel industry. During hotel renovation projects, hotels sold their used furniture and televisions at significantly reduced prices to their employees. Secondhand goods could also be found at the weekly neighborhood tianguis. Although most items sold at tianguis were not secondhand, the prices at which they are offered were cheaper than their official designated market value.

Social networks provided another informal source of cash for migrants. Due to their limited salaries and minimal access to formal credit, migrants must plan their conspicuous consumption. Migrants turned to their extended kin network for money and social support, which included fictive kin from the compadrazgo system. Asking for a loan from one's social network required establishing a good credit history, making family ties evident, and naming a valid reason for the request. Consequently, these loans cemented social relationships (see Stack 1974; Zavella 1987). For example, Mariela borrowed money from Saúl Chi Be', her brother-in-law, to complete the $300 she needed to purchase a television, which was a gift for her father. The following year during the low tourist season, Saúl borrowed money from Mariela to complete the $110 he needed to purchase his son's stroller. Employers and work colleagues also provided personal loans for migrant consumption and remittance practices. For example, after building a relationship of trust, domestic servants were able to ask their employers for loans, while work companions were asked to become godparents in the compadrazgo system. Tandas were also based on trust; migrants advised me that one cannot participate in an informal system of credit without confianza. The social life of remittances depends heavily on the maintenance of biological and fictive kin networks.

## Earmarking Funds

If the poor aspire to own, Francisco May Pat informed me, then they must learn to save. To do so, migrants earmarked a specific amount of money from their salary on a bimonthly or monthly basis and/or earmarked discretionary incomes, such as tips and money collected from tandas. The needs of each migrant determined the categories for discretionary funds, but these allocations could be compartmentalized into three broad categories of expenses: (1) a pueblo fund; (2) a gustos fund; and (3) an establishment fund. For conceptual clarity, I rely on these categories to explain migrants' "funding intentions" (Zelizer 1994). Migrants established a pueblo fund to cover expenses related to Kuchmil. Migrants used this fund to send money home, to purchase goods to be sent home, to pay for religious *promesas* (promises) and cargos, and to pay for travel and other expenses incurred during visits to Kuchmil. In addition, since migrants wanted goods, particularly high-quality goods, the gustos fund paid for stereos, televisions, stoves, armoires, dressers, dining room tables and chairs, cell phones, and refrigerators. Finally, to save the money necessary to establish oneself in Cancún or any other city, Kuchmil migrants allocated money to their establishment fund. Monies were used to buy land, to build a house, to invest in a business, to pay for a wedding, to buy a car, and to cover rent and daily expenses when money was scarce during the low tourist season. This fund was sacrosanct because its intent was to provide future economic stability. Physically distinguished from the pueblo and gustos funds, this fund was rarely touched, even during emergencies. For example, Horacio May Kauil quit drinking with his buddies in order to divert this income into the construction of his new home. In contrast, the pueblo and gustos funds are fungible; that is, if necessary, they can be used for emergencies. Illness, legal troubles, emergency travel, and social network claims divert the purpose of these funds to cover such crises. Health problems, migrants reminded me, can bankrupt you because of their unexpected nature and the expense required to cure them. Treatment by a private doctor costs at least $50 ($30 for the doctor's visit and $20 to hundreds of dollars for medications).

All three funds must be continually replenished. Unlike the establishment fund, which required saving consistently for several years, the pueblo and gustos funds were continually reborn year after year; they contracted and expanded, depending on the intentions that spurred their creation. These funds disappeared at certain moments in time, particularly during an economic crisis or as soon as they were spent on their intended purpose. This "social earmarking" of monies allowed migrants to save large quantities of money (Zelizer 1994, 24). Earmarked money was rarely touched because it was parceled into categories that symbolized salient relations, needs, and gustos in people's lives (see Lave 1988). While most migrants did not name their stashes of money, especially when the money was usually kept in one lump sum, they conceptually distinguished the amount of money they intended to spend on a particular purchase or event.

Migrants stored these savings primarily in cash. A few migrants opened individual savings accounts with banks and hotel companies. To save money to purchase an additional plot of land for his business, Jesús May Pat opened a savings account with a local bank. Minerva Can Uc, who worked as a domestic servant, also relied on a bank account to protect her money. Since her sister subsidized most of her expenses, she spent very little money in Cancún. Her cousins informed me that she had over $5,000 in savings. Hotel employees could put aside money from their paychecks on a monthly basis; the hotel transferred the amount requested into an interest-bearing savings account. This money, along with the interest, was handed over to the employee at the end of the year.[15] However, not all migrants had access to a savings account, and even those who did, did not necessarily take advantage of this option.[16] The majority of migrants kept their money the old-fashioned way.

## What Is Given?

One of the challenges to studies of remittances is tracking remittances, particularly those that travel through informal channels (Lozano Ascencio 1993). To track remittances, I interviewed both migrants about their remittance practices and Kuchmil households about the remittances they received. I also traveled with migrants on their visits home, and visited migrants' homes when family members from Kuchmil arrived in Cancún. Cash and goods constituted the most visible forms of migrant remittances.[17] In contrast to remittance transfers by international migrants, 90 percent of which are characterized by the use of electronic transfers or money orders (Lowell and de la Garza 2000), remittance transfers among internal migrants occurred predominantly through informal channels. In 2001, the relative isolation of Kuchmil from banks, the lack of knowledge about the banking system, and the limited use of bank accounts by migrants made it difficult for migrants to transfer money electronically to their hometown and families. Cash and goods were sent home with relatives and close friends, carried personally by migrants, or picked up by family members visiting Cancún. In a few instances, I carried letters, money, and goods between Kuchmil and Cancún. Within such a system, goods could travel safely and thus constituted a significant portion of the constant flow of remittances. This reliance on informal channels shows how deeply remittances were embedded in social relationships.

At least half of the Kuchmil households had *direct* access to migrant contributions. Thirteen of the twenty-nine households in Kuchmil included members who migrated to cities, principally Cancún. The remaining households had *indirect* access to migrant contributions via their extended kin networks. Since minimum-wage salaries and busy schedules limited the amount and frequency of migrant remittances, natal families did not receive a "salary" from their migrant children.[18] Instead, unmarried migrants delivered on average $50 dollars every two to three months. The amount remitted did not vary much among unmarried migrants, but it did among married migrants. On average, married migrants' remittances ranged from $15 to $30 every few months. Emergencies or special events, such as weddings, the village fiesta, and other ceremonies, demanded larger contributions, up to $200, from all migrants. The heads of households in Kuchmil stressed that they were not dependent on migrant contributions for their sustenance. Since only half of these households had direct access to remittances, they proudly reminded me that they took care of their households' daily expenses. The ejido continued to provide a family's basic staples. More important, government subsidies, not migrant contributions, formed Kuchmil households' primary source of income (see Table 2). Remittances, nonetheless, played a critical role within rural households because this cash covered extraordinary expenses, that is, expenses incurred beyond daily sustenance like the cost of rituals, additional labor in the milpa, secondary and postsecondary school fees and tuition, health care, and clothing for special events. While remittances were not necessary to sustain rural households, they nonetheless played a critical role in their social reproduction. Remittances were also used to solidify kin networks and expand social networks, increase leisure time, and purchase additional labor, thereby accumulating social and economic capital for households with access to migrant wages.

Durable and consumable goods also formed an important component of migrant remittance practices. Contributions of durable goods included items such as gold jewelry, *electrico-dómesticos* (electrical appliances for the home), kitchenware, and housing construction materials. Consumable goods consisted of food, clothing, and medicines. Migrants purchased goods they believed would enhance their parents' quality of life by decreasing their labor output (e.g., washing machines and blenders), by improving their health (e.g., vitamins, food, and water-purifying tablets), or by offering entertainment and rest (e.g., fans, televisions, and compact disc players).

TABLE 2

**Total average monthly and annual household revenue in Kuchmil, 2001 (in U.S. dollars)**

| | WITHOUT MIGRANT CHILDREN | | WITH MIGRANT CHILDREN | |
|---|---|---|---|---|
| | MONTHLY | ANNUAL | MONTHLY | ANNUAL |
| Household income | $37 | $444 | $18 | $216 |
| Subsidies | $65 | $780 | $93 | $1,116 |
| Remittances (cash only) | — | — | $18 | $216 |
| Total household revenue | $102 | $1,224 | $129 | $1,548 |

For village fiestas, migrants supplied the meat, liquor, and religious icons and materials needed for the decorations.

## The Order of Things

The order in which goods were purchased reveals decision-making processes within migrant and rural households. This order demonstrates which items were considered essential, which items fulfilled gustos, and which items were purchased out of obligation to the rural family, even though in some cases goods fulfilled all three purposes. Tracing the order of goods also reveals gender differences in migrant consumption practices; men and women did not purchase goods in the same order, nor did they always purchase the same goods.

When migrants first arrive in Cancún, they purchase goods "essential" for subsistence in Cancún. Cultural understandings of essential items for living vary within the Kuchmil–Cancún migrant circuit. While a stove was not considered an essential item for living in Kuchmil, it was in Cancún. As such, I refer to essential items as items that Maya migrants purchased because they fulfilled a basic need. Unlike most rental housing in the United States, in which landlords equip a rental unit with a stove and, in some cases, refrigerators and washing machines, rental housing in Mexico is stripped of these amenities. Occupants provided their own stoves, refrigerators, air conditioners, and washing machines. Furnishing a rented room or house in Cancún entailed purchasing the following essentials: a hammock for sleeping, a stove and tank of gas for cooking, an iron to keep one's work uniform neatly pressed, kitchenware, a *batea* (basin) to hand-wash clothes, and a table and chair for meals. Maya migrants brought their hammocks from home and purchased the remaining items in Cancún. Recent migrants, who shared housing with a relative, were able to avoid purchasing many of these items until they established their own household. After equipping themselves with these basic items, Maya migrants purchased items based on their gustos or on the demands placed on them by their families in Kuchmil.

Gender affects the logic of consumption and remittances. The first purchases made by Maya women differed from those made by men. Women purchased gold jewelry with their first few months' wages, an item traditionally expected to be given to them by their future husband. This purchase served as an investment. Jeni Moo Chi's narrative illustrates the importance of gold. Jeni bought *oro bueno* (fourteen-karat gold) while she worked as a domestic servant in Cancún. After marrying a Kuchmil migrant, Jeni remained childless. Miraculously, a few years later, she became pregnant and bore a daughter who was very sick. The local doctors could not cure her illness, and her husband did not have enough money to pay for a private doctor. Jeni refused to leave her daughter's fate to God's will. She pawned all of her jewelry. With this money, she traveled with her daughter to Mérida to visit a well-known pediatrician who successfully treated her daughter. Jeni continues to invest her money in gold jewelry. Rural families did not criticize their migrant daughters for purchasing gold because the purchase of gold jewelry reflected their gustos and represented a sound investment.

Migrant women also purchased gold for their mothers and siblings. In many instances, migrant women allowed their mothers in Kuchmil to "borrow" their gold; this practice prevented the possible theft of gold on the street and in the homes in Cancún while at the same time improving their mothers' "visible" investments. I was deeply touched when Paula gave me a gold ring as a birthday present. During my time in Mexico, I wore very little jewelry, occasionally a pair of gold-hoop earrings. The absence of gold on my person prompted Maya women to advise me on the economic benefits of owning gold, where to purchase it, what kind to buy, and the like. These discussions were held waiting in line for government subsidies, at weddings, at baptisms, and in people's homes. Even young children knew the value of gold. One afternoon during a visit with Isadora

Can Uc and her young children, Isadora's three-year-old son asked me, "Where is your *sogilla* (gold necklace)?" I informed him that I did not have one. In response, he asked me "*Yàan öoȼil?*" (Are you poor?). Since even he owned a sogilla, he presumed I must be poor. Maya women worried about my lack of gold because, for them, it translated into a lack of future economic security.

Men, in contrast, first purchased a television or a bicycle, items that entertained them or increased their physical mobility in Cancún. Francisco May Pat explained the important role a television served in an urban setting. "Sometimes we arrive at home [from work] only to look at each other's faces. We didn't have anything to do, or we would sit and watch the street. We would get bored. Because of those experiences, we got the television." The television also entertained the wives and children of married migrants. Rental housing for the working poor in Cancún consists primarily of single rooms measuring four meters by four meters that lacked a private patio. To avoid break-ins, child abduction, and other perils of the street, married women and their children spent their daylight hours enclosed within their rented rooms. *Gustando* (watching and enjoying) television helped Maya men, women, and children transition into an urban lifestyle of solitude, tight living spaces, and locked doors. It is important to note that when Kuchmil women migrate to Cancún, they move into already established households belonging to a relative or a husband, most of which include televisions to which they have access, allowing them to divert their income to the purchase of other goods.

Cell phones were another item that Maya men purchased prior to women. In Mexico, rented rooms and apartments rarely included telephone landlines. Since the waiting list to install a landline takes several months, Kuchmil migrants relied on cell phones, in spite of the expense, as a way to communicate with each other and their families in Kuchmil. Initially, men purchased this item at a higher rate than women did because single migrant women usually lived in established households with cell phones or access to landlines, while married migrant women were given cell phones by their husbands or shared their husbands' cell phones. However, as cell phones have become more affordable and ubiquitous, women now purchase them as often as men.

Like male migrants, migrant women also purchased televisions, bicycles, stereo systems, and furniture. However, they diverged on kitchenware. Men purchased a stove before women did. Since migrant women shared living quarters with married relatives who already owned this item, they did not need to invest in a stove. But women were first to acquire items like washing machines that helped ease domestic chores. Maya women were usually in charge of the washing, regardless of whether they were employed or not, in both migrant and natal communities. Washing machines reduced their labor significantly in both settings. Thus, consumption practices were gendered.

## Making Labor Visible

The money migrants sent home, in most cases, was invested or spent on goods or services that the community did not necessarily associate with migrant labor, especially if the money was spent on food or clothes. In contrast, many of the goods migrants sent home were directly associated with migrant labor because of their conspicuous nature. By conspicuous, I am referring to the exorbitant cost of these goods. Few families from Kuchmil could afford the electronic goods migrants sent home. The presence of these goods in rural households served as visible displays of migrant labor contributions, similar to their participation in the village rituals and the purchase of a land plot. These goods were displayed in prominent positions in rural homes, like the location of Horacio's television on the altar. Since migrants' visits to Kuchmil were limited by their work schedules, these goods reminded families of their children's presence and of their devotion, particularly during an absence of many months.

For migrants, making their labor visible also constituted an attempt to refashion local conceptions of work and gender. Although parents preferred that their children obtain service jobs because it was not as tiring as milpa work, service work did not automatically generate social status the way milpa work did. Unlike milpa cultivation, which was considered back-breaking work, Kuchmil residents considered hotel work to be easy because it did not involve physical labor under a hot sun. Similarly, domestic work in Cancún also did not require the repetitive stress of domestic work in Kuchmil. This image of easy work was cemented when migrants returned home for vacation. No longer accustomed to farmwork and household work, they found it difficult and tiring to help their family members. Service work became associated with women's work because, like women, men worked indoors and participated in activities considered to belong to a woman's domain, such as cooking and serving. To reassert their masculinity and make their labor visible, returning and visiting male migrants came home with expensive durable goods and spent a lot of money during these visits. Similarly, conspicuous goods served as visible displays of female migrants' labor and femininity. Like male migrants, female migrants used these goods to establish or maintain a reputation as a resourceful and dedicated worker. These qualities were highly desired in a wife and reflected positively on these women's reputations. The purchase of gold, for example, was considered a wise investment by Maya women. Men also invested in gold for their wives, female relatives, and, on occasion, for themselves. Gold was worn daily on the bodies of Maya women and children as advertisements of their own labor (in the case of women), of a migrant's labor, and of familial devotion (when gold was a gift). Through this presentation of the self, female migrants attempted to counter the rumors of sexual promiscuity attached to female migration. By visibly displaying their labor through conspicuous goods, male and female migrants represented themselves as hardworking, devoted daughters and sons, and active community members.

The display of gold jewelry, cell phones, and video cameras signaled at the wealth in migrant remittances and generated respect for migrants among rural households. By displaying the luxury goods they purchased with their wages on their bodies, their relatives' bodies, or in their homes, migrants increased the value of their labor in the eyes of the rural community (cf. Bourgois 1995). At the same time, through these goods, migrants also transformed the meaning of work and local expressions of femininity and masculinity (see Finn 1998).

### Gustos and Goods

In addition to serving as a substitute for and visible display of labor, durable goods also constituted a physical representation of gustos. Mass-produced commodities represented the gustos of the person who purchased the items or the gustos of the recipient of these gifts. While migrants purchased many of the same goods, they pointed out that the style, size, and quality of the good and their assemblage served as an expression of their individual tastes. The goods crammed into Horacio's tiny house served as a display of his individuality, aesthetics, tastes, and intelligence. They narrated his personal migration experience in Cancún, his struggle to survive in the service industry, the relationships he sustained and forged within the Kuchmil–Cancún migrant circuit, and the knowledge, experience, and maturity he acquired as a result of these experiences. The presence of particular name brands, such as Sony, which was considered to be of the highest quality, demonstrated Horacio's breadth of knowledge of the quality of such commodities and his astuteness in negotiating the complexity of Cancún's commercial district. In sum, these goods served as a performance of Horacio's moral character.

Unmarried Maya migrants were expected to contribute economically to their rural households, but what they contributed was not regulated. They could contribute items purchased out of desire, which may not have been as useful to the rural household. It was not uncommon for migrants to contribute expensive goods that their families may not necessarily need, such as a compact disc stereo system and another television, even though a more utilitarian object such as a stove may be less expensive to purchase. It is important to note that what is considered utilitarian in one culture, may not be so in another. I categorize a stove as utilitarian because it would reduce the labor expenditures of the household. At least 90 percent of Kuchmil residents cooked over open fires, which required the daily collection of firewood and constant exposure to smoke inhalation. While a stove may require less labor and be better for one's health, it also requires gas, an added expense that reduces its possible utility and converts it into a luxury item. Desirable goods did not always help reduce labor outputs in rural households, but nonetheless they were coveted by rural households and migrants alike because they provided entertainment or reduced labor expenditures and thereby improved the quality of life (without always necessarily increasing expenditures), and thus illustrated the "essentially usurious and sumptuary" facet of the gift economy (Mauss 1990, 6).

Migrant children sent home goods that fulfilled their parents' gustos, not just their own. Gold jewelry is an example of a commodity that fulfilled gustos and was used to distinguish the individual within systems of reciprocity in Maya society. For example, doña Pati used the money I paid her for housing and food to cap several of her teeth with gold because she had always wanted a golden smile. In Maya culture, gold has significant value. Silvia Terán points out that "the language of gold, among them [the mestizas of Yucatán], is not just aesthetic. In their culture, gold signifies the solidity of an engagement and marriage, the security of savings, the brilliance of the fiesta and the only real property of the mestiza" (1994, 10, my translation).[19] In the past when women married, they received a muhul negotiated by their parents that typically included gold jewelry, clothes, and shoes. Falling wages and the increased cost of gold, however, have resulted in smaller gifts of gold jewelry. Today, there is no guarantee that a woman will receive this gift. When don Dani and doña Pati negotiated the muhul for their youngest daughter, they did not specify the amount to avoid appearing demanding. "Whatever is in your heart to give" was their stipulation to their future in-laws. They were shocked when the muhul they offered did not include jewelry. Doña Pati was so angry that she refused to let Fátima marry. "You won't take her," she informed Saúl. Since doña Pati never received a proper muhul upon her marriage, she wished her daughter to avoid this fate. Fátima, however, refused to terminate the engagement because Saúl had given her a gold necklace, bracelet, and earrings a few months before the wedding. For don Dani and doña Pati, these gifts did not count because they were given before the bridewealth negotiations began. At Fátima's insistence, they were forced to give the couple their blessing, and the wedding was held as planned.

As women increasingly participate in migration, women marry at a much later age than in the past and thus delay receiving a muhul.[20] Yet, Silvia Terán observes, "for women, wedding gold is extremely important because it is practically the only thing that they own and over which she has absolute discretion. It forms the cornerstone of her autonomy" (1994, 25, my translation). Given gold's significance, migrant women purchased their own gold jewelry instead of waiting for their future husbands to do so. Mariela gave her mother, doña Pati, a thick gold bracelet that she purchased from a relative because her mother was missing such an item from her collection of gold jewelry. Money was not wasted if you bought gold, women constantly reminded me, because gold could be used as collateral during a financial crisis. Otherwise, money disappears on small delights, like clothing, makeup, recreational activities, and so forth. Gold was expensive but accessible; red gold bracelets and necklaces could be obtained for a minimum of $20 each, a price that can easily be saved up after a few months of work.[21] What type of gold one purchased marked one's gustos (see Villagomez and Pinto 1997, 151). Rural residents preferred red gold shaped into traditional designs and settings by local jewelers: earrings in the shape of calabazitas (pumpkins) or with floral motifs, thick braided necklaces called sogillas, and rings stamped with multicolored designs spelling amor (love). After living in Cancún, migrants learned that red gold marks them as mestizas, or Indians, because indigenous women from the countryside preferred these traditional designs. In contrast, yellow gold (14K), with its modern designs and "Made in Italy" stamp, was associated with a cosmopolitan, urban lifestyle. Since yellow gold was more expensive than red gold, wearing yellow gold marked men and women as upwardly mobile. By choosing yellow gold over red gold, migrants demonstrated their gustos for modern styles and found it easier to express these gustos because yellow gold was fashioned into more varied contemporary designs. The red/yellow gold distinction illustrates how goods mark individual, class, and racial differences.

Although the consumption and promotion of electronic goods is a common phenomenon of the global economy, Kuchmil migrants' consumption practices were rooted in more than just a desire to become modern subjects and to own the goods displayed on television and store windows in Cancún's global market. Certainly, ideas of progress and modernity did guide migrants' consumption practices. For Maya migrants, the acquisition of expensive durable goods was associated with success in the labor market. As Franciso Maya explained, "Aspiramos a tener" (We strive to own). At the same time, the consumption of goods whose cost far exceeds migrants' monthly income also challenges capitalism's emphasis on the good consumer as the primary facet of the model citizen. Indigenous migrants' conspicuous consumption did not necessarily stem from the desire to become autonomous individuals. Such an explanation occludes the complexity of how people are made to feel individual (Rouse 1995). Instead, I propose that indigenous migrants incorporated the trappings of capitalism to reinforce their individuality in the capitalist sense of being economically successful and in the Maya sense of gustos. Through this process, migrants were able to maintain their cultural membership in an indigenous community, could attempt to succeed in Cancún's labor market, and constructed alternative ways to engage with modernity.

## Parental Demands and the Distribution of Goods

Given Cancún's dense population, migrants could "disappear" within the myriad of unmarked streets of Cancún's regiones. The extended kin network, however, kept a close watch over its members. While the nuclear family formed the basic unit of social organization in Kuchmil, the extended kin network took precedence in Cancún. This shift harkens back to older models of social organization within Maya society. Prior to the

Spanish conquest, the extended family and multiple families served as the predominant structure of social organization in Maya society (Villa Rojas 1985, 97). The restructuring of the extended family into smaller nuclear units resulted from the forced separation of extended kin families through the imposition of colonial practices, such as the peonage system of the hacienda and the emphasis on marital unions, which were taxable, by a Catholic state (Farriss 1984; Villa Rojas 1985). Maya communities reacted to these practices by fleeing in nuclear units from Spanish, and later Mexican, rule (Farriss 1984). Today in Cancún, structural constraints have reshaped how Maya households are organized. The constricted housing market has resulted in escalating rental and housing costs that few migrants can afford with their minimum-wage salaries. To pay rent and save money, migrants reorganized themselves into extended or multiple family households.[22] Before and after marriage, migrants shared housing with cousins, aunts, uncles, grandparents, madrinas, and friends. Through this kin network (biological and fictive) and as members traveled within the migrant circuit to celebrate birthdays, baptisms, and weddings, Kuchmil families remained in constant contact with their migrant children.

During the course of these interactions, Kuchmil parents actively reminded their children of their obligations to their nuclear families. When migrants were absent, they made these requests via emissaries and letters. I was present when César and Javier Can Poot received a letter from their mother requesting money for her medicine and their sisters' school supplies. The letter was brought over by a friend who had just returned from a visit to Kuchmil. César read the letter first, then handed it over to Javier, who commented that he had just given his mother money during his visit a week ago. César eventually circulated the letter among his other two unmarried brothers. He explained that the three of them would decide how much to give. When remittances took too long to arrive, their parents, don Hector and doña Antonia, would travel all the way to Cancún, a half-day's journey, to request funds. "When I need a little bit of money, I go look for it," remarked don Hector. At first, they made these trips infrequently, but as the years went by and their sons' lives became more entrenched in Cancún, these reminders became more frequent; they traveled to Cancún once a month. Their sons no longer sent remittances because they expected their parents' visit every month. Don Hector's eldest son lived next door in Kuchmil. He was willing to take care of their animals and milpa during their absence, alleviating their responsibilities.

Families who could not get away so easily relied on technology: phone calls and bank cards. Mariela Can Tun's parents called her cell phone whenever they needed money or assistance. In fact, Mariela bought her cell phone for this very purpose: to remain in close contact with her parents, particularly since her mother was constantly ill. Don Dani contacted her via telephone whenever the family needed money or her mother needed physical assistance. Leonardo May Kauil relied on his bank check card to fulfill his filial duty. Every month at a branch in Valladolid, Leonardo's mother took her "salary" from the ATM, while Leonardo lived off his tips. As hotels increase their reliance on electronic banking systems, migrant children and husbands may turn to this secure, yet impersonal, method, to provide remittances. Through extended kin networks and new technologies, Kuchmil parents remind their children of their obligation to give.

## Retaining Ownership

Sending goods to rural households did not translate into a loss of capital for migrants in Cancún. Migrants retained ownership of the goods they purchased for their families. When I conducted a household census in Kuchmil, I asked each household to list the items that they owned. During my first interview, I noticed that the family did not list the refrigerator taking up space in the main house. Doña Dora informed me that the refrigerator did not belong to her, but to her daughter, who left the household to work as a domestic servant over two decades ago. I learned quickly to ask each household for the goods they owned and the goods given to them by their children. They classified each good under the following categories: "es prestado" (it's a loan); "es de mi hija" (it belongs to my daughter); and "yo lo compre" (I bought it). Each household, except for the homes of newly married couples, contained items owned by migrant children that were on "loan" or in "storage," such as gold jewelry, televisions, fans, stereos, and dishes. Sometimes, the homes themselves were on loan from migrants.

Goods retained ownership, even when they were deliberately given to Kuchmil residents. For all intents and purposes, a refrigerator that has been in residence for twenty years will not be demanded, or expected to be returned, by its original owner. Ironically, doña Dora's daughter informed me that she gave the refrigerator to her mother "to fulfill her gustos." Regardless of the recipient of the gift, the original giver remained the owner of the gift. Gifts remain the property of the original giver because the value of the gift lies in the labor required to purchase it, not just in its function. These gifts symbolized visible representations of a person's labor, in addition to the reciprocal relations that bound children to their parents. The retention of original ownership reminded migrant children that their labor was not forgotten and, most important, continued to be productive. As representations of their children's gustos, these gifts embodied their children's personalities, desires, and individuality. The placement of the television on the religious altar represented not the worship of capitalism, but the worship of the embodiment of the migrant child.

During visits to Kuchmil, migrants also received pleasure from and made use of the items they gave. They watched television, consumed ice from the refrigerator, listened to music from stereos, cooked meals with the kitchen supplies and electronics, and cooled off with the aid of fans. In addition to providing pleasure for their parents, the gifts given by migrant children constituted goods that made their own visits more pleasurable, attracted migrants to return to their village, and modernized the countryside by providing some of the pleasures of an urban lifestyle in the campo.

It is important to note that migrants maintained reciprocal relations not just to fulfill social obligations, but also for pragmatic reasons. The instability of tourism's labor market is counterbalanced with the availability of ejido land in Kuchmil. Considering that many Kuchmil migrants claimed they planned to return to live in Kuchmil after a few years, sending goods home sustained this dream. Four male migrants built homes in Kuchmil, even though they reside full-time in Cancún. After working for five years in Cancún, César Can Poot quit his job and returned to "rest" for several months in Kuchmil. Women also returned to bear their children in Kuchmil, and, in some cases, to bury them.[23] A few migrants have returned to live in Kuchmil, but the majority continues to reside permanently in Cancún. The circulation of goods strengthens social relations between village residents and migrant wage laborers, ties that are crucial to their economic and cultural survival.

## Transforming the Moral Economy

Not all migrants felt obligated to give. Although unmarried migrants did not stop giving altogether, the reduction or an extended absence of remittances caused conflict within Kuchmil families. Such behavior was usually ascribed to alcohol. Since many of the male migrants worked as bartenders, they had easy access to alcohol and spent the majority of their free time drinking with their friends. Most migrants outgrew this behavior after a few years, especially once they married and became fathers. A few, however, became alcoholics. Their addiction clouded their priorities to their natal families. In spite of this addiction, they continued to contribute remittances, but significantly reduced compared to the amounts they sent prior to the onset of their addiction. Children who failed to remit money were accused of compromising their growth into full persons and of being selfish, disrespectful to their parents, and irresponsible community members.

Certainly, power relations within rural households can be reproduced in migrant sites (Malkin 2004), but they can also be transformed. As young Maya women increasingly participate in migration, their contributions have altered household power and gender dynamics. Mariela Can Tun's migration experience illustrates how these transformations influence what is given and consumed. With the help of her aunt Luci, Mariela "escaped" from her pueblo at the age of nineteen.[24] During a visit to Kuchmil, Luci convinced Mariela that with her support she could find a job in spite of her limited Spanish language skills. Although Mariela desired to earn money and experience the world beyond her village, her duty to her mother and family made it difficult for her to leave. Who would haul the twenty-four buckets of water needed to fill the household cistern every day? Who would wash the clothes that piled up every few days? Were her sisters strong enough to take over her chores? More important, were they mature enough to provide their mother with the companionship she needed? In addition to these concerns, Mariela worried about her family having enough to eat. Her father's injured arm kept him from planting enough corn to supply their family with food until the next year's harvest. Mariela also faced future visits by a possible suitor; courtship required a new wardrobe, makeup, and gifts for her future in-laws, all of which cost money.

In spite of the very real economic hardships her parents were facing, don Dani and doña Pati resisted Mariela's plans, but they had little money with which to convince Mariela to stay. They finally succumbed to her pleas. In actuality, Mariela hid her packed suitcase before she negotiated her departure with her parents. She looked forward to wage work not only because she could help her family economically, but also because she could purchase the goods necessary for a girl facing her courtship years. Mariela did not earn much as a domestic servant, about $60 a month in 1992. Due to her low wages, she could not afford to send much money home. Instead, she allocated her first couple of months' salary toward the purchase of clothes, makeup, and shoes, goods with which to mark her individuality. She also purchased jewelry that reflected her gustos, and increased her economic and social capital. After these initial expenditures, Mariela sent around $15 to $25 dollars every month. Eventually, as her wages increased, so did her contributions to her family, up to $40 per month (from a monthly salary of $200) in 2001. Mariela and her fiancée (a migrant from Kuchmil) have postponed their nuptials because their economic responsibilities to their families limit the amount of money they can save to pay for a church wedding (a huge expense) and to prepare for their own future.

As gender ideologies and power relations shift as a result of migration, the gift economy is altered. Indeed, children are not submissive contributors to the household, particularly once they become wageworkers. Among Kekchi communities in Belize (an indigenous group within the same linguistic family as the Yucatec Maya), Richard Wilk demonstrates that this struggle for wages between parents and children results in a "traditional and pragmatic" solution of investing "surplus cash into the house and furnishings" (1989, 311).[25] This solution allowed Kekchi children to invest in electronic goods they desired and ensured their families of their continued contributions to the household. As a result of income differentials from wage work, parental authority over unmarried migrants has diminished among Maya households, especially among female migrants. Many of these women became the main sources of income for their families. As a result, parents have begun to defer to these women's opinions over those of their married sons.[26] This shift in power relations has forced parents of migrant children to become active in soliciting money from their unmarried children and to reinforce their authority over their children via telecommunication technology and existing social networks in Cancún. Mariela's parents, for example, relied on telephone calls to transmit their demands for wages.

Remittances also increased the social capital of particular households, resulting in increased class stratification among rural families. Only half of the households in Kuchmil had access to migrant wages. These households consisted primarily of members of the community who had children old enough to migrate. These households hired workers to labor in the cornfields and thus were able to farm more land and generate a surplus of produce that could be sold for cash. Remittances made it possible for these households to sponsor religious festivals and accumulate more prestige. Conspicuous consumption served as a demonstration of wealth and increased social status (Veblen 1967). For Mariela's family, remittances allowed her family to partake in activities and consumption practices they could not afford in the past. Mariela paid for her younger brother to study the bachillerato and for the construction of a new block house. This bifurcation between households with remittances and those without created tensions within the political life of Kuchmil because it shifted the balance of political power in the community, which had previously been oriented around the leadership positions established by the communal landholding system. Remittances transformed local practices by infusing cash into the local economy, increasing class stratification, and altering gender ideologies in Kuchmil.

## Conclusion

In spite of their limited salaries, Kuchmil migrants desired expensive items for themselves and for their families because these items fulfilled gustos, were more durable, and/or represented success in the labor market. While what was owned mattered, the ability to acquire these goods and allocate resources to rural families also mattered. The multiple meanings ascribed to remittances within a local context (a migrant circuit) illustrate Maya migrants' active engagement with modernity and its resources. Indeed, how Maya communities positioned themselves within Mexico's vision of modernity was influenced by an indigenous sense of personhood that acknowledged the importance of the individual within a dense set of obligatory social relations. As migrants have learned to become a different type of individual, an autonomous individual, consumption and remittance practices helped them mediate the contradictions that resulted from the multiple spaces they inhabit and the multiple roles they must play. Migrants learned to embody the modern, disciplined worker, to embody gender roles that influence where they can work and how they move within Cancún, to embody gustos, and to embody being good sons and daughters. Remittances and consumption practices allowed them to visibly address all of these roles and even transform the ways in which these roles can be fulfilled and performed.

# 6

# Becoming *Chingón/a:* Maya Subjectivity, Development Narratives, and the Limits of Progress

Faced with limited social mobility and job opportunities, Maya migrants have not uniformly experienced the salvation inherent in Cancún's tale of development. Not surprisingly, the new locations (social, economic, and political) that Maya communities find themselves in can be disorienting and depressing. Cultural critics Lisa Lowe and David Lloyd suggest that placing these (dis)locations within the frame of the "progressive narrative of Western developmentalism" results in the perpetuation of assimilation models that cannot explain nor contain the social formations actually produced (1997, 5). Rather, it is more productive to examine the "contradictions that emerge between capitalist formations and the social and cultural practices they presume but cannot dictate" (ibid., 25). To interrogate the progressive narratives embedded in projects like Cancún, where an international development logic is converted into a nationalist one, I analyze migrants' subjective experiences as they participate in a global tourist economy.

Until recently, the emphasis on structural explanations in migration studies ignored migrants' self-awareness and worldviews (Napolitano 2002). Considering that migrants' responses to economic transitions are also visceral and embodied, new forms of subjectivity arise in reaction and in contestation to these homogenizing processes. For indigenous communities, becoming modern citizens entailed a shift in self-perception and the acquisition of new attitudes and behaviors, many of which clashed with previous models for self-actualization and collective engagement. Under these circumstances, Maya migrants from Kuchmil appropriated the Mexican discourse of being *chingón* (aggressive and astute) as a way to survive in the new economy with a sense of dignity and agency: When they speak of being chingón, Maya migrants offer a gendered and racialized critique of the global economy.

## Unpacking Progressive Narratives

After World War II, development as an applied approach for understanding and organizing social change in impoverished countries gained currency. But the roots of this approach run deep, to anthropological models of social evolution based on stages of development in which "savage" and "civilized" peoples fall at opposite ends of a linear continuum. As a result, the premise of such development theories is that discrete societies are made of autonomous rational individuals whose social development follows a universal path—albeit not always at the same pace (Ferguson 1997). Critics point out that the discourse of development is ahistorical and reinforces an uneven system of value in which certain cultures, people, and economic systems are unfairly valued over others (Cooper and Packard 1997; Escobar 1995). Nonetheless, bounded, static, and racialized conceptions of peoples (as primitive/civilized, childlike/adult, Indian/non-Indian), societies (traditional/modern), space (rural/urban), and time (ahistorical/historical) popularized by nineteenth- and early twentieth-century models of social evolution have persisted (Fabian 1983; Frye 1996; Gupta and Ferguson 1992). This ahistorical, racialized discourse can also be found in development projects like Cancún that target for social improvement "untouched" spaces and the "traditional and authentic" Indians who reside there.

Social transformation is central to ideas of development, so it is not surprising that development discourse has impregnated theories of migration. Structural explanations invoking evolutionary models have dominated academic discussions of why people move. Robert Redfield's "folk-urban continuum" model of social change provided a framework for early understandings of Maya migration. As Maya peasants migrated between rural communities to urban centers, they adopted modern cultural traits (e.g., individualism and rationalism), which, once infused into rural communities, provided the catalyst for their eventual metamorphoses from "folk" to "urban" (Redfield 1941). Like the folk-urban continuum, the neoclassical migration model of "push-pull" was predicated on assumptions of a universal linear progression and assimilation. Beginning in the 1960s, social scientists challenged depictions of isolated communities by historicizing them within colonial projects and capitalist systems (Cardoso and Faletto 1979; Frank 1967) and questioned portrayals of migrants as rational male actors guided by cost-benefit analyses by focusing on female migrants and by highlighting the significance of households and social networks in determining migration patterns (Arizpe 1981; Lomnitz 1977; Rouse 1989). Migration, however, continued to be envisaged as linear. To displace this deep-seated paradigm, some scholars conceptualize migration as a circuit (Levitt 2001; Rouse 1991).

Considering that human transformation and agency is central to development theories, it is not surprising that scholars have begun studying migration as a subjective and embodied experience (see Malkin 2004; Rouse 1995). In her study of migrants who moved from rural communities to Guadalajara—one of Mexico's largest cities—anthropologist Valentina Napolitano (2002) calls our attention to how migrants narrate this movement. Her subjects frame these experiences (perhaps subconsciously) within an evolutionary discourse of the rural as backward, primitive, and lacking consciousness. Napolitano argues that for many migrants, migration was viewed as a process of enlightenment because "the transition from rural to an urban environment is perceived as a step from an unconscious to a conscious life, and is represented in terms of both self-empowerment and the loss of that power" (2002, 53).[1] This move from the unconscious to consciousness echoes development models of subjectivity that privilege the autonomous, conscious individual as the archetype for all members of premodern societies (Saldaña-Portillo 2003).

This teological view of human agency does not account for subjectivities and social formations that aim to disrupt these narratives. What does it mean when migrants narrate their migrations as a process of enlightenment? Scholars suggest that the movement from pueblo to *ciudad* (city) has become a "rite of passage" for young men and women.[2] This metaphor reinforces a linear progression of migration as a process of moving from one state of being to another. What behaviors and ideas, what kind of consciousness does this process reinforce, establish, undermine? We cannot presume this rite of passage is experienced homogeneously across ethnic, racial, gender, and class lines. Therefore, understanding the subjective and embodied experiences of migrants requires paying critical attention to the historical, economic, cultural, and racial roots of the moral and theoretical frameworks that structure these experiences.

## Maya Subjectivity in a Global Economy

Kuchmil migrants who moved to Cancún experienced migration as a learning process that awakened their senses, their knowledge, and their understanding of the world. Among the Maya, this developing consciousness was not something particular to an urban experience but formed part of the process of becoming a person. Experiencing migration became a life stage in addition to marriage and parenthood, among other stages, by which Kuchmil residents acquired the knowledge and experience that allowed them to achieve full maturity or personhood. But becoming a full person was not contingent on migration: Kuchmil residents who did not migrate acquired this knowledge through the life stages of rural life (e.g., *quinceañeras* [ritual celebration of a girl's fifteenth birthday], marriage, parenthood, making one's own milpa, holding public office).[3] Kuchmil residents spoke of these stages as part of the learning process of becoming a person. The Maya phrase, "Má' tin ná'atik" (I am not learning it) was commonly used to refer to one's lack of experience and knowledge and referred to the initial stage of exposure to a new practice, activity, or knowledge. Initially, I considered this assertion a sign of humility, but I soon recognized it to be a proclamation of the learning process in becoming a person. The noun *ná'at* refers to intelligence, reason, and knowledge (Bricker, Po'ot Yah, and Dzul de Po'ot 1998), and to proclaim "má' tin ná'atik" represents one's awareness that life is a continuous journey toward maturity, knowledge, and full consciousness—which can only be obtained through practice and observation.

In Cancún, Kuchmil migrants took advantage of social gatherings to build on and impart the knowledge and experience defining adulthood. During ritual celebrations and casual gatherings, they continually compared wages and work experiences and shared information on medical care, child rearing, and employment opportunities. Through these discussions, migrants acquired and shared knowledge that would help each other become more socially and politically conscious of the systems of power they lived under. Eventually, through such exchanges and the practice of everyday life, one becomes more *despierto* (awake) and adept at maneuvering these systems of power.[4]

To acknowledge the new experiences migrants faced, the community incorporated these activities and practices into the recognized life stages commonly experienced by men and women. Some of these practices replaced traditional markers of personhood rooted in an agricultural-based economy. For example, the practice of going to Cancún to spend the summer working—as early as age eleven—became a marker of adolescence and part of the transition to full personhood. This insertion into the Cancún labor market exposed youths to the demands of this market, which, with time, demanded more schooling. In addition, children's interest in school and their households' economic needs prompted parents to educate all their children. As children began to spend more years in school, the age of marriage was expanded, creating a longer adolescence.

Youths who attended boarding schools and migrated to Cancún and other neighboring cities found that space, place, and community—and how to be a person within such temporal and moral frameworks—were "imagined" differently as they established connections within and across this expanded space (see Anderson 1983) (see chapters 4 and 5). This imagining cannot be explained simply as a linear process of enlightenment, as a form of acculturation, but must be understood as part of a long history in which "'indigenous cultures' have been historically produced in a dialectical relation of resistance and domination with the Mexican nation-state" and capitalist structures (Hernández Castillo 2001, 233). Unlike the consciousness promoted by development models of the rational actor unencumbered by social ties, this type of awareness was grounded in a collective and racialized experience.

As we construct regional histories of these embodied processes, we cannot ignore the interconnectedness and interdependence of the city and the countryside. Migration in Mexico has become part of the rural experience, making the *ciudad* central to the rural imaginary, not only as a foil to the rural but also as an expanded sense of place. If place is a mediated experience forged from social relations through which it is understood (Massey 1994; Olwig 1997), then claims to geographical distinctions, particularly between the rural and the urban, must be reevaluated. Yet binaries (tradition/modernity, rural/urban, Indian/non-Indian) serve as central tropes in theories of migration. In her study of the Maya community of Chan Kom, anthropologist Alicia Re Cruz (1996a) relies on the dichotomies of the peasant/capitalist, rural/urban, and tradition/modernity to explain the conflict engendered by Maya migration. She argues these dualisms not only reflect the political divisions within this community but also are deployed strategically by Maya political factions in their attempts to take control of community resources. These categories are fraught terms because they reinforce a racialized discourse that presumes they are natural and spatial (Gupta and Ferguson 1992) and that one can become more or less Indian based on distance traveled. Being Maya, however, is not based on living in a particular place or location but is grounded in the social and historical relations and collective experiences of a particular community and people. As indigenous peoples move to urban spaces, social scientists should be less concerned with processes of acculturation and more concerned with how these new articulations disrupt naturalized categories and create new categories of difference.

Even as migration and displacement blur the edges of concepts previously considered bounded categories, such as the pueblo, the city, and the nation, Akhil Gupta and James Ferguson (1992) suggest paying attention to the hierarchical relations between these concepts and spaces, particularly as they become "*re*territorialized" and reconceptualized with time and as a result of changing practices. "For if one begins with the premise that spaces have *always* been hierarchically interconnected, instead of naturally disconnected, then cultural and social change becomes not a matter of cultural contact and articulation but one of rethinking difference *through* connections" (ibid., 8). These spaces are also deeply gendered places that are not always gendered in the same way across different sites (Massey 1994). Through a thick description of a migrant circuit situated within local, regional, and international spaces, I map out the complex ways Maya migrants negotiate the power hierarchies of these interconnected spaces.

## Becoming Chingón

Through their work in Africa, John and Jean Comaroff (2001) illustrate the inextricable ties between personhood, labor, and production, while reminding us of the importance of understanding the historical and cultural specificity of personhood. Within the context of the Yucatán Peninsula, the new global economy not only affected agricultural production, but also affected the performance of personhood among Maya peoples. This shift, however, did not happen smoothly, but required a deliberate break with past customs, the solidification of others, and the patient fashioning and performance of new ways of being Maya in relation to the social and economic changes facing the Mexican countryside. Judith Butler suggests that performance is "never fully self-styled, for styles have a history, and those histories condition and limit the possibilities" (1990, 139). According to Butler, gender is a social construction established through a "stylized repetition of acts" that "seek to approximate the ideal of a substantial ground of identity, but which, in their occasional *dis*continuity, reveal the temporal and contingent groundlessness of this 'ground'" (ibid., 140–41). Similarly, changes in the political economy of the Yucatán Peninsula resulted in the interruption of previous acts of repetition that modeled gender, race, class, and ethnicity. New acts and discourses initiated by local communities, government institutions, and economic systems intended to teach rural and indigenous communities how to become modern individual citizens. These acts and discourses did not always complement each other, nor did they change many of the class, gender, and racial parameters within which indigenous communities were located. Not surprisingly, at times the process of nation building boils down to how to produce liberal citizens without destroying local cultural practices and without rupturing the social ties binding communities together (see Williams 1991). This tension is evident in the performance of Maya personhood.

For Kuchmil parents, teaching their children to be *despierto* (in this context, "astute") in this age of global capitalism becomes central to guiding their children's mental, physical, and religious development.[5] Parents hope that with such guidance their children will learn to handle government bureaucracy, the oppressive aspects of wage labor, and their social and economic obligations to their community. Paul Sullivan (1989) points out that in contrast to earlier years (from the 1920s and the 1940s) in which "notions of justice, fair exchange, divine will, and political alliance in terms of 'goodness, love, and propriety'" marked Maya interactions with foreigners, "nowadays injustice, unequal exchange, and political subordination seem to them [the Maya of Quintana Roo] like nothing so much as 'getting fucked' in the social intercourse of daily life" (ibid., 175–76).[6] Sullivan suggests that like the Spanish word *chingar,* whose usage predominates in Mexican society, the Maya word *top* (to fuck, to screw, but also to harm, to bother) "sums up contemporary assessments of the results of those dealings" with foreigners, including Mexican officials (ibid., 176).

Indeed, scatological references provide Maya migrants in Cancún with a way to critique their subordinate positions and oppressive conditions within the tourist economy. Instead of using the Maya word *top,* they adopt the Spanish term *chingar* but imbue it with the multiple meanings of *top:* to fuck, to be brave, to be beautiful. Likewise, José Limón suggests the usage of the term *chingar* by working-class Mexican Americans constitutes "symbolic expressions of an essentially political and economic concern with social domination, not from below . . . but from above—from the upper levels of the structure of power" (1994, 131). Similarly, for

Maya migrants, the verb *chingar* offers a way to critique the global economy and also provides a way for migrants to reposition themselves within this economy.

The word *chingar* is a raw, brutal word with multiple meanings. Octavio Paz (1985) suggests that its origins are in the Nahuatl language spoken by the Aztecs. Paz characterized this word as an "aggressive" word that "we utter . . . in a loud voice only when we are not in control of ourselves" (ibid., 74). Paz also recognized its magical and lyrical nature in Mexican usage. "It is a magical word: a change in tone, a change of inflection, is enough to change its meaning" (ibid., 76). Use it with a flirtatious tone, and *chingar* means to tease, to make merry, to be great, to be manly, to defy. Use it soberly, and it implies failure, neglect, and frustration. Use it aggressively, and it has a deadly and violent ring: to be deceptive, to contradict, to sexually penetrate, to rape, to destroy.

*Chingar* is also a gendered and sexualized word. *La Chingada*—the fucked one—the noun form of *chingar,* refers to Malinche, Malintzin, or doña Marina, the Indian woman who served as translator and mistress to the Spanish conquistadors and is historically recognized as the mother of the first mestizo. Gloria Anzaldúa suggests that among Mexicans and Chicanos, *chingar* cannot escape its gendered and sexualized origin. "She has become the bad word that passes a dozen times a day from the lips of Chicanos" (1987, 22). For Anzaldúa, this contempt is indicative of the resentment Mexicans and Chicanos feel toward their indigenous selves and toward women in general. "The worst kind of betrayal lies in making us believe that the Indian woman in us is the betrayer. We, *indias y mestizas* police the Indian in us, brutalize and condemn her. Male culture has done a good job on us" (ibid., 22). Likewise, Paz reflects that La Chingada is the "cruel incarnation of the feminine condition" (1985, 86).[7] In many ways, this racialized metaphor includes all Indians, not just women.

In contrast, to be chingón—to commit the sexual act, violence, deception—represents an "active, aggressive and closed person," the macho in opposition to the inert female body of La Chingada (Paz 1985, 77). According to Paz, power "sums up the aggressiveness, insensitivity, invulnerability and other attributes of the *macho*" or chingón (ibid., 81). Matthew Gutmann suggests that being a working-class macho has been "a male Mexican project," a project central to defining Mexico as a nation (1996, 241). In spite of this national reification of the working class macho as representative of *lo mexicano,* Gutmann reminds us that the meanings of *macho* are multiple, shift with time, and thus cannot be "justifiably called exclusively national in character" (ibid.). Gutmann's critique is useful in deconstructing what it means to be chingón among Maya men and women who use this term to refer to themselves. I suggest that adopting a national discourse, rather than a regional one through the use of *top,* allows Maya migrants to participate in a shared sense of oppression with their fellow citizens. In my analysis of its usage among Kuchmil migrants, I rely on Mexican, American, and Chicano authors' analyses of this word as a way to think through how this term and its meanings relate to people's lives. However, I do not presume that the meanings Chicanos and working-class Mexicans attach to this word are automatically applicable to Kuchmil migrants.

According to Octavio Paz, humor serves as a weapon by which to display the macho's power:

> The *macho* commits *chingaderas,* that is, unforeseen acts that produce confusion, horror and destruction. He opens the world; in doing so, he rips and tears it, and this violence provokes a great, sinister laugh. And in its own way, it is just: it re-establishes the equilibrium and puts things in their places, by reducing them to dust, to misery, to nothingness. The humor of the *macho* is an act of revenge. (1985, 81)

In his ethnography of working class Mexican American men in South Texas, José Limón examines these chingaderas as a "discourse of the dominated" (1994, 125). The homoerotic meanings inherent in the term are obvious and frequently used by Mexican American men to assert power through humor. Limón argues that humor in the form of "doing or saying *chingaderas* (fuck ups)" creates a "powerful yet contradictory sexual and scatological discourse" rooted in a Mexican working-class folk tradition (ibid., 127, 129). Additionally, Limón suggests that the verb *chingar* is used in "speech body play" that constitutes "dynamic forums that interactionally produce meaning, mastering anxiety by inverting passive destiny through active play" (ibid., 125, 133). Regardless, the gendered and sexual nature of the term imbues it with contradictory meanings that resonate with the contradictions working-class machos face in an industrialized postmodern South Texas. Limón suggests,

> Here humor becomes not existential angst and cultural ambivalence but carnivalesque critical difference, though never without its own

internal contradiction, for the fact that here . . . I deal with a world of men from which women are excluded qualifies the "positive" and "resistance" character of this humor. (ibid., 125–26)

While Limón cautions that the male carnivalesque reproduces female sub-jugation, I argue that the internal contradictory nature of the term *chingar* allows it to be used as a critical space for expressions of power by other sub-jugated groups, in particular indigenous peoples and women. More than just play, this speech becomes part of an active refashioning of people's subjectivities in actual life. Indeed, the desire for their children not to be screwed or harmed in life constitutes one of the main reasons Maya parents constantly push their children to be alert. Néstor Canul Canche explained, "[Growing up] I was somewhat dumb. It took a lot of effort for me to learn." By teaching his son Raúl to be more despierto (more self-aware), Néstor expected this awareness to help Raúl not only with his schoolwork, but also to help him to avoid being *tóop* (the passive of *top;* that is, to be fucked, to be harmed) in life. Self-awareness leads to a greater awareness and sensitiv-ity to the social condition of the world in which one lives. More important, being despierto transforms Maya people from victims to agents. Being despierto makes one chingón: aggressive, assertive, capable of understand-ing how power works and using it to one's advantage.

The term *chingón* was employed by both Maya men and women in everyday talk. While *chingón* traditionally and in many places continues to be a reference to a "masculine actor" (Alarcón 1989, 61), among Maya communities, this actor need not be male. Instead, men and women can both be chingón because this term is used as the Spanish equivalent of the Maya word *top,* which is gender-neutral. For Kuchmil residents, the mean-ing of *top* depends on its usage. Used pejoratively, it implies to be fucked or harmed. Used positively, it implies to be intelligent, beautiful, and brave. By infusing *chingar* with the multiple meanings of *top,* Kuchmil migrants expand its meaning to reflect their particular racialized experiences. In the process, becoming or being chingón has become flexibly gendered in its daily use and reference. *Chingón* retains a masculine sense of power be-cause it is a reference to power, a concept that continues to be rooted in masculinity, because for many Mexicans, reality represents power as such. This reference to power is what makes becoming chingón an attractive po-sitionality for Kuchmil migrants. Becoming chingón requires Maya men and women to position themselves within national identity discourses.

When children are taught to be despiertos, they learn to be chingones in the aggressive sense of the term. Violeta May Chen described her one-year-old daughter Yasmín as chingona because she used her observation skills to quickly solve problems. Violeta's proclamation occurred after Yasmín outsmarted me, the anthropologist. On a hot September afternoon, Violeta was busy preparing the midday meal of pork with beans while I sat in a hammock that traversed her tiny kitchen. Yasmín sat on a nearby chair and watched me intently as I pulled out my writing materials from my shoulder bag. As Violeta talked about her experiences as a young mother in Cancún, I jotted a few notes. Yasmín was fascinated by my notebook and kept trying to get hold of it. With each attempt, I moved slightly out of reach. I soon became engrossed in the conversation and stopped paying attention to Yasmín, who took advantage of my absorption to snatch the notebook from my lap. Once I noticed the missing notebook, I reached out to recover it, but Yasmín smiled, slid off her chair, taking the notebook with her, and scampered behind the chair. Her mother applauded and cheered her daughter's fearlessness, inventiveness, and problem-solving skills. "Mi hija es chingona!" (My daughter has got balls), she exclaimed. On other occasions, when Yasmín failed to solve a problem and cried in frustration, her mother and uncles jokingly teased her, "Ya te chingaste!" (You've been screwed). Yasmín was being taught at a very young age to use her intellect and spunk to solve life's dilemmas.

As another way to describe being despierto, Kuchmil migrants used a term that also has roots in violence and aggression: *abusado* (from the verb *abusar,* to abuse, mistreat, take advantage of, or impose on). This term was used because it offered a less vulgar way of describing women who were chingonas. Mariela Can Tun described her sister Jovana as being abusada because she learned how to do things quickly. For example, she quickly learned to get around the entire city of Cancún by bus and lobbied successfully for her land plot. These examples demonstrate that the meanings of being chingón and abusado were tied not always to a particular gender, but to a gendered behavior in which aggressiveness, but not aggression, and creative problem solving were considered attributes necessary for both men and women to live with dignity within changing fields of productive relations.

Being despierto, abusada, and chingón indicate a strong sense of self, but these attributes are also gendered depictions of a powerful self located within a masculine world. Octavio Paz (1985) points out that the aggressive, masculine nature of the verb *chingar* hints at an underlying violence (physical, sexual, and psychological). Ruth Behar suggests that this desire to take on a "male role" and "desire to be a *macha*" represent for women, particularly indigenous women, a desire to be "a woman who won't be beaten, won't forgive, won't give up her rage, a *macha*, too, in the sense of wanting to harness a certain male fearlessness to meet evil and danger head-on." (Behar 1990, 242, 249). Behar identifies *coraje* (rage)—a state of emotion and illness generated by strife between kin or other inequities— as a "culturally forceful state of consciousness, whether it refers to feminist rage or the diffuse anger that oppressed people feel in colonial settings" (ibid., 241). The concepts of being despierto, abusada, chingón, or a person full of coraje are rooted in masculinity because power is usually depicted as masculine and legitimated through a masculine discourse. However, the awareness generated by such emotional states gives people knowledge of how to resist and/or claim power for themselves (see Behar 1993).

*Chingón* also encompasses the "logic of the absurd," because the underlying violence in this word is accompanied by humor (Limón 1994; Paz 1985, 81). Indeed, Renato Rosaldo notes that "culturally distinctive jokes and banter play a significant role in constituting Chicano culture, both as a form of resistance and as a source of positive identity" (1989, 150). The same has been said for Mexican culture (Gutmann 1996). Through such humor, the use of the verb *chingar* "reestablishes the equilibrium and puts things in their places, by reducing them to dust, to misery, to nothingness" (Paz 1985, 81). When the Maya point out how chingón they are, there always exists a tongue-in-cheek effect to this assertion, particularly among women, because they are conscious of the limitations to their "contestative discourse" (Limón 1994, 139), limitations rooted in the gender, class, and racial hierarchies in which indigenous peoples are situated. This discourse and positionality contains excesses too: One can be seen as too chingón.

## Becoming Too Chingón

When Kuchmil parents teach their children to be chingón, they are nurturing their children's sense of individuality. However, the Maya concept of the person or individual is not equivalent to the Western concept of the autonomous individual who seeks to advance the self as a way to achieve modernity (see Comaroff and Comaroff 2001). Maya persons are taught that self-awareness is rooted in a collective identity. This sense of the collective creates the framework through which personhood is enacted and gustos fulfilled. Most important, this moral framework keeps people from becoming too chingón. Individuals who made attempts to become successful by abusing their relationships with their neighbors and relatives were quickly sanctioned by the community. For example, in 1996, don Teo May Balam was evicted from Kuchmil because he failed to meet the mandatory work requirements imposed by the ejido system, and because he overcharged the residents for the use of his mill. He lost his house, his mill, and his land. Becoming rich at the expense of the needs of the community was considered a shortsighted act that demonstrated a lack of a social and political conscience. Don Teo was accused of being too chingón.

Migration can also lead to excess. In Cancún, Kuchmil migrants are taught by multinational corporations to become the autonomous individual who, "now conceived as a subject, independently of social context," pulls himself up by his bootstrap and is alienated from his labor (Sayer 1991, 58). I purposely mark this individual as male because more men than women work for these corporations. Migrants are taught that in order to succeed economically and socially, they need to become modern individuals. The struggle for remittances described in chapter 5 offers a clear example of the problems that result from embracing the liberal individualism promoted in modern citizenship. When migrants follow this dictum they run the risk of becoming too chingón.

Let's take the case of twenty-five-year-old Javier Can Poot. Javier purchased a car because his busy work schedule necessitated a secure form of transportation in the evenings. The car also made it possible for him to secure employment in managerial and supervisory positions that required extensive travel to visit corporate franchises. After buying a car, Javier was criticized for being too chingón by Kuchmil residents. Each time he drove into town, his neighbors (most of whom were kin) treated him hostilely. They were upset because Javier no longer spent time in the community. During his visits, Javier spent a few hours with his immediate family and left for Cancún soon afterward. Before he purchased a car, Javier arrived by bus. The public transportation schedule was organized in such a way that one was required to spend the night in Kuchmil; even the bus driver slept in the village located at the end of his route. In the past, Javier spent this time hanging out in the park, playing basketball, or visiting friends. The hostility directed toward him and his new car motivated Javier to keep his visits brief, but he truly missed the social gatherings among his

*A migrant prepares to leave Kuchmil in his car after the fiesta in honor of Santa Cruz.*

peers in Kuchmil. Although Javier's family appreciated the comfort, convenience, and social capital that came with access to an automobile, they also considered Javier's visits to be too short. Access to a car allowed Javier to make more frequent trips but spend less time in Kuchmil. Additionally, his family was also upset by this purchase because to save for the car, Javier stopped sending remittances. This struggle over remittances hints at the problems that result from the clash between community and familial expectations and labor market demands.

Assertive, independent women also faced the risk of being sanctioned for being too *abusadas*. Fernanda Can Hernández's experience with migration illustrates this process. Fernanda migrated to Cancún in 1996 at the age of sixteen. She worked as a store clerk six days a week, making it difficult for her to travel to Kuchmil. Fernanda's parents did not worry about her because she lived with her mother's uncle and his family. She periodically sent money home through her mother's relatives. On the few occasions that she traveled to Kuchmil, she was stylishly dressed and brought presents and money. However, since the residents of Kuchmil and the migrants living in Cancún rarely saw Fernanda (she was absent from community events for several years) and did not know the uncle with whom she was living, they became suspicious of how she was earning her money. "No one knows about her. She hardly ever returns to the village," Kuchmil residents and migrants exclaimed. The community's concern with Fernanda's absence from community activities reflected their anxieties about women's new economic roles. As a result, questions of Fernanda's morality began to circulate between Kuchmil and Cancún. According to the gossip, a family feud caused Fernanda to move away from her aunt and uncle. I was told that her *padrino* (godfather), a local schoolteacher, went to Cancún to search for her. He cried when he discovered that she worked as a waitress in a bar, which the residents of Kuchmil equated with prostitution. Her padrino could not believe that she had fallen "so low." Stories like these circulate quickly within the regional network in which Kuchmil is embedded. To counter this narrative, Fernanda began spending more time with her family in Kuchmil. Fernanda invited me to visit her at work because she knew that as a frequent traveler between Kuchmil and Cancún, I could witness and testify to her virtue and her housing accommodations.

Through these visits to Kuchmil, Fernanda contradicted the narrative of her downfall and demonstrated that she was a good daughter and a morally upstanding woman. It was during one of these visits that she agreed to be a *madrina* (godmother). She also asked to accompany me when I visited the homes of Kuchmil migrants in Cancún. During these visits, she was treated warmly by the migrants, many of whom were kin, and made arrangements to visit again. Fernanda never hinted that she knew about the gossip, but her socializing began soon after the gossip commenced. A few months afterward, people stopped telling this story.

In April 2001, Fernanda returned to serve as madrina of *héeȼ-méek'* for friends of the family who lived in a *ranchería* near Kuchmil. She brought the child diapers, a set of clothes, a plastic baby bottle, a pair of shoes, baby wipes, and moisturizing lotion. Godparents are responsible for guiding a child's religious education and intellectual development. As such, these roles were traditionally filled by a married couple. As an unmarried migrant, she earned a healthy income, thus Fernanda's unmarried state was overlooked because of her relative wealth. Her younger brother Matías played her counterpart in this ritual. This display of goods reinforced Fernanda's success in Cancún. Migrant women's purchasing power has elevated their social status within the community. Regardless of their marital status, female

*A héec-méek' ceremony with gifts.*

migrants are now viewed as attractive choices for *comadres* (ritual co-motherhood). In this instance, this success was not perceived as being too chingón because Fernanda was redistributing resources through culturally appropriate channels. Money from migration was frequently channeled into making rituals more elaborate in size and complexity, thereby increasing the prestige of families in the community.[8]

Paula, introduced in chapter 5, was also considered *muy abusada*. She met Macario while they both studied at the boarding school near Valladolid. After she left the boarding school, Paula took a seamstress course to improve the basic sewing skills she had learned in boarding school. She was very talented and soon established an informal sewing business within her home in Cancún. Her talent, her prices (she charged less than a tailor, about $5 per tailored piece of clothing), and her warm gregarious personality kept her constantly busy with *pedidos* (requests). Kuchmil women were very impressed with Paula because she earned her own money and was not afraid to attend fiestas without her husband and dance all evening with her young son. Paula allocated the money she earned to her elderly mother, who cared full-time for Paula's epileptic sister.

However, Macario, Paula's husband, took advantage of Paula's extra income to reduce his own contributions to their nuclear family. He accused Paula of being too chingona, too independent, of being too vocal about how much money she earned. "If you earn so much money, then you can take care of your children!" he accused Paula when she requested money for the children's school uniforms and supplies. Yet he never complained about Paula's trips to the village fiestas because she was accompanied by her children and Macario's relatives. Although he was very proud of his wife for being a modern, independent woman (he imagined himself as a modern, independent man), Macario had a difficult time accepting the behaviors that came with this type of persona.

Being too chingón also created problems in the workplace. Many of the hotel and nightclub employers appreciated the energy, hard work, and strong educational backgrounds of the Kuchmil migrants. As a result, these migrants were promoted quickly, in many cases before employees who had more seniority. However, because most migrants acquired jobs through their social networks, these promotions caused friction among friends. Néstor's experience provides a clear example of the struggle between collectivism and individualism in the workplace. Before getting married, Néstor spent time working as a steward alongside his friends in a nightclub in Cancún. The manager really liked Néstor because he had *estudios* (an education), so he promoted him to chief steward. His friends with more seniority were upset that he was promoted before them and that he accepted the position.

To put Néstor in his place, they accused Néstor of stealing an American guest's purse, and convinced the American woman that Néstor was the perpetrator. The manager fired Néstor on the spot. Néstor's brothers and a neighbor who was a policeman suggested that he file a complaint against his accusers, but Néstor refused because they were his *paisanos* (countrymen from the southeastern peninsula) who came from *la misma ruta* (literally "the same road," but also refers to being from the same place or on the same path). In spite of the incident, both Néstor and these young men remained on friendly terms because they needed each other for future job references and soon would become kin by marriage. A year later, when Néstor returned with Ramona to Cancún, these friends helped him obtain a job in a hotel.

## Challenging Capitalism's Inequities

The person who is despierto and challenges the structural relations of power in which they are embedded also faces the risk of being sanctioned by employers and corporations. Ramona's narrative reflects this process. Ramona quit her job in the luxury hotel in the Zona Hotelera in part because she discovered a "help wanted" sign while shopping in the *crucero,* the busiest commercial area downtown. Many businesses were hiring temporary staff for the winter holiday season. Ramona applied to be a sales clerk at Santiago,[9] a popular national clothing store chain, because she would earn commission for every item she sold. She also liked their clothes and could use her discount to stock up on clothes for herself and her family. The schedule was more demanding than hotel work, but the pay was supposed to be much better. Ramona worked seven days a week from 8:00 a.m. to 11:00 p.m., with a lunch break at 2:00 p.m. The store was extremely busy, so the temporary staff was the first to arrive, the last to leave, and the last to eat—if they received a break at all. To accommodate this schedule, Ramona sent her son to Kuchmil, where her mother cared for him.

Ramona, who was gregarious, quickly made friends with the other staff. She hoped they would like her and keep her on at the end of the season. In spite of the long hours, which kept her from spending much time with her family and young son, she enjoyed the freedom of working independently and talking to customers (the majority being working-class Mexicans, many of whom were Maya). Her colleagues were primarily female from the states of Veracruz and Tabasco, while the supervisors were all male. However, when Ramona received her first paycheck, she was devastated. "$195! Wasn't it a paycheck?" she thought. "I couldn't make heads or tails of it." She showed it to her brother who exclaimed. "What's this? This isn't a check." Her husband made a similar comment. Both Néstor and Francisco had spent the past fifteen days helping with the cooking and cleaning so that Ramona could work. When I visited Ramona, she complained to me about the check. She was upset that Santiago had not paid her the commissions she earned, while other employees earned an extra $100 for the same fifteen-day period. She was also concerned about not receiving pay for ten working days that fell within the pay schedule. Finally, the manager did not give her the check until after the banks closed, so Ramona could not send money home to her mother with the *combi* driver who was traveling to Kuchmil.

Ramona decided she would not continue working for such low wages and immediately asked the assistant manager for the wages for the ten days. She owed her brother $50 for a doctor's visit and her mother $30 for her son's *gastos* (expenses), his diapers, food, and clothes. The assistant manager refused to pay her, even attempting to take her check back, and demanding she return a $30 loan she cosigned when she started (which she used to send her son to Kuchmil). Ramona was furious about the ten days' salary being withheld and that she was now being forced to repay the loan. "You can sue me, but I won't pay you. I don't plan to come back to work!" she exclaimed, and left the store.

Ramona acknowledged she was being punished for refusing the assistant manager's sexual advances. After he made repeated attempts to touch her, Ramona told him "she would never fail to respect her husband." On the other hand, her coworkers did not resist his flirtations because they needed their jobs. According to Ramona, these women had few work options: They did not have the proper paperwork to work in a hotel corporation or a more discriminating business. The employee who earned the highest commission, close to $300 (not including the daily minimum wage), was married but spent afternoons with the assistant manager away from work, explaining to Ramona that this was the best way for her to improve her son's life.

I suggested Ramona speak to the manager about the deductions in her paycheck. She asked me to accompany her, so we visited the clothing store that afternoon. Ramona greeted the secretary warmly and introduced me as a friend, asking to speak to the manager. Her request stifled the secretary's lighthearted attitude. After stonewalling us for about fifteen minutes, the second assistant manager, accompanied by a security guard, offered to answer Ramona's questions. His answers frustrated us. Commissions, according to this manager, were up to the discretion of each assistant manager and not based on personal feelings. Regardless, he claimed that Ramona missed several days of work when she was sick and did not merit commission for the entire pay period. Santiago employees' paychecks were also automatically deducted $5 per pay period, money that was transferred into a savings account offered by the company. Because she quit her job, Ramona would not be able to access this money. We left the store with the frustrating feeling of exploitation and injustice. Ramona never recouped the money she was owed and was blacklisted from working in Santiago franchises.

In spite of her negative experiences in Cancún's labor market, Ramona made another attempt to enter the workforce a few months later. She submitted an application to work in her profession (accounting) for a local private hospital. One of the secretaries was out sick that day, so the hospital needed someone to answer the phones. "Can you handle the switchboard?" the manager asked. "If you show me how, I can," Ramona said. Short-staffed, they hired Ramona as a receptionist. The manager agreed to let her spend part of her workday working in accounting. Ramona enjoyed her work immensely, especially now that she was actually working in her profession, but was not pleased with the limited benefits the job provided or the lack of job security. "After my experience with Santiago," she reminded me, "I know that I have to keep fighting for my rights." For Ramona, in spite of these problems, becoming chingona made her aware of her rights.

## The Limits of Progress

Maya migrants moved to Cancún expecting to benefit from the national rhetoric of progress and modernization. But for those with minimal education (most migrants had only a high school diploma), tourist jobs were poorly paid and failed to provide more economic stability than agricultural work. To advance the tourist economy (and to advance in it), corporations trained workers to adopt a new attitude and work ethic based on the dedicated, self-reliant, and flexible worker. However, Maya migrants like Ramona, Javier, and Fernanda did not fully embrace this mindset because doing so would devastate familial, social, and cultural ties that nurtured their sense of self and well-being. Instead, Maya migrants relied on a nationalist and masculine discourse of *chingaderas* (bullshit, acts of mischief and treason) to resist development's alienating discourse of liberal individualism. Becoming chingón made it possible for Maya migrants to withstand the racial and economic discrimination directed toward indigenous peoples within a tourist economy and to maintain a sense of agency without shedding the collective orientation promoted in rural life.

As migrant workers learn to become autonomous individuals, some resist this imposition. Others, however, embrace it because they equate liberal individualism with progress. These migrants use the rhetoric of modernity to criticize the collectivist orientation of their pueblo. Rubén Can Kauil, who has worked as an accountant for a multinational hotel for over a decade, offered such a critique. He considered Kuchmil's emphasis on communal rights and privileges as infringing on people's individual rights. "The people don't let you improve yourself," he explained. As an example, Rubén argued that envy was at the root of don Teo's expulsion, envy of his ambition and wealth. Don Teo owned a store and a corn mill, lent money to neighbors, and cultivated more than four hectares of land. Don Teo accused the comisariado ejidal of limiting his wealth, and those of the other residents who were seeking to improve themselves, by imposing a four-hectare limit on milpa cultivation (even though this decision was approved by a two-thirds vote by ejidatarios). "They want everyone to be the same," proclaimed don Teo. "But they are all chingones!" laughingly exclaimed his wife Lucrecia, implying that equality was impossible because everyone spends time trying to screw each other. For Rubén and don Teo, this desire for equality inhibits progress in Kuchmil, limits its physical growth, the development of its infrastructure, and the ambition and drive of the villagers themselves.

Don Teo and Rubén point out that this notion of equality and collectivity was not supported by all the residents of Kuchmil, just a few of the more powerful leaders of the community. Nonetheless, their leadership has resulted in the exodus of families and young people who disagreed with a collectivist orientation. For political refugees like don Teo and migrants who have embraced Western modernity and evangelism like Rubén, this outcome was crippling Kuchmil's future prospects. Rubén explained that all the "tenacious, intelligent, and positive people" are leaving because Kuchmil lacks a "sense of vision, of progress," leading him to the prediction: "If that village [Kuchmil] continues the way it is, it's going to become a *fantasma* [ghost]."

These progressive (or regressive) narratives are quite powerful. They resonate even with migrants who continue to champion Kuchmil's communal ethic and who challenge modernity's inequities. Javier Can Po'ot associates youth migration with the phantasmic effects of modernization. "The village is very sad, like it's missing something. It's missing people," Javier explained. Like Rubén, Javier thought the steady migration of Kuchmil's young people was slowly eroding the tight-knit community. They felt that the presence of young people transformed the community into a dynamic and entertaining place to live, and without this presence the residents no longer socialized with each other on a daily basis. Families looked inward to their nuclear unit and outward toward extended migrant networks for resources and support instead of relying on other community members, thereby weakening social ties developed over time. For returning and visiting migrants, the absence of these youths and their peers accentuated the ruptures in the social fabric of community life. For Javier Can Po'ot and Leonardo May Kauil, as the cohesion and embeddedness of community life began to disappear, village life began to resemble the socially fragmented life representative of Cancún. In this narrative of loss and impending dissolution, migration continues to be predicated on a linear continuum.

These narratives suggest that the lack of population growth and a disarticulation with modernity will transform Kuchmil from a living community to a dying one. Of course, this is one vision of the negative implications resulting from both resisting and embracing modernity. Following the Can Tuns and the May Kauils, I articulate an alternative version, in which the residents of Kuchmil rely on both a collective and an individual approach to criticize modernity and its limitations and to reinforce community ties across the space-time divide.

# 7

## The Phantom City: Rethinking Tourism as Development after Hurricane Wilma

They had been warned. Trucks with loudspeakers had driven through the regiones a few days before. Disembodied voices advised people where to go for refuge if they did not live in concrete-block homes. Radio broadcasts, televised news programs, and leaflets distributed throughout the regiones provided detailed instructions on how to prepare for the hurricane. Residents were advised to stock up on canned foods, bottled water, batteries, and candles. They were reminded to seal windows and doors. Some people heeded these warnings. Others did not.

Residents who live in hurricane-prone regions can become desensitized to such warnings. In September 2000, while I was living in Kuchmil, Hurricane Keith threatened the peninsula. I helped don Dani and doña Pati cover and tie down most of their belongings and move all their electronics and dishes to their son's concrete-block house. We sat up all night listening to the radio, waiting for the hurricane to arrive, fearing the worst. Although the sky darkened, the wind howled, and it rained heavily, the hurricane weakened to a tropical storm before reaching Kuchmil. Every year during the Atlantic hurricane season (June 1 through November 30), hurricane predictions fill the airwaves.[1] According to the U.S. National Climatic Data Center, on average at least one hurricane hits the Caribbean annually.[2] However, it had been over a decade since a Category 5 storm—Hurricane Gilbert (1988)—hit the region.

During the 2005 hurricane season, three hurricanes threatened the Yucatán Peninsula: Emily, Stan, and Wilma. In July, Hurricane Emily began as a Category 4 storm (135 mph), but its wind speed decreased to 115 mph after landfall in the peninsula. Emily did cause some damage in Cancún, but its greatest impact was further south in Playa del Carmen and in the countryside. Although short-lived (the storm passed through in four hours), Emily damaged approximately 11,000 homes and destroyed 58,000 tons of crops (Osbahr and Few 2006). In early October, Hurricane Stan's torrential rains caused severe flooding and landslides in Chiapas and Central America. Once again, Cancún was spared. As the end of the hurricane season came closer, residents did not expect another hurricane forecast.

Based on experiences with Emily and Stan, in 2005 most Kuchmil migrants did not take the predictions of Hurricane Wilma too seriously. Migrants who lived in homes with corrugated cardboard roofs and walls made of wood planks did not follow the government's advice to evacuate because they feared that vacated homes would be looted during their absence. After the government announced that the electricity would be shut off during the hurricane, most migrants purchased provisions for a day or two. But they did not heed the warnings to stock up on enough food and bottled water for three to five days. They preferred to save their money rather than spend it on goods they might not use. Once this prediction became true, residents quickly depleted the stocks of the commercial grocery stores.

On Friday, October 21, Hurricane Wilma hit the Yucatán Peninsula late in the evening. It was a Category 4 storm with a wind speed of 150 mph. (For comparison, Hurricane Katrina began as a Category 5 storm, but by landfall had weakened to a Category 3 storm with a wind speed of 125 mph.) By the following afternoon, Wilma had weakened to a Category 2 storm, but it did not move on until Sunday morning. In contrast to most hurricanes, Wilma hovered over the peninsula for over twenty-four hours. Wilma only caused a handful of deaths, but due to its duration, it devastated Cancún's infrastructure. Over two-thirds of Cancún's hotels and several thousand homes were damaged.[3] The winds snapped off traffic lights and electricity posts and stripped the trees and shrubs of 40 percent of their foliage. Flooding damaged the drainage system and the asphalt roads, creating large potholes every few feet. This debris was scattered everywhere, ruining the Zona Hotelera's lush landscaping and making it difficult to maneuver through the city by car or on foot. As a result of this devastation, the government took much longer than expected to reinstate basic services. It took five days for potable drinking water to circulate and one week for electricity to be restored to 80 percent of the city's residents.[4] Some regiones went without electricity and water for over two weeks. Because of this destruction and chaos, national news coverage declared Cancún to be a "ciudad fantasma."[5]

## Rebuilding the Phantom City

After Wilma, tourists continued to flock to the Riviera Maya, to the tourist towns of Puerto Morelos, Playa del Carmen, and Tulum, which experienced less damage and hence recovered quickly from the hurricane. In December 2006, these towns had an occupancy rate of 90 percent.[6] In contrast, Cancún's hotel occupancy rate hovered at 40 percent because over two-thirds of the hotels and most of the businesses in the Zona Hotelera were closed for reconstruction or renovations.[7] Of the 27,848 hotel rooms in Cancún, approximately 10,000 were available for occupation in January 2006. Two-thirds of the damaged businesses did not re-open until April 2006, while a third of the hotels remained closed until June 2006.[8] Considering that Cancún's economic livelihood depends on tourism, the lack of tourists devastated the local economy. It also negatively impacted the national economy. Tourism is one of the top three generators of foreign exchange and employment for Mexico.[9] In 2004, Mexico received over twenty million foreign visitors who injected over $10 billion into the national economy.[10] Since its resorts were the destination for over six million tourists, nearly a third of these dollars were spent in the state of Quintana Roo.[11] As Mexico's most popular tourist site, Cancún generated over $2 billion in revenues in 2005.[12] In 2006, Mexico lost approximately $7 million daily as a result of hurricane damage (Cortellese et al. 2006).[13]

The price of rebuilding Cancún was estimated in the millions of dollars. Since this region attracts half of the tourists visiting Mexico and generates over 30 percent of tourism's dividends (Cortellese et al. 2006), the federal government proclaimed reconstruction a national priority. The municipal government calculated the costs for repairing the city's infrastructure, excluding damage to the Zona Hotelera, at $9 million. International bank loans, insurance claims, and the federal government's Nacional Financiera (NAFIN; National Development Bank) and Fondo Nacional de Desastres Naturales (FONDEN; Fund for Natural Disasters) provided the bulk of the funds to rebuild Cancún.[14] NAFIN set aside $345 million for small-business loans. FONDEN paid out $142 million in claims for damages caused by Hurricane Wilma and Hurricane Stan.[15] The World Bank and the Inter-American Development Bank (IDB) granted a credit line of $500 million for the region.[16] Additionally, Cancún hotel owners, commercial businesses, and homeowners filed approximately $1.7 billion in insurance claims.[17] Finally, FONATUR allocated $10 million to rebuilding Cancún's beaches, to which the federal government added $20 million.[18] Over $30 million was spent to pave, to landscape, and to replace the street lighting along Kukulcán Boulevard, the main street that runs through the Zona Hotelera.[19] The federal and municipal governments allocated another 500 million pesos (approximately $50 million) for infrastructure development in 2007.[20]

Considering the large sums of money invested to rebuild Cancún, this tragic story appears to have a happy ending. The speed with which the city recovered has been praised globally, especially in light of the slow reconstruction of New Orleans. The United Nations World Tourism Organization commended Cancún for its swift recovery.[21] Unlike the Bush administration after Hurricane Katrina, the Mexican government responded within fifty-two hours of the disaster, providing funds, supplies, and manpower in the form of its army and navy. Architect Ricardo Alvarado Guerrero, FONATUR's general director in Cancún, explained that this tragedy provided a great opportunity for Cancún's tourist industry to "remodel completely" in order to "construct a new image" at home and abroad. Prior to the hurricane, FONATUR's study of the tourist industry in Cancún showed "noted signs of overdevelopment, in its infrastructure, in its activities, in its buildings."[22] Hotels and commercial businesses took advantage of the devastation to enact extensive renovations. However, these renovations involved more than a physical reconstruction. They also involved bureaucratic and workforce changes. Cancún shed stagnant businesses, weary facades, and surplus workers. Indeed, Cancún was rebuilt into a shiny new version, transforming itself from a phantom city to a fantastic one.

The story of Cancún's successful recovery ignores Wilma's impact on the city's largest population, its migrant workers. During the aftermath of the hurricane, workers were retained to clean up the mess. But soon after, as hotels foreclosed or switched ownership, their staff was let go. According to the municipal government, only an estimated 6,000 migrants left the city, even though most of the hotels and businesses shut down for four months.[23] However, given the chaos after Wilma, it would not be surprising if more migrants left town. The municipal government claimed that these migrants were not firmly rooted in Cancún, that their departures did not impact the city because other migrants arrived to take their place. But their absence remains visible in the tragic carcasses of their abandoned homes. The workers who remained rebuilt Cancún. In the process, they suffered through hunger, inadequate shelter, and physical and economic insecurity. The millions of dollars funneled into Cancún's reconstruction were initially oriented toward the Zona Hotelera and eventually to its commercial center. But very little money was allocated to rebuild roads, fix damaged homes, provide additional security, or gather trash in the regiones. These tasks were left in the hands of local residents and grassroots organizations. The May Pats' and the Can Tuns' experiences before and after Wilma illustrate how this grand narrative of success masks the problems involved with promoting tourism as a development model for Mexico.

## On Suffering

Jovana Can Tun's experience is representative of how migrants passed their time in the hours before the storm. The day the hurricane was scheduled to land, Jovana purchased enough groceries to sustain her family of four for two days. She did not expect to need more supplies because in the decade that she had lived in Cancún, most hurricanes landed and passed through the region within a day. The government warned its citizens that the electricity would be shut down as a preventive measure against accidental electrocutions from downed power lines. Because the blackout would interrupt the water supply, residents were advised to stock up on water. Heeding this warning, Jovana topped off her water tank and filled extra buckets with water. Fortunately, Jovana's home was sturdy enough to withstand a hurricane. The two bedrooms in her house were made of concrete block. This is where her family planned to wait out the storm, accompanied by her brother-in-law and his family. However, Jovana was concerned with the inaccessibility of her bathroom and the instability of her kitchen. Although the bathroom was made from concrete, its entrance was located outside, which would make access difficult during a hurricane. She improvised by creating portable toilets. There was nothing she could do about her kitchen, which was flimsily built with wood planks as walls and a corrugated cardboard roof. When her husband, Juan, came home from work in the late afternoon, they moved the stove, china cabinet, cooking supplies, and dishes into one of the bedrooms. They boarded up the windows, tied down the cardboard roof as tightly as possible, and wrapped the dining room table, chairs, and refrigerator with plastic and rope. The only thing left to do was wait.

With tears in her eyes, Jovana described the fear and panic generated by the force of the hurricane. "We locked ourselves inside. [The hurricane] lasted a long time. Three days with wind." Because her stove was attached to its own gas tank, Jovana continued to prepare hot meals by candlelight during the storm. But the wind and rain made their life very difficult. The wind forced the rain through the windows, which lacked panes and shutters, and the walls absorbed the downpour and became wet.[24] Water seeped under the doors, flooding their home. Immediately, Jovana and her family "began to scoop the water out. But we realized that although we dumped it out, the water flowed back inside." As the storm continued, pools of water began to form in the bedrooms because these floors were slightly lower than the rest. Jovana recalled,

> We placed concrete blocks on the floor, so that we could walk. All we could do was lay down. There was nothing else for us to do. . . . I have to watch over the [children] when they wake up because I don't want them to step down into the water. After sleeping, they are too warm [to be exposed to cold water].

Her family did not own a battery-operated radio, so they were unaware of the storm's trajectory and duration.

When the storm ceased the following day, Jovana thought the ordeal was over. As everyone exited their homes to assess the damage, her neighbors informed her that they were in the eye of the hurricane. Although the eye provided a respite for people to restock supplies and contact family members, Jovana was disheartened by the news. To get through the next few days, she purchased more food and Maseca (a brand of corn flour) with which to make tortillas at the corner grocery store. When the wind and rain returned, Jovana's five-year-old daughter exclaimed, "We are going to die, Mamá." Traumatized by this ordeal, Jovana said after, "We suffered a lot. A lot of water came in. We couldn't [scoop up the water] anymore."

After the hurricane departed, the fear remained. Similar to New Orleans after Hurricane Katrina, the radio announcers focused on the looting of businesses and homes. Who was looting became a central concern in the regiones, especially since many of these neighborhoods lacked electricity for over two weeks. Jovana's neighbors told her that the perpetrators were escaped prisoners. This rumor spread quickly from neighborhood to neighborhood. During the first week after the hurricane, the majority of calls made to the municipal government's emergency office were security related. The municipal government claimed that the majority of the stories circulating after the storm were rumors rather than facts, generated by the fear and "psychosis" that gripped the city after such a traumatic event.[25] Regardless, the government made an attempt to respond to these claims, but it did not have enough equipment to traverse the littered landscape and the manpower necessary to investigate each claim. In response to this fear and the government's inability to police the regiones, each neighborhood set up its own nighttime security detail. To illuminate the streets, the residents in Jovana's neighborhood built fires on every corner. Jovana explained how the community patrol worked.

> We would go out at midnight and return at two [in the morning].
> Then another family would come out to tend the fire. Each family
> had to find what they were going to burn at night in order to keep
> the fires going. Because everything was dark. There was no light.
> You only hear people talking to each other, yelling. Only noise. Later
> you hear that someone is trespassing. Only once did we hear that
> someone was captured. But no, we didn't see it. We went outside
> to see what was happening because there is so much shouting. . . .
> Every night we went out to patrol the streets.

Families tended the fires, rotating every two hours. The community patrols also provided protection to workers, like Juan, who were able to return to work within a week of the disaster and who had to walk home or bicycle in the dark because their shifts ended late at night. The community patrols facilitated these workers' safe passage home. According to the municipal government, the community patrols did a superb job in preventing physical harm; after the hurricane, no one filed an official complaint of physical aggression or rape.

As a result of the hurricane, many people, in particular minimum-wage service employees, lost their jobs or experienced a sharp decline in wages due to the lack of tourism. A quarter of the Kuchmil migrants lost their jobs, while those who remained employed had their salaries reduced. The immediate consequence of this unemployment and lack of tourism was hunger. Most migrants did not purchase enough food and water to tide them over for two weeks. Some, like Horacio May Kauil, had emergency money set aside in their bank accounts, but the blackout made it impossible to access these accounts. In addition, the outlets for purchasing food were limited. Corner grocery stores, the place where most residents buy their groceries, ran out of supplies within a couple of days. Due to hurricane damage, only one commercial grocery store opened immediately after the hurricane. To prevent chaos and looting, management restricted the number of shoppers allowed inside and provided its personnel with baseball bats and rifles.[26] Long lines formed outside this store.

In response to this scarcity, during the first twenty days after the storm, the municipal government, with the aid of the federal government, set up twenty soup kitchens and distribution centers for *despensas* (food supplies) and delivered water via trucks carrying water tanks throughout the city. Although concerned citizens, state governments, and the federal government supplied three tons of despensas to this region, these resources were not evenly distributed. For example, as a rebuke for the looting of a local commercial grocery store, the municipal government did not hand out despensas in Jovana's working-class neighborhood. But in some regiones, the absence of the state was never explained, as was the case in Ramona May Pat's working-class neighborhood. Ramona heard about this aid from televised news reports, but she bitterly exclaimed, "We got nothing." In contrast, in Horacio May Kauil's neighborhood, which is a new private/public housing development promoted by former President Vicente Fox, several food kitchens were set up. According to Horacio, "You could eat breakfast, lunch, and dinner free. . . . This lasted for twenty days I believe. Every day, one could get food and bring it home." In addition, government bureaucrats passed through daily to offer help to residents in this neighborhood, while the police patrolled the streets day and night. Working-class residents blamed this uneven distribution on greedy politicians who used the despensas to secure votes in the upcoming election.

To address the physical and economic issues facing Cancún's citizens, the federal government disbursed economic and home reconstruction subsidies and required banks and organizations, such as the Instituto de Fomento a la Vivienda y Regularización de la Propiedad (INFOVIR; Housing Development Institute), to postpone mortgage payments and freeze interest payments during the two-month period following the hurricane. Once again, this support was not evenly distributed among the families most afflicted by the hurricane or was slow in coming. For example, the federal government handed out a one-time subsidy of 2,000 pesos (the equivalent of $200) for working families, but it was based on a lottery system rather than on financial need. As a result, not everyone received this subsidy. Among the Kuchmil migrants, only a handful received it, all of whom were employed. Those who lost their jobs, like Néstor Canul Canche (Ramona's husband) and Eduardo Can Tun, were not beneficiaries. In addition, corruption limited the impact of this subsidy, as is evident in Juan's experience. Juan felt extremely lucky to receive this subsidy until he received his bimonthly paycheck. It was reduced by 500 pesos, more than half of his bimonthly salary of 900 pesos. When Juan questioned this discount, his employer informed him that they classified half of the subsidy as a loan, which Juan was obligated to pay back to his employer, not to the government. Of course, Juan knew this was a scam. He was told that if he disputed this claim, he would lose his job. Finally, although the government set aside money to help people rebuild damaged homes, the bulk of these funds had yet to be disbursed six months after Hurricane Wilma. INFOVIR declared that it could not disburse funds until it had evaluated and approved every applicant's claim.[27] Thus, although the federal, state, and municipal governments did allocate resources with which to help its working-class citizens, these resources were limited and unevenly distributed. The bulk of this aid was not directed toward Cancún's largest population—its working-class migrants—but rather toward the Zona Hotelera.

In the absence of the state, Cancún's working-class migrants relied on each other and their extended social network for emotional, social, and economic support. Neighborhoods organized community patrols. Local grocers distributed food. And everyone helped clean up the debris. In Kuchmil, families like the May Pats immediately gathered supplies to send to their children. Three days after the hurricane (after the roads had been cleared), a truck filled with Maseca, candles, flashlights, powdered milk, rice, beans, cookies, and canned foods arrived in Cancún. A few migrants also sought help from tourists or foreigners they had befriended. Horacio and Leonardo called up their friends in England and Canada, respectively, to let them know they had survived the hurricane. These friends generously offered to wire money to help them. Likewise, when I contacted Ramona after the hurricane and she told me that her kitchen roof was severely damaged, I sent her money to help pay for the repairs. But these contributions were short-lived. Consequently, Eduardo Can Tun described the six months following Wilma as a period of "great suffering" because some days his family ate only tortillas and other days they ate only beans.

## Tourism as Development

In spite of the devastation caused by natural disasters and of its vulnerability to economic recessions and political instability, tourism remains an attractive, if not the most attractive, alternative for developing countries. Global tourism is one of the largest industries in the world (Cothran and Cothran 1998). In the Caribbean, for example, tourism receipts constitute 25 percent of total exports and, in 1999, 21 percent of its gross domestic product (Pattullo 2005). Not surprisingly, critics suggest that tourism promotes a new type of economic dependence between rich and poor countries (Enloe 1989; Gregory 2007; Nash 1989; Pattullo 1996/2005; Wilson 2008). Amalia Cabezas further argues that tourism "deskills and devalues" workers and "sexualizes their labor" (2008, 22). Given that this dependence resonates with these countries' histories of colonialism and slavery (ibid.; Pattullo 1996/2005), Maya migrants' declarations of service work as *la nueva esclavitud* (the new slavery) makes sense.

Notwithstanding these critiques, Felipe Calderón Hinojosa, soon after beginning his tenure as Mexico's president (2006–12), declared tourism a national priority. In his message to the *Secretaría de Turismo* (Ministry of Tourism, or SECTUR), Calderón proclaimed tourism as critical to Mexico's economic growth because it generates the third largest foreign exchange dividends (after oil and remittances). In 2004, Mexico was ranked the eighth most popular tourist destination in the world, attracting over twenty million tourists annually.[28] Tourism generates approximately 1.9 million direct jobs and many other indirect jobs as a result of its multiplier effects and its ability to make linkages with marginalized communities and other economic sectors.[29] According to Calderón, tourism is the optimal means by which to combat poverty because of its capacity "to produce jobs for a large proportion of women, . . . to promote the development of regions that lack an export industry, [and] to make active use of natural resources and culture (of which marginalized groups have an abundance)."[30] Applauding tourist centers like Cancún, Los Cabos, and Huatulco, Calderón recommended these centers as models for future development. Following previous government administrations, Calderón places Mexico's economic future squarely within the export and service industries. For the nation-state, tourism's ability to generate jobs makes it a success and its international character helps solidify Mexico's membership in the new global economy.

Equating tourism with jobs as President Calderón has done, however, is not the best strategy for economic development. Tourism accounts for only 10 percent of jobs in Mexico (Cothran and Cothran 1998).[31] Indeed, the fickle tastes of tourists make tourism one of the most unreliable methods by which to acquire foreign exchange (Madeley 1992). Since the bulk of these jobs provide minimum-wage salaries with limited access to economic mobility, tourism does not encourage investments in human capital (e.g., education). Rather, profits are contingent on keeping labor costs low (Enloe 1989). Although tourism generates high foreign exchange earnings, the bulk of this income is reduced by "leakages" in import costs associated with tourism (e.g., food, furniture, equipment, building materials). In the Caribbean, leakages consume 70 percent of every dollar earned through foreign exchange (Pattullo 1996/2005). These leakages can be a result of stipulations imposed by foreign investors and financial institutions. For example, the $150 million loan FONATUR received from the IDB in 1993 for tourism development was contingent on instituting international competitive bidding for contracts including large construction projects (over $5 million) and expensive materials (over $250,000) (Wilson 2008). The bulk of tourist dollars are funneled first to corporations, then to states, and very little trickles down to city governments and locally-owned businesses (Castañeda 1996). In addition, tourism requires vast amounts of capital for infrastructural development (e.g., electricity, airports, roads, telephones, water and sewage treatment facilities), the bulk of which is underwritten by local governments (Gmelch 2003). In Mexico, between 1974 and 1998, FONATUR invested $12 billion in capital and credit (Clancy 2001). In 1982, the growth of private investment made it feasible for the Mexican government to begin to withdraw its economic support of the tourist industry, but it continued to fund the marketing and promotion of tourism (ibid.). Finally, Cancún's location in a hurricane-prone region makes it vulnerable to future devastating and extremely costly natural disasters like Wilma.

In his message to SECTUR, Calderón acknowledged that government intervention was "fundamental" for tourism's success. The Mexican government's response to Hurricane Wilma illustrates its continued financial commitment to this industry. To speed along Cancún's recovery, the governor of Quintana Roo and the municipal president of Benito Juárez traveled extensively throughout Europe and the United States to promote the region as safe and secure for tourists. To fund this international marketing campaign, the state government requisitioned the city's 2 percent hotel tax.[32] Their objective was to replace images of a destroyed Cancún with those of a new and improved Cancún. This rebranding campaign presented an opportunity to dispel Cancún's reputation of catering to all-inclusive tour packages and as a mecca for spring breakers. In a sense, Cancún was perceived as a luxury brand in need of reinvention. This campaign reflects the continued collusion between governments and transnational corporations in their effort to promote tourism as a form of development.

The devastation caused by Hurricane Wilma created an opportunity for the Mexican government, whether at the local, state, or federal level, to address the problems associated with tourism, such as leakages, lack of job security, and wage depression. While the state and municipal governments, with the aid of federal funds, took advantage of this disaster to make infrastructure improvements in the Zona Hotelera, they did not tackle most of the other issues. Instead, the government's solution to Cancún's economic stagnation was to focus on capturing a new segment of the tourist market. Cancún is being oriented toward a new type of client—the wealthy tourist—a strategy that may lead to an increase in capital gains but not necessarily to job growth. To appeal to a selective and wealthy clientele, FONATUR, working in conjunction with the municipal government, has proposed three new development projects: Riviera Cancún, Puerto Cancún, and Tajamar.[33] All involve building luxury condos next to businesses catering to the rich. Riviera Cancún, located by the airport near the southern entrance to the Zona Hotelera, will be oriented around a golf course. Currently, Cancún operates three golf courses; the government plans to develop an additional ten. Puerto Cancún, located between the commercial center and the entrance to the Zona Hotelera, will convert 808 acres into a private enclave consisting of 2,100 luxury condominiums and apartments located around a golf course, shopping center, and marina. Finally, Tajamar will be oriented around a boardwalk facing Laguna Nichupté. This promenade will become the city's new "classic" downtown, displacing the "deteriorated" downtown.[34] All the projects are currently under construction and are being underwritten by FONATUR and by the Banco Nacional de Obras y Servicios Públicos (BANOBRAS), another state development bank in Mexico. As soon as the infrastructure (sewage and drainage system, electricity, etc.) needed to support these projects is complete, FONATUR will sell the land to private investors for development. These projects have been promoted as generating greater foreign exchange than the current emphasis on time-shares and all-inclusive hotels and as being environmentally friendly due to their low-density approach. Regardless, this type of "boutique" and "retirement, second home" tourism tends to remain under the economic control of foreign elites (Pattullo 1996, 207).

Tourism's dependence on foreign capital and tourists makes it vulnerable to global economic crises and health pandemics like the 2009 H1N1 flu outbreak. In addition, tourism does not necessarily produce more jobs for local residents or benefit local businesses. Nor does it address Cancún's vulnerability to natural disasters and their devastating consequences. Tourism continues to generate exorbitant costs for national economies, the brunt of which is born by the workers employed in this industry. The havoc wrought by Hurricane Wilma underscores the fragility of Mexico's modernity and its dependence on transnational capital and foreign tourists.

## The Hidden Costs of Tourism

The May Pats' and the Can Tuns' experiences with Hurricane Wilma underscore the limits of modernization projects, neoliberal ideologies, and transnational capitalism. Although much of the focus has been on its destruction of Cancún, Hurricane Wilma also made a lasting impact on the countryside because it arrived a few months after Hurricane Emily had battered the cornfields and right before the corn harvest. The force of the winds flattened the cornstalks and the heavy rains inundated the fields. Mold spread quickly, decomposing the crops (corn, beans, and squash) remaining after Hurricane Emily. In the state of Yucatán, Wilma damaged approximately 28 million hectares of corn and 300 hectares of vegetables (primarily chiles and tomatoes).[35]

In Kuchmil, although a few ejidatarios managed to save half their harvest, the majority lost the bulk of it. The May Pats and Can Tuns were no exception. Don Dani, for example, managed to save thirty-two bags of maize. In response to this loss, the government provided campesinos with a one-time subsidy of 900 pesos per hectare (limited to five hectares) for damages caused by Wilma.[36] This cash allowed families to purchase seed to sow their next harvest and corn to feed their families and to sustain their livestock (pigs, chickens, and turkeys) for a few months. However, during the summer months households ran out of cash and corn. To add to this distress, the Mexican government began liquidating its farm subsidy program, PROCAMPO, in 2006, two years before this program was scheduled to be terminated in accordance with NAFTA. Farmers were given the option to receive the remaining subsidies in one lump sum, rather than annually over the next three years. Each program participant was to receive 370 pesos per hectare under cultivation (limited to five hectares per year) for a period of three years. According to don Jorge, the municipal government promised that the newly elected president would create a new program to replace PROCAMPO. Based on this promise and in order to recover from Wilma, the ejidatarios in Kuchmil agreed to liquidate their PROCAMPO accounts. By doing so, they now lack a safety net against future ecological problems and environmental disasters. Thus the liquidation of PROCAMPO was directly linked to the imposition of neoliberal projects and to the upcoming elections.

The May Pats' and Can Tuns' migrant children were also deeply affected by Wilma. Before Wilma, both Jesús and Francisco May Pat and their wives converted their homes into corner grocery stores. This type of business made a profit after Wilma, but the recent increase in licensing fees and the global fiscal crisis is threatening their existence.[37] To make ends meet, Jesús and Francisco continue to work in the hotel industry while their wives manage the stores. Although the older children were able to gain a stable economic foothold in this tourist center, their younger siblings, in spite of their college degrees, continue to live in economic insecurity. After completing his master's degree in education, Tómas May Pat continues working for his brother because he does not have the political connections to obtain a teaching post. Similarly, Mario Can Tun, who recently graduated with a bachelor's degree in tourism administration, has been unable to find hotel work. As an accountant, Ramona May Pat has stable employment, but after Wilma, it took her husband Néstor six months to find a job as an assistant bartender, even though he has extensive experience as a bartender. Among the Can Tuns whose educational background was limited to the secundaria, Eduardo, Saúl (Fátima's husband), and Jovana also became unemployed after Wilma. It took them six months to get back on their feet.

Tourist centers like Cancún were intended to modernize and industrialize the countryside, to transform indigenous peasants into modern, urban service workers. However, the bulk of tourist jobs, which are low wage and based on seasonal short-term contracts, do not provide greater economic security than agricultural work, especially in a city based on a dollar economy. Environmental changes and the fickle taste of tourists make this type of service work unpredictable and as prone to crisis as farmwork. Despite government expectations, service jobs have not replaced farm work. Rather, due to its seasonal nature, tourism has become dependent on the countryside, as is evident by the constant movement between Kuchmil and Cancún. This dependence has led the residents in Kuchmil to question the merits of a tourist economy. At least half of the ejidatarios have spent time working in Cancún or the Riviera Maya. Return migrants point out that both economic systems (tourist and agrarian) provide similar experiences of economic insecurity and poverty. Carlos May Chan, don Jorge's nephew who returned to live in Kuchmil after spending a decade in Cancún, explained:

> It's the same. Here [in Kuchmil] you don't spend as much as you would [in Cancún]. You may eat less than over there because [in Cancún] one eats more meat. . . . Here no one earns an income, but they survive on something. Everyone sells something—habanero chiles, tomatoes. We exchange among ourselves in order to live. Here you don't have to buy lemons, chile. . . . [In Cancún] you measure everything you earn. . . . Everything surpasses [your income]. It is never enough. You can live this way year after year, and it's always the same.

This critique identifies the very real limitations of tourism and of agriculture in reducing poverty among indigenous communities. Even as the Mexican government praises the economic growth generated by tourism, Maya people's experiences remind us of its uneven distribution.

# Resurrecting Phantoms, Resisting Neoliberalism

I would like to conclude this book by addressing Rubén's and Leonardo's concerns about the future viability of rural indigenous communities, especially in light of neoliberal projects like NAFTA and the Proyecto Mesoamérica (formerly known as the Plan Puebla Panamá).[1] Will they become fantasmas (phantoms)? This process of assimilation has been critically debated over the last fifty years by Mexican anthropologists and institutions working with indigenous communities, particularly as indigenous migration to Mexican cities and the United States has increased steadily. Yet this may be the wrong question to pose. Rubén's concerns are grounded in a deterministic evolutionary model of capitalism in which modernity replaces all other customs, attitudes, and behaviors not associated with the free market exchange of goods, autonomous individualism, and maximal economic utility. But capitalism does not treat all individuals equally (Sayer 1991). As such, people's responses to capitalist structures vary; they constantly negotiate their relationship with the structures of power in which they are embedded. Nor does capitalism dissolve cultural difference entirely. Rather, as Néstor García Caclini reminds us, "capitalist modernization, particularly in case of dependent capitalism with strong Indian roots, does not always destroy traditional cultures as it moves forward; it can also appropriate them, restructure them, reorganize the meaning and function of their objects, beliefs, and practices" (1993, viii). By tracing the ghosts of these appropriations, we can disrupt evolutionary narratives grounding theories of modernity, assimilation, and migration that attempt to erase or essentialize indigenous peoples' past, present, and future. Thus what we should be asking is what do these resurrections tell us about modernity's and neoliberalism's limitations and how can they shape their future possibilities?

This book suggests that indigenous peoples have always been central to Mexico's efforts to become modern. Tourism projects like Cancún are nothing more than the latest manifestation in a long history of modernization projects intended to make this transformation happen. Modernity, as an ideology put into practice through development projects like Cancún, asks indigenous peoples to alter their sense of time, space, place, and self. To some extent, it has been successful. Maya campesinos continue to arrive daily in Cancún and the Riviera Maya. They make up a significant portion of Cancún's workforce and are sought after by hotel management. Maya migrants themselves desire to be "modern." But to acquire the accoutrements of modern life (e.g., home, car, and electronics) and survive economically, Maya migrants must take on debt, a practice that increases the insecurity of life in Cancún, especially when this money is borrowed from private corporations rather than from social networks and public institutions. Among the working class in Cancún, access to credit has been a recent phenomenon, but it forms part of finance's growing emphasis on predatory lending to the poor (Williams 2004). Debt has become an integral part of being modern in Cancún, especially among working-class migrants. Jovana Can Tun explained that to have things, to own things, requires that you "expose yourself to risk in order to buy [things]." This declaration, which was repeated by other Maya migrants, contrasts sharply with migrants' prior understandings of the meanings of money and consumption (see chapter 5). Maya migrants' willingness to take on large amounts of debt represents a shift in their relationship to transnational capital and neoliberal reforms. This shift is due in part to the government's response to Hurricane Wilma, which reminded migrants of Cancún's economic significance. According to Horacio, "Cancún will always be Cancún. It's a place that is internationally well-known . . . like Paris." His brother Leonardo affirmed, "Whatever happens, there will always be investment." That is, capital will never abandon this translocality. Bearing this in mind, Jovana and Juan are contemplating renting out their current self-built home and taking out a twenty-five year mortgage for a modern one-bedroom home in a new housing development (a prefabricated block home priced initially at $23,000 but costing $300,000 over the life of the mortgage). For Jovana and Juan, in spite of the fact that their monthly income does not exceed $600, this vision of progress and social mobility remains extremely alluring. It also places them at great risk of becoming the next casualties of our current global fiscal crisis.

These transformations can never be complete. The success of modernization projects like Cancún and NAFTA presupposes access to government subsidies, cheap goods and land (usually in the global South), and disposable labor (in many cases that of youthful ethnic bodies). In the end, these projects propagate greater inequalities. As the value of farmers' produce has declined as a result of NAFTA, Cancún's population has grown exponentially. This growth has led to a rise in urbanization, the bulk of which is concentrated in informal, self-built, and rental housing. This "overurbanization," according to Mike Davis, "is driven by the reproduction of poverty, not by the supply of jobs" (2006, 16). Cancún's surplus labor is illustrative of this very problem. More important, in spite of the Mexican government's effusive praise for tourism as an economic engine of growth, it cannot absorb everyone. Tourism is dependent on the countryside to defray migrants' and their families' reproductive costs and as a source of surplus and reserve labor. Thus Cancún and the countryside have become interdependent (Castellanos 2009b). As Carlos May Chan observed, farm work and tourist work are not fundamentally different for Maya people; they both involve an impoverished, precarious existence. What modernity produces in many cases for indigenous peoples is a sense of cultural loss and marginalization—that is, ghostly experiences—that is anathema to the very idea of modernity and the nation-state, to ideas of progress, growth, and development.

As Stephen Gregory (2007) demonstrates in his study of tourism in the Dominican Republic, the asymmetries symptomatic of tourist sites breed diverse forms of opposition toward neoliberal policies and transnational corporations. Indeed, Maya families and their migrant children show that there are multiple ways to cope with and resist this structural violence and the cultural loss it engenders. In the past, just as the ejido and the Cultural Missions required indigenous communities to establish a new type of relationship with the Mexican government, the collapse of agriculture and the transformation of the peninsula into an international tourist hot spot in the late 1960s demanded that Maya communities once again negotiate the types of relationships they will have with these new economies, the state, and each other. Presently, in light of the dissolution of agrarian reform and the decline in government subsidies (both consequences of NAFTA), the ejidatarios of Kuchmil face pressure from government bureaucrats and individual members to privatize ejido land. To resist neoliberal policies, the community of Kuchmil recalls memories of past oppressions and reinforces customs grounded in a Maya spiritual worldview. The ejido, they proclaim, "is nature. It cannot be sold." Given this understanding of land as inherently sacred and inalienable, parceling the ejido is considered an irreverent and sacrilegious act. By retaining communal ownership of their land, they aim to prevent the return of slavery. To avoid fleeing the countryside permanently, Kuchmil households have begun investing time and labor into projects that will diversify their production. As ejidos are pressured to privatize and Maya migrants take on debt, the present has come to look a lot like the past—landlessness and debt also marked the epoch of slavery (see Sullivan 1989). Not surprisingly, Maya migrants refer to this moment as a new epoch of slavery.

At the same time, Kuchmil parents teach their children to be more assertive and attentive to their surroundings. This emphasis on the individual, along with exposure to wage work in Cancún, results in a shift in how personhood is performed among Kuchmil migrants. In the past, Maya men and women belonged to a moral community that recognized their individuality within a sexual division of labor marked by the home and the milpa. As migrants, like Rubén, have learned to become a different type of individual—a liberal individual—they embrace modernity, but this does not mean that they embrace it fully or that their interpretation of modernity is similar to national and corporate metanarratives (see Rofel 1999). Most Kuchmil residents recognize modernity as a subjugating discourse and a set of structures that require one to be chingón and despierto to successfully maneuver them. Even as they acknowledge their dependence on tourism, they also recognize that tourist jobs, in the form of low-wage, contract labor, were not enough. To improve their children's opportunities within a system increasingly polarized by class and racial distinctions, Kuchmil families have begun to send their children to university. To date, this positionality is considered the best way to adequately prepare their children to face the challenges ahead.

Given the rise in unemployment and strict border policing in the United States, going North remains an unattractive proposition for Maya migrants. Instead, Maya migrants who equate service work with slavery, like Ignacio and Carlos, are moving west, back to Kuchmil. Ironically, these return migrations show that Cancún needs indigenous peoples more than they need Cancún. These return migrants reinvigorate life in Kuchmil. In addition, Maya migrants' frequent visits, gifts of goods, and remittances infuse Kuchmil with life and aid. Living in Cancún and observing tourists' fascination with their culture—and of course hanging out with an anthropologist—continually reminds them of the beauty and importance of Maya customs and practices. Migrants return to Kuchmil with video camcorders and digital cameras to record daily activities and special events. Their remittances and promesas pay for grander fiestas in honor of the Santa Cruz and the Virgin de Guadalupe. They now hold wedding ceremonies in *traje* (traditional clothing), a practice that was phased out twenty years ago. As a result, when I spoke with Leonardo recently, he corrected his assessment of Kuchmil. "Many people like [Kuchmil] and now stay to live. It's not disappearing. Every year they have more children and the pueblo continues to grow. Of course, many [of these children] will come here, but many remain." Through these practices and positionalities, Maya migrants imagine new spaces that permit a continual and palatable engagement with the modern nation-state and transnational capital, even if these terms are not equal to or better than previous circumstances. Although Leonardo no longer believes his community will disappear, this does not mean that, barring minor glitches, modernization projects have been successful. Rather, this observation suggests that modernity as a project and ideology involves a continual struggle between various forces, including indigenous peoples, governments, and hotel corporations, to shape its meanings and outcomes.

# Kin Chart of Can Tun and May Pat Families

**Can Tun Family**

Francisco Can Chi
m. Florencia Pat Kinil

José Can Pat
m. Matilde Balam Uc

Dani Can Balam
m. Patricia Tun Pech

Nicolas Can Tun
Mariela Can Tun
Jovana Can Tun
Eduardo Can Tun
Fátima Can Tun
Mario Can Tun

*Cousins*

Rubén Can Kauil
Jimena Can Kauil
César Can Poot
Javier Can Poot
Carla Be' Can
Ignacio Be' Can
Fernanda Can Fernández
Julia Can Uc

**May Pat Family**

Pablo May Poot
m. Rogelia Cocom Pol

Pedro May Cocom
m. Juana Cituk Jimenez

Jorge May Cituk
m. Berta Pat Kauil

Jesús May Pat
Francisco May Pat
Ramona May Pat
Tómas May Pat
Cristián May Pat
Nora May Pat
Andrés May Pat

*Cousins*

Horacio May Kauil
Leonardo May Kauil
Enrique May Kauil
Reynaldo May Kauil
Celia Kauil May
Laura Kauil May
Gustavo Kauil Tun
Macario Kauil Tun

# Notes

## Introduction

1. "Kuchmil" is a pseudonym used to protect the identity of my informants. It is similar in its etymological roots and linguistic significance to the name of the village where I did my research. In Yucatec Maya, *kùuč* means "a load" or "to be carried" (Bricker et al. 1998, 135). *Mil* comes from the Nahuatl language spoken in Central Mexico. It refers to "a field" or "cultivated land" (Karttunen 1983, 147). When *mil* is joined to *kùuč,* it can be loosely translated as "the place of the load or cargo." Thus, I translate "Kuchmil" as "the place that demands devotion through the performance of ritual." The mixture of Nahuatl with Yucatec Maya is characteristic of the Postclassic period, during which the pre-Hispanic site of Kuchmil was occupied.

2. By car, this trip takes three hours. The bus, however, stopped in every village along the way, significantly lengthening the voyage.

3. According to Instituto Nacional Estadístico, Geográfico e Informático (INEGI; National Institute for Statistics, Geography and Data Processing), the 2005 population of the *ayuntamiento* (municipal government) of Benito Juárez, where Cancún is located, was 572,973. Its average annual population growth is 5.63 percent. See INEGI (2006). The ayuntamiento, however, claims that INEGI undercounts its population. They estimate their population at 750,000 people. Personal communication, Lic. Jorge Fregoso Toledo, Sub-Director de Proyectos y Estrategias de Turismo Municipal (2005–8), H. Ayuntamiento de Benito Juárez, Cancún, Quintana Roo, January 9, 2006.

4. This number may include indigenous peoples from Chiapas and Oaxaca, who also work in Cancún. Juan Arvizu, "El éxodo a ciudades no les ha dado acceso a servicios básicos: Conapo," *El Universal,* May 19, 2005, http://www2.eluniversal .com.mx/pls/impreso/version_imprimir.html?id_nota=125236&tabla=nacion (accessed March 4, 2007).

5. To convey the multiple meanings associated with the Spanish term *el pueblo,* I leave it untranslated. El pueblo can refer to a town or a village, but it can also refer to a local and national community. Leonardo uses this term to refer to his village and to a sense of local community.

6. See Bonfil Batalla (1996), Hernández Castillo (2001), and Oehmichen Bazán (2001).

7. For a discussion of the disappeared in Latin America, see Arditti (1999), Carmack (1988), Hernández Castillo (1998), Jonas (1991), Stephen (2006), and Taylor (1997).

8. June Nash's work in Chiapas is rich and extensive. Here I cite her key works. See Nash (1970, 1993, 2001).

9. Here I invoke Arjun Appadurai's use of *deterritorialization* as the process by which goods, money, people, and ideas from disparate places come into contact as they circulate globally (1990, 301–3). The "deterritorialized social space" is the place where these flows come into contact. Yet even as communities are displaced, place does not lose its importance. As I show throughout this book (see chapter 6 in particular), place still matters. Also see Nash (1995).

10. Robert J. Dunphy, "Why the Computer Chose Cancún," *New York Times,* March 5, 1972.

11. In the *Yucatán Peninsula Handbook,* Chicki Mallan (1994) claims that in 1967 a computer program designated the small fishing village on the peninsula's northwest corner as the next tourist hot spot. Alternatively, the Lonely Planet's *Yucatán* guidebook proposes that Cancún was built to replace the faded glamour of Acapulco (Greensfelder 2003). Also see the Cancún Convention and Visitors Bureau's Web site, http://cancun.travel/en/.

12. For a discussion of tourism as a nationalist cultural project, see Saragoza (2001). For a discussion of tourism as a state-led modernization project, see Berger (2006).

13. Heritage tourism may be initially oriented toward a domestic audience, but in the case of Mexico, the promotion of *indigenismo* (indigenism) and *lo mexicano* (typical Mexican goods) was directed at both domestic and international audiences (Berger 2006; Saragoza 2001). Heritage tourism can be imbued with multiple meanings; it can be used to represent a local or national identity or to promote political socialization (Richter 1997).

14. For a discussion of the folklorization of Maya culture by the nation-state and scientists, see Castañeda (2001).

15. Regardless of President Alemán Váldes's efforts, Mexican tourism continued to be defined in part by heritage tourism because Mexico's archaeological sites and colonial cities remained popular tourist sites (Saragoza 2001).

16. The Bracero Program (1942–64) was a temporary foreign worker program operated jointly by the Immigration and Naturalization Service, the Department of Labor, the State Department, and the Mexican government. This program supplied workers for the agricultural and meatpacking industries. For a discussion of this program, see Calavita (1992) and Galarza (1964).

17. By 1978, the IDB had invested an additional $50 million in Cancún's infrastructure (Clancy 2001).

18. This number is based on annual reports of hotel and motel occupation tallies for 2006 and 2007. See http://www.sectur.gob.mx (accessed January 15, 2006 and January 19, 2009).

19. Founded in 1970, Grupo Posadas is a Mexican-owned and publicly traded company. It operates ninety-two hotels in Mexico, South America, and the United States.

20. Since the mid-1990s, social scientists have appropriated this concept in an effort to understand global flows of people, capital, technology, and ideas. Not surprisingly, these studies have been criticized, on the one hand, for being too narrow in scope because they focus on a limited group of people engaged in such activities, and on the other hand, for becoming an all-encompassing catchphrase for economic and social practices associated with recent globalizing trends. For examples of these debates, see Grewal and Kaplan (1994), Guarnizo and Smith (1998), Kearney (1991), Mahler (1998), Mintz (1998), Portes (2001), and Rouse (1991).

21. Appadurai 1996, 192. Also see Smith (1998). For a discussion of translocal cities in Latin America, see Reguillo and Godoy Anativia (2005).

22. I rely on David Harvey's definition of "neoliberalism" as "a theory of political economic practices that proposes that human well-being can best be advanced by liberating individual entrepreneurial freedoms and skills within an institutional framework characterized by strong private property rights, free markets, and free trade" and limited state intervention in the market (2005, 2). Neoliberal structural adjustments refer to the process by which international lending organizations, like the World Bank and the International Monetary Fund, restructure the economies of poor and indebted countries to insure debt repayment. These countries are mandated to deregulate their economies by privatizing state-owned companies and reducing expenditures on public services.

23. Of these foreigners, a large number of them are Argentineans who moved to the Riviera Maya prior to and after their country's economic crisis.

24. Unless stated otherwise, all amounts listed are in U.S. dollars. During my fieldwork period, September 2000 to September 2001, the exchange rate fluctuated between 8.98 and 10 Mexican pesos per U.S. dollar. The average exchange rate was 9.2 pesos per dollar. In 2005, the exchange rate hovered at 10 pesos per dollar. I use the average exchange rate in 2001 for all dollar amounts listed here, except in chapter 7, which relies on the 2005 average exchange rate.

25. The other half of the migrant population in Cancún originates primarily from the states of Veracruz, Tabasco, Campeche, Chiapas, Oaxaca, Guerrero, and Mexico City.

26. In 1970, fewer than a thousand people lived along the Riviera Maya (Van Bramer 1997). By 1995, Cancún had flourished and grown into a city of 297,183 people (INEGI 2000a). These population growth statistics should be taken with a grain of salt because it is difficult to track population movements in a city dependent

on the highs and lows of the tourist seasons. For example, the Consejo Municipal de Población (COMAPU; Municipal Population Council), the census bureau of the Benito Juárez municipio, disagrees with the demographic statistics compiled by INEGI. COMAPU claims that INEGI underreports the actual population of Benito Juárez's municipio, the county to which Cancún pertains.

27. See *Il Conteo de población y vivienda 2005* at http://www.inegi.gob.mx. Although Maya speakers can be found throughout Mexico, the bulk of Maya speakers reside in the three states (Yucatán, Quintana Roo, and Campeche) that make up the Yucatán Peninsula (INEGI 2001).

28. In 2005, the Mexican state of Chiapas's population included 957,255 people who spoke over twenty-eight indigenous languages. See http://www.inegi.gob.mx.

29. See Castañeda (2004), Castillo Cocom (2004), Eiss (2004), Fallaw (2008), Gabbert (2004a, 2004b), Restall (2004), Rugeley (1996), Thompson (1974), and Watanabe and Fischer (2004).

30. For a discussion of the linguistic purity of the Yucatec Maya language, see Berkley (1998).

31. I conducted ethnographic and archival research during the summers of 1991, 1992, 1994, 1997, and 2002; January to August 1999; September 2000 to September 2001; January 2004 and 2006; and May to June 2006.

32. *Gringa* has multiple meanings. It is primarily used by Mexicans to refer to foreigners from the United States, but it can also refer to foreigners in general. This term also indexes racial difference because it usually refers to a "white" foreigner. For a critique of the power relations between ethnographers and informants, see Rosaldo (1989).

## 1. Devotees of the Santa Cruz

1. The honorifics *don* and *doña* are given to all married men and women in Mexico. In Maya society this honorific is not always placed before the names of married adults, although it is always placed before the names of married adults with adolescent or adult children. I follow this practice throughout this book. In 2004, ninety-five-year-old don José Can Pat passed away.

2. In the southeastern part of the peninsula, unlike in Chiapas and the northeastern part of the Yucatán Peninsula, indigenous communities have retained their ancestors' surnames. Men and women take on the paternal surnames of both parents. Women do not change their name upon marriage. The surnames used here are pseudonyms, but they are drawn from common surnames found in this region.

3. *Milpa* is the Nahuatl word for maize field (Morley and Brainerd 1946/1983). The term is commonly used in Mexico to refer to a cornfield. Among Yucatec Maya speakers, "to make milpa" refers to the cultivation of corn.

4. *Cenote* is also spelled "dzonot," as in *Ke'eldzonot*. The site of Kuchmil includes at least three pyramids, three platform mounds, and multiple graves filled

with pottery. Since Kuchmil is not listed as a pre-Hispanic site in historical re-cords, it has not been officially dated or studied by archaeologists. I date it within the Postclassic period based on pottery decorated in Postclassic designs (Joyce Marcus, personal communication, Ann Arbor, April 2000); the provenance of its name, which is derived from Yucatec Maya and Nahuatl languages; the discovery of conch shells used to communicate across ancient trade networks or as musical instruments in the performance of rituals (Morley and Brainerd 1946/1983); and its location near the ancient *sak-b'eh,* an artificially raised causeway connecting the Postclassic site of Coba with Yaxuna.

5. The footprint of Maya homes may vary. In Quintana Roo, for example, a *choza* measured sixteen meters by five meters, which is substantially larger than homes in Kuchmil. See Villa Rojas (1978).

6. Until 1997, James Fox brought other students to visit Kuchmil. Their visits were brief, lasting no longer than two months, and occurred in between my visits.

7. Alfonso Villa Rojas points out that this practice of building one's home next to one's father's house is a vestige of pre-Hispanic Maya patrilineal descent and social organization practices (1985, 98; see also Wilk 1989). Under certain circum-stances, a daughter and her husband may remain in the daughter's parents' home after marriage. For example, a married daughter may live with her new husband in her parents' home if her mother is ill and the household lacks the presence of a second daughter or a daughter old enough to take on domestic responsibilities.

8. Gisel Henriques and Raj Patel, "NAFTA, Corn, and Mexico's Agricultural Trade Liberalization." Special Report, Americas Program of the Interhemispheric Resource Center (IRC, online at http://www.irc-online.org), February 13, 2004 (accessed November 7, 2006).

9. Monica Campbell and Tyche Hendricks, "Cheap U.S. produce pushes down prices under free-trade pact." *San Francisco Gate,* Monday July 31, 2006, http://sfgate.com/cgi-bin/article.cgi?file=/c/a/2006/07/31/MNGIVK8BHP1.DTL (ac-cessed November 7, 2006).

10. This was the price of corn in Kuchmil on January 1, 2009.

11. In 2001, Mexico's Secretaría de Salud (Ministry of Health) established the Seguro Popular program to provide health care for those not covered by employer-provided insurance.

12. Most roofs in Kuchmil are made of *guano* (palm thatch). Guano used to be plentiful in the surrounding forest, but as it has become scarce in the region, resi-dents must purchase this commodity. This demand increased its value and its cost. Black corrugated cardboard has become a cheap substitute.

## 2. Modernizing Indigenous Communities

1. Initially, the household survey consisted of a few questions I posed during informal visits with families, questions regarding the births, deaths, and educational

backgrounds of family members. As I added more detailed questions about household economic activities (e.g., number of hectares cultivated, types of crops planted, and durable goods present in each household), collecting this information became difficult to accomplish during informal visits. In 1998, I created a formal open-ended questionnaire, which I translated into Yucatec Maya and Spanish. I set up formal appointments to collect this data.

2. Even after schools were built in Quintana Roo, the Maya rebels' antipathy toward the Mexican government and the region's isolation made it difficult to recruit teachers. In response, the military staffed the schools. Thus Maya communities in the region came to associate teachers with the military (Ramos Díaz 2001).

3. These recordings were taken with the permission and in many cases at the explicit request of the subjects. I made copies of these tape and video recordings to give to the participants as a small token of my appreciation.

4. See works by Hernández-Castillo (2001), Tsing (1993), and Wolf (1982).

5. The Caste War was not an isolated event but formed part of a history of Indian insurrections. For a history of other Indian rebellions, see Bricker (1981) and Viquiera (1997).

6. In 1786, the encomienda system was terminated in the peninsula (Farriss 1984).

7. In 1832, the majority of the inhabitants were of Maya descent; only 14 percent of the population had Spanish surnames. AEGY, *Poder Ejecutivo, Censo y Padrones, Padrón de habitantes del pueblo de Ke'eldzonot, noviembre 8 de 1832.* The census of 1929, however, counted only sixteen people living in Ke'eldzonot, all of them with Maya surnames. This shift was the result of the Caste War.

8. The commercial production of sugar was established in the early nineteenth century under colonial rule. By 1818, sugar was traded in Valladolid, Mérida, and Bacalar with the help of *arreiros,* peasants who worked as sugar transporters (Rugeley 1996). Soon after, to reduce competition among its colonies, the Spanish Crown prohibited the commercial production of sugar in Mexico (Reed 1964). After independence, the Mexican government no longer had access to Cuban sugar and thus encouraged the production of this lucrative cash crop (Cline 1948; Strickon 1965). In 1823, large sugar plantations were established in the southern and eastern parts of Yucatán (Reed 1964). The enactment of the 1825 law provided greater access to land for sugar production in the frontier zone (Cline 1948). The rise in sugar plantations over a short period of time significantly decreased the land available for corn cultivation by local residents and resulted in a system of peonage and slavery in the previously unfettered frontier zone (Strickon 1965). In contrast to sugar production, the extent and economic importance of tobacco, rice, and cotton production is not well documented in this region.

9. For further readings on the causes of the Caste War, see Berzunza Pinto (1965/1981), Bricker (1981), Farriss (1984), González Navarro (1970), Patch (1979), Reed (1964), and Rugeley (1996).

10. The resettlement history of Kuchmil was reconstructed from conversations with don José, his sons Victor Can Pech and Dani Can Balam, and archival records from the Catholic diocese and Civil Registry of Valladolid, and the Archivo de la Secretaría de Reforma Agraria del Estado de Yucatán in Mérida.

11. Throughout his narrative, don José attributed human qualities of resistance to the monte; the war wiped out human populations in the region, but the monte remained and continued to provide sustenance and protected those who managed to escape the atrocities of the war.

12. At the time of the Spanish conquest, the Yucatán Peninsula was divided into sixteen independent provinces, each of which was controlled by a ruling lineage (Roys 1957).

13. Most of the fighting during the Revolution occurred outside the peninsula (Joseph 1982/1995). Maya peasants, however, joined the army or, more likely, were conscripted to fight in the Mexican Revolution (see Redfield 1950).

14. The Spanish crown established the *república de los indios* in order to facilitate the payment of tribute. In return, the local indigenous leaders administered their own lands and people (Guardino 1996).

15. SRAY, *Ejidos Dotaciones* (Local), Box 357, *Censo general agrario de la ranchería de Chan-Sahkay,* 1930.

16. The 1940 agrarian code included one exception: Female ejidatarias with small dependents were permitted to rent or sharecrop their ejido plots and even hire wage workers so that they could attend to domestic duties (Baitenmann 1997).

17. The general assembly, made up of the ejidatarios, serves as the supreme authority. The comisariado ejidal, the official representative of the general assembly to the state authorities and CNC, includes three elected members—president, secretary, and treasurer—serving three-year terms. A *comité de vigilancia* (supervisory committee), with the same organizational structure as the comisariado, supervises and audits the activities of the comisariado.

18. For examples of this variation, see Baños Ramírez (1996); de Janvry, Gordillo, and Soudalet (1997); Stavenhagen (1986); and Warman (1985).

19. For an analysis of how these regional characteristics shaped the implementation of agrarian reform under the Cárdenas administration, see Fallaw (2001). Under the Cárdenas administration, ejido land in the northwestern Yucatán was organized into henéquen cooperatives. However, the ejidatarios eventually rejected this model because this system was not financially viable, generated too much conflict within and among villages, and excluded them from the decision-making process regarding production and marketing (Joseph 1982/1995).

20. The 1917 Constitution legally abolished faenas. However, due to indigenous customary practices and the postrevolutionary state's lack of funds, faenas endured as a way to secure labor for public works (Acevedo Rodrigo 2004).

21. For an extended analysis of this case, see Castellanos (2010).

22. E. P. Thompson (1971) first used the term "moral economy" to question

the depiction of markets as abstractions in Europe. James Scott expanded the concept to understand the "normative roots of peasant politics" and to critique neoclassical economic models of individual profit maximization (1976, 4). Scott argues that peasant societies, given their subsistence character, rely on a moral economic framework in which a subsistence ethic, norms of reciprocity, and moral expectations of what is socially just guide peasants' economic practices. Scott's definition of a moral economy offers a framework for understanding local responses to individual and state efforts to transform the ejido.

23. By the early 1970s, 84 percent of ejido plots were categorized as subsubsistence (Stavenhagen 1986).

24. In 1939, all four communities requested that each village receive its own communal land grant title. SRAY, *Organización Antigua, Reforma Agraria Nacional,* Packet 591, *Comisariado Ejidal de Kuchmil, Carta,* 25 September 1940.

25. In the mid-1970s, soon after the sparsely populated territory of Quintana Roo became a state, its government advertised the availability of ejido lands with monte alto as a way to attract new residents. As a result, new communities cropped up in the southern part of the state. Rather than cultivate corn, many new settlers exploited the forest for lumber (Villa Rojas 1977).

26. For critiques of Salinas's economic plan, see Gledhill (1995); Tarrío, Steffen, and Concheiro (1995) (with respect to decreasing agricultural production and poverty); Fritscher Mundt (1995) (with respect to declining corn subsidies); and Hernández Castillo (2001) (with respect to PRONASOL).

27. Protests were launched by the Movimiento Nacional de Resistencia y Lucha Campesina (MONARCA; National Resistance Movement and Peasant Struggle) and the Taller Universitario de Asesoría a Campesinos (TUAC; University Workshop to Help Peasants). See Botey (1998) and Harvey (1998).

28. During the 2006 election year, the Mexican government offered farmers the opportunity to cash in their subsidies for 2007 and 2008. The farmers in Kuchmil agreed to do so and thus stopped receiving PROCAMPO subsidies by 2007.

29. Procuraduría Agraria, "*Ejido Tipo* 2004," http://www.pa.gob.mx/publica/PA07.HTM.

30. Gail Mummert (2000) documents a similar discussion among ejidatarios in Michoacán who feared land concentration.

31. In some cases, ejidos were made up of previously entrenched communities (Boyer 2003; Mallon 1995; Nugent and Alonso 1994; Purnell 1999).

32. Residents could not recall the exact date the mission arrived, but they did remember their age at the time. I calculated the date of arrival of the missions based on their ages, so it may not be exact. Since the SEP archives regarding the Cultural Missions are stored in Mexico City, I was unable to verify this date.

33. Interview with Rafael Osorio Hurtado, director, Cultural Missions, Mérida, March 2001.

34. Ana Rosa Duarte Duarte, personal communication, Cancún, May 2001.

## 3. Indigenous Education, Adolescent Migration, and Wage Labor

1. In 1909, workers had much to protest. The fall of henéquen prices generated poor economic conditions that forced the closure of haciendas, caused a reduction in wages, and prompted the withdrawal of credit for workers (Wells and Joseph 1996).

2. Regardless of this decree, few schools were built in Yucatán prior to 1915.

3. In protest against Yucatán's promotion of the *escuela racionalista* and its anticlerical stance, the SEP withdrew federal aid to Yucatán from 1920 to 1924 (Vaughan 1982).

4. Paul Eiss (2004) posits that the Casa may have been modeled after the Ciudad Escolar de los Mayas.

5. For a discussion of this debate in Yucatán, see Eiss (2004).

6. This CEI was later moved to Chichimila, Yucatán (Fallaw 2004).

7. The failure of the CEI did not deter the Cárdenas administration and Indigenist scholars from promoting intregrationism (Díaz Polanco 1997).

8. In the 1960s, by reinforcing cultural differences among indigenous communities in Chiapas, the INI attained political control over these communities, which were becoming increasingly marginalized, disenfranchised, and poorer as the state diverted its resources from small farming in its southern, predominantly indigenous regions to commercial agricultural production in the north (Collier 1994/1999).

9. This absenteeism prompted Kuchmil parents to petition the supervisor of the elementary schools in Yucatán to replace the teacher in Kuchmil. ACK, Letter to Romualdo Che Tuz, Supervisor of Elementary Schools, September 26, 1991, Petition to change teacher due to absenteeism.

10. "La política indígenista," *Acción Indígenista* 166 (1967): 264.

11. The exact date the casa escuela of Maxcanú closed is unclear. I have been unable to find archival materials referencing this closure, therefore I rely on the date provided by its former pupils.

12. My numbers are based on interviews with the families residing in Kuchmil and Cancún only. Since I was unable to interview several families from Kuchmil who relocated during the 1980s, more kids may have attended internados.

13. As more commerce came through on the newly built road, a wider variety of foods became available, e.g., fresh fruits, meat, and canned fruits and vegetables. After purified drinking water became available, the gastrointestinal diseases that had previously afflicted the residents diminished. Households with access to remittances had more money to spend on these products, whereas households without access to remittances continued to participate in temporary migration and in multiple state subsidy programs through which they improved their access to cash. By 1999, children were stronger, fatter, and healthier because they ate more frequently and were given money with which to purchase candy and junk food at local stores.

14. Male adults educated in Kuchmil prior to the 1960s were functionally literate, but few had the skills and educational background required for many service jobs in the tourism industry today.

15. Based on time allocation studies of Maya children's labor, biological anthropologist Karen L. Kramer (2005) shows similar expectations and practices among Maya households in southwestern Yucatán. According to Kramer, Maya children begin helping their parents with household chores at age three. Between seven to eleven years of age, their work contributions double. Between eleven to fifteen, this allocation doubles again.

16. Around the age of six months, parents consider babies capable of stating their tastes through body language, even if these tastes are limited to food, music, and television programs. After the child's first birthday, parents begin to accommodate these tastes. As evidence of her son's growing individuality, Fátima Can Tun informed me that her ten-month-old son cried for hours if she failed to take him for a stroll in the park or to the store every day.

17. Up until the early 1980s, children spent much of their time working: pulling water, cutting firewood, clearing fields, etc. After the mid-1980s, some of these responsibilities were reduced as a result of the introduction of new technologies (e.g., potable water system, stoves, and washing machines), the growing emphasis on school attendance, and the presence of migrant remittances that allowed households to hire workers to clear fields.

18. In Kuchmil, boys added tassels and shiny stickers to distinguish their bicycles from one another's.

19. These girls' ages ranged between twelve and twenty-four.

20. After her first year, Selena dropped out of the university because her parents could not afford to pay her expenses. Selena works as a supervisor in a textile factory in Valladolid where she earns a good salary.

21. Redfield and Villa Rojas (1934/1990) acknowledged that this understanding of social organization in Chan Kom was idealized. Reality presented a much more complex set of social relations. In the initial phase of my fieldwork, my unmarried state called forth the following proverb—"para que sirve la mujer si es para casarse" (the purpose a woman serves is to marry)—a proverb intended to remind women of their place in society. Contradicting this proverb, Mary Elmendorf (1976) suggests that a gendered division of labor fostered a system of interdependence between Maya men and women, in which men and women respected each other's roles and worked to complement one another. Alternately, Lourdes Rejón Patrón (1998) explains that this interdependence was contingent on a gendered division of labor; as long as women continued working in specific gendered trades, they were respected. For example, Maya women's participation in commercial agricultural programs promoted by the state in the early 1970s resulted in conflict within households (e.g., Nadal 1995; Pinto González 1998; Villagómez and

Pinto 1997). In the case of Kuchmil, the community's roots as migrants, the declining productivity of the milpa, and parental concern with educating their children all made it difficult to maintain this ideal form of social organization (also see Redfield 1950).

22. The concept of the life course emphasizes individual trajectories as they develop over time and recognizes the fact that regardless of gender, life course experiences are not homogeneous. See D'Aubeterre Buznego (2000). The individual was appreciated within this life course, in recognition that not all boys and girls were interested in the same activities or fulfilled the life course in the same manner. For example, not everyone was expected to marry (such as children with birth defects and the youngest daughter, who was expected to remain at home to care for her parents). Unlike the marriages of the early 1900s (Redfield 1950; Redfield and Villa Rojas 1934/1990), marriages were not arranged but were agreed on between families, usually with the consent of the couple. For further discussion of the evolution of Mayan marriages, see Juárez (2001). To attract the attention of the opposite sex, adolescents refined their skills in one aspect of the gendered division of labor. Mariela Can Tun, for example, dedicated much of her time as a young girl to hand embroidering the finest huipiles in the area. Tómas May Pat developed his skills as a storyteller and his knowledge of the Yucatec Maya language. Through such distinctions, these young men and women marked their individuality and advanced their opportunities to become full persons in the eyes of the community.

23. In the early 1900s, all Maya men were required to perform *faginas* (public service without remuneration also called faenas) for their community (Redfield and Villa Rojas 1934/1990). One such service was *guardia*—the policing of the village square on a rotating basis. It is possible that prior to the 1920s, boys became men upon performing guardia for their community (Ben Fallaw, personal communication, September 16, 2008). Although this practice has disappeared, men are still required to perform faginas today, but this responsibility is assigned only to those who are enrolled as ejidatarios.

24. This statistic is based on the economic information I collected from both Kuchmil and migrant households.

25. Nancy Modiano (1973) also notes that indigenous families in Chiapas allowed boys to keep the money they earned.

26. Jesús had reached the wage ceiling for his official qualifications as a licensed electrician. In spite of his knowledge and skill, an increase in salary or a promotion required a university degree or the support of the manager of the hotel.

27. Rachel Sherman (2005) shows that luxury hotel employees also adopt this congenial demeanor as a form of protection against their subordinate position and as a way to mark themselves as superior to the people they serve.

28. These requirements were provided by Luis Escada Roman (pseudonym) a

hotel supervisor of a four-star hotel in Cancún (personal communication, Cancún, October 20, 2000).

29. For other examples of this form of sexual control in Mexico, see Malkin (2004), Mummert (1994), and Rouse (1995).

## 4. Civilizing Bodies

1. In Yucatec Maya, *šíimbʾal* means "to walk" or "visit." In Kuchmil, it commonly refers to the act of visiting people or taking a stroll.

2. In her study of displaced southern people in an urban Washington, D.C., neighborhood, Brett Williams (1988) discusses these families' attempts to bring the texture of their rural lives into their urban lives. By "texture," Williams means "dense, vivid, woven, detailed narratives, relationships, and experiences" (47). Since Kuchmil migrants experienced a similar sense of dislocation in Cancún, they were also concerned with maintaining or creating this texture in their urban lives.

3. It is important to note that the working class is incredibly diverse. I acknowledge here that Mexico's working class is not a homogeneous group, but one whose experiences are rooted in race, gender, generational, and regional differences. Kuchmil migrants entered the working class once they migrated to Cancún. As they moved up the labor hierarchy, one could argue that Kuchmil migrants became lower-middle class because their professional positions gave them more control of their labor than migrants who worked in entry-level service positions. Nonetheless, I include all Kuchmil migrants within the working class because even those with professional positions do not have the income and resources typical of Mexico's middle class.

4. For examples, see Fernández-Kelly (1983), Freeman (2000), Iglesias Prieto (1997), Ong (1987), Salzinger (2003), and Wolf (1992).

5. Juan Robles Terán (pseudonym), personal communication.

6. Linda Fermín Cantú is a pseudonym.

7. Once these middle-class women discovered that my informants were Maya women, they asked me to recruit maids for them. This desire for particular bodies, however, did not erase negative stereotypes of indigenous women among elite Mexicans. Praise was accompanied by racist commentaries. For example, one employer told me that her maid Nanci was very honest, but later on during the conversation, she complained that Yucatecos, like Nanci, "did not have any culture" because they did not know how to speak Spanish correctly or to clean properly. Maya domestic workers underwent a civilizing process in which their employers taught them to speak Spanish, maintain a certain level of cleanliness, perform work in a particular fashion, adopt an attitude of submissiveness, and display a willingness to work long hours. These observations are based on my experiences living with and befriending Mexican middle-class families in Mérida and Cancún.

I overheard and engaged in numerous conversations with them about their live-in and live-out servants. They were eager to talk to me because many considered me a great conduit by which to gain access to indigenous maids.

8. Michelle Madsen Camacho's work (1996, 2000) is one exception. She addresses the strategies multinational hotels use to control workers and the resistance strategies employed by these workers in the tourist zone of Huatulco in Oaxaca, Mexico.

9. Cuahtémoc Cardiel Coronel (1989) suggests that this increasing inequality is manifested in the proliferation of non-Catholic churches, which are predominantly located in the poorest regiones of Cancún.

10. Richard J. Dunphy, "The Computer That Chose Cancún," *New York Times,* March 5, 1972.

11. The 2005 census calculated the county's population at 572,973, of which 526,701 resided in the city of Cancún (INEGI 2006).

12. Juan Arvizu, "Urban Migration Can't Alleviate Poverty," *El Universal,* May 23, 2005.

13. Cancún residents constitute 95 percent of the municipio's population.

14. By 2007, Cancún could accommodate 2.4 million tourists (in 161 hotels, which had a total of 30,000 rooms). See http://www.cancun.gob.mx (accessed December 10, 2008).

15. In 2009, Cancún's minimum daily wage was increased to 49.50 pesos (approximately $5).

16. Mario Ernesto Villanueva Madrid, ex-governor of Quintana Roo, was involved in drug trafficking (200 tons of cocaine) with a Colombia drug cartel. Villanueva Madrid fled the state in 1999. On January 8, 2002, he was indicted for narcotics trafficking and money laundering in the Southern District of New York. For a discussion of child prostitution and sexual abuse in Cancún, see Cacho (2005).

17. Interview with Lic. José A. Bayon Ríos, Director of FONATUR, Cancún, July 30, 2002. According to Lic. Bayon Ríos, FONATUR shifted its focus from middle-class American tourists to European and wealthy tourists to capture the growing market in adventure tourism.

18. The Ruta Maya is a tourist corridor that includes ancient and contemporary Maya sites located in Belize, El Salvador, Guatemala, Honduras, and Mexico. In 1989, *National Geographic* magazine created and promoted this "route" as a way to funnel resources to local businesses and to generate support for further development. Similarly, the governments of Belize, Honduras, El Salvador, Guatemala, and Mexico are promoting tourism development through the Mundo Maya project developed in 1992 (Brown 1999).

19. In Latin America, the single largest job category for women is domestic service (Enloe 1989).

20. For a discussion of how beauty and youth shape employment practices in

the tourist center of Huatulco, one of Mexico's five tourist poles, see Madsen Ca-macho (2000).

21. Luis Escada Roman is a pseudonym.

22. Workers are also taught a new vocabulary for the workplace. For example, Horacio May Kauil learns that *tablones* refer to *mesas* (tables) and that different table settings are labeled by particular names (i.e., *mexicana, caribeña, italiana, china*).

23. John Urry borrows the phrase "sensuous geography" from Paul Rodaway (1994). For Rodaway, a sensuous geography "refers to a study of the geographical understanding which arises out of the stimulation of, or apprehension by, the senses" (5).

24. According to the male camarista who cleaned my hotel room, the pay is abysmal and the work schedule too demanding; they were frequently asked to clean more than the standard twelve rooms daily. As a result, there is a high turn-over rate among women in this department. After Hurricane Wilma damaged two-thirds of Cancún's hotels and led to layoffs in 2005, male camaristas stepped in to fill these vacancies.

25. Maya migrants who interacted with tourists outside the work site did so via long distance. Given their tight work schedules, they did not socialize with tour-ists while in Cancún, but rather kept in touch with hotel guests via mail and tele-phone calls. For further discussion of more intimate tourist relations with locals, see Adler and Adler (2004), Brennan (2004), Cabezas (2004), and Padilla (2007).

26. The all-inclusive program forms part of the effort to increase tourism by allowing tourists to purchase a prepaid package in which all meals and drinks are paid for in advance. The wristband helps service employees determine who is al-lowed to eat, drink, and use hotel facilities.

27. After NAFTA, the Mexican government deregulated and thus privatized its banking system. Even though multinational hotels rely on foreign banks to pay their employees, the use of bank accounts forces employees to become visible, countable, and taxable citizens in Mexico and thereby this practice supports the ideology of the modern citizen promoted by the nation-state.

28. For a detailed analysis of the structure of hotel employment hierarchies and duties, see Rachel Sherman (2007).

29. Unfortunately, this phone did not always work, particularly after a storm.

## 5. *Gustos,* Goods, and Gender

1. According to the Comisión Nacional de Salarios Mínimos, the state of Quintana Roo's minimum daily wage was 35.85 pesos in 2001.

2. In Cancún, few secondhand stores exist, but pawnshops and *tianguis* abound.

3. For examples of studies of mass consumption that take this approach, see

Appadurai (1986), Douglas and Isherwood (1979/1996), Miller (1987), Mintz (1985), Rutz and Orlove (1989), and Sahlins (1972).

4. In Chiapas, as Coke and Pepsi have replaced liquor in religious and secular rituals, access to these soft drinks reinforces political and class distinctions among indigenous communities (Nash 2007).

5. For examples, see Archer and Tritter (2000), Fischer and Dornbusch (1983), and Green and Shapiro (1994).

6. The verb form, *gustar* (to taste, to like), is commonly used throughout the Yucatán Peninsula to refer to activities involving audio and visual pleasure. Alison Greene (2001a) discusses the use of *gustar* in reference to television viewing. However, the use of this verb is not limited to television viewing but includes listening to music on the radio *(gustando la radio)* and observing baseball games and other sports activities *(gustando beisbol).*

7. For a similar critique of the emphasis on a communitarian Africa, see Comaroff and Comaroff (2001).

8. Mariachi music was more popular among tourists than the ballads the trio initially sang.

9. Enrique Iglesias, the son of singer Julio Iglesias, is a popular rock singer.

10. This shift in allegiances does not mean that married children end all contributions to their parents, but the contributions of cash, food, and labor diminish with the presence of a wife and a child.

11. I did note several exceptions. In these cases, the children's remittances decreased but did not stop altogether, usually as a result of an alcohol addiction. My documentation of these contributions reveals that migrants who have settled in Cancún, the majority of whom are married, contributed consistently to rural households.

12. Kuchmil migrants complained that the IMSS did not prescribe or provide the most effective drugs on the market, while independent medical practitioners did. They also complained of the inefficiency of the system, the long waiting list regardless of the hour you arrive. The treatment they received from the doctors and nurses also left a lot to be desired because these practitioners were influenced by negative class and racial stereotypes; they critiqued migrants' parenting skills and beliefs in healing practices that deviated from Western medicine or the local humoral system. Migrants therefore preferred to pay the extra $30 to visit a private doctor.

13. See Lomnitz (1977) for an analysis of the role of trust in the tanda system among the urban working class.

14. Price, access to credit, warranty programs, and product selection also influenced where migrants purchased their goods. When they could afford to, Maya migrants preferred to purchase name brands they knew to be of good quality or easy to repair, as a way to guarantee their investment. Migrants, for example, preferred

to purchase Sony stereos because the sound was sharper and they were cheaper to repair. Philips-brand televisions were also considered to produce a better quality image and brighter colors. Migrants purchased goods at Elektra, in spite of its higher prices, because they offered Milenia, an extended-warranty service program. Migrants felt more secure purchasing an item that came with a service contract. Those not eligible for store credit flocked to Telebodega, which did not offer credit but offered lower-priced goods. Since being debt free was an important concern among Kuchmil migrants, many bought their goods at Telebodega.

15. Employees preferred hotel savings accounts over private bank accounts because the savings were automatically deducted from their paychecks and hotels imposed restrictions on when and how much money they could withdraw and thus guaranteed that a certain amount would be saved.

16. Although Mexico's banking industry was privatized soon after the 1982 oil debt crisis, banks did not make a concerted effort to target the working class until recently. By 2009, the majority of migrants kept their money in bank accounts.

17. Kuchmil migrants contributed more than just cash and goods to their natal families. They made social and emotional contributions that have not been captured within the remittance concept used by social scientists. Sentiments such as love and affection, which I call "sentient resources," also play a critical role in sustaining community and kin ties across space and through time and maintaining the emotional and physical health of both Kuchmil residents and migrants. See Castellanos (2009a).

18. The infrequency of migrant remittances makes it difficult for rural households to count on them for their household budgets.

19. In Yucatán, *mestiza* refers to Maya women who reside in the countryside and follow Maya customs and practices. In greater Mexico, it connotes being of mixed racial heritage and therefore less Indian.

20. In the early 1990s, young women typically married by nineteen years of age, and young men did so by the age of twenty-two. By 2001, it was common for young women to marry around twenty-two years of age and for men to marry around twenty-four. But these are ideal ages. In practice, the age at marriage varied.

21. During the colonial period, artisans used yellow gold. However, the maquila system of subcontracting jewelry production to individual artisans, and the escalating price of gold, affected the number of karats used (Terán 1994, 104). To reduce costs, artisans use as little as 8K of gold in each piece. Rural residents prefer red gold because of its price; red gold contains fewer karats of gold than 10K gold, even though it is labeled as 10K gold. Artisans usually shape red gold into the most traditional designs, such as calabazitas and ramilletes, in an effort to cater to the tastes of rural residents.

22. For further discussion of Cancún's housing market, see Castellanos (2008) and Kray (2006).

23. Funerals and interment were expensive in Cancún. Although it was against the law to transport a dead body across state lines, a young couple living in Cancún buried their stillborn child in Kuchmil instead of Cancún because they did not have much money for the burial.

24. The concept of escaping has several meanings. During the Caste War, which began in 1847, *escapar* (to escape) meant to flee peonage on haciendas (a practice referred to as *púuɉ' ti' kǎaš*) or it referred to running away from or with a man (Lorena Martos Sosa, personal communication, Stanford, California, November 1992). Likewise, during the 1970s and 1980s in Kuchmil, the term *escapar* referred to young women who, without their parents' permission, ran away with their boyfriends. With the commencement of young women's and girls' migrations in the 1990s, the concept of escapar was expanded to incorporate these migrations (Castellanos 2003). Mariela hesitated before migrating because she did not wish to tarnish her parents' good names and risk her reputation as a hard worker. To establish this reputation, she had worked diligently, finished chores before most girls, and was the most accomplished embroiderer of huipiles in town. Luci risked her reputation when she eloped with her boyfriend, but she reestablished her good name after she married him. Luci's gregarious personality and self-assuredness gave Mariela the confidence to ask her parents for permission to visit her aunt.

25. Richard Wilk contends that Kekchi Maya households in Belize are "deeply concerned with keeping their children in the natal household as long as possible, and must strike a balance that allows the younger worker to retain a portion of cash as disposable income" (1989, 309–10).

26. Mary Beth Mills (1999), Aihwa Ong (1987), and Diane Wolf (1992) demonstrate a similar struggle for wages and authority between parents and daughters in Southeast Asia.

## 6. Becoming *Chingón/a*

1. Napolitano acknowledges that migration is not always experienced as a process of enlightenment and empowerment. For many migrants, it can be a harrowing, violent experience that serves to reinforce their vulnerability and marginality and that ruptures native understandings of the self, of the other, and of their conception of progress (e.g., Conover 1987; Hernández Castillo 2001; Ibarra 2003; Urrea 2005).

2. Arnold van Gennep (1960) first coined this term in his classic book *The Rites of Passage*. Victor Turner's use of the concept in his essay "Betwixt and Between: The Liminal Period in *Rites de Passage*" (1967/1989) made its use popular in anthropology. For a discussion of migration as a rite of passage, see Chavez (1992) and Kearney (1991).

3. In 2001, I attended a quinceañera to celebrate the birthdays of a girl and

a boy. In this case, to save money, the family took advantage of their daughter's birthday to celebrate her male cousin's birthday as well.

4. In her analysis of Maya subjectivity in K'anxoc, Yucatán, Ana Rosa Duarte Duarte (2006) refers to this sense of exploration and experimentation as an *espíritu de lucha* (an internal desire to know and seek knowledge).

5. For a discussion of the role religion plays in rural Maya communities, see Redfield and Villa Rojas (1934/1990). For a discussion of the role religion plays in migration, see Castellanos (2007). For a discussion of the role Protestant and Evangelical churches play in the development of the *regiones* of Cancún, see Cardiel Coronel (1989).

6. Lorena Martos Sosa (1994) critiques Paul Sullivan's interpretation of the Cruzob Maya as victims of the Caste War. Instead, she suggests that contemporary Cruzob Maya use oral histories to continue to oppose the Mexican government because these histories recall the government's misdeeds and proffer millenarian prophecies that depict its demise.

7. The depiction of Malintzin as "evil goddess," "mother-whore," and traitor has been contested by Chicana feminists. See Alarcón (1981), Anzaldúa (1987), Candelaria (1980), Gonzáles (1980, 1989), Moraga (1983), and Villanueva (1985).

8. Presently, rituals such as baptisms, *héeč-méek'* ceremonies, novenas, and weddings are elaborate affairs. In the past, the absence of cash kept rituals simple and modest because people could not afford to purchase lavish goods for them. Migration, however, has increased rural residents' access to cash. To pay for these rituals, people borrow money from migrants and ask them to be padrinos of these events. Some of these rituals now take place in Cancún because the facilities are grander and the location makes it easier for migrants to attend.

9. Santiago is a fictitious name.

## 7. The Phantom City

1. The state government of Quintana Roo formally recognizes hurricane season as beginning July 15 and ending November 15. Personal communication, Lic. Jorge Fregoso Toledo, Sub-Director de Proyectos y Estrategias de Turismo Municipal (2005–8), H. Ayuntamiento de Benito Juárez, Cancún, Quintana Roo, January 9, 2006.

2. See http://www.ncdc.noaa.gov/oa/ncdc.html (accessed February 1, 2007).

3. According to architect Ricardo Alvaro Guerrero, the director general of FONATUR in 2006, over 90 percent of Cancún's hotels suffered some damage, but the extent of the damage varied. A few weeks after Wilma, only 2,000 rooms were available for occupation. By January 2006, one-third of hotel rooms had become available for occupancy. By May 2006, one-third of Cancún's hotel rooms remained closed for renovations. According to INFOVIR, 1,139 people completely

lost their homes because they were made from flimsy materials (corrugated cardboard, thatch, tin roofs, and wood planks). INFOVIR has designated funds to help nearly 3,000 families reconstruct their homes. Personal communication, Lic. Bertha Valderrama Iturbe, Subdelegado de Vivienda y Desarrollo Social, Delegación Benito Juárez, Instituto de Fomento a la Vivienda y Regularización de la Propiedad (INFOVIR), May 23, 2006.

4. Personal communication, Lic. Jorge Fregoso Toledo. However, according to the Kuchmil migrants who lived in the regiones, restoring these services took longer than claimed by the municipal government.

5. Victor Ballinas, "Cancún, convertida en ciudad fantasma," *La Jornada,* October 25, 2005, http://www.jornada.unam.mx/ultimas (accessed October 25, 2005).

6. Barnard R. Thompson, "Cancún and Mexico's Maya Riviera Resurrected," December 19, 2005, http://www.mexidata.info/id719.html (accessed February 9, 2007).

7. Personal communication, Lic. Jorge Fregoso Toledo. There are approximately 110 hotels in Cancún's Zona Hotelera.

8. Personal communication, architect Ricardo Alvarado Guerrero.

9. Oil and remittances are the greatest generators of foreign exchange for Mexico.

10. *"El turismo como prioridad nacional,"* Message by President Felipe Calderón Hinojosa, posted on the Secretaría de Turismo's Web site in 2007, http://www.sectur.gob.mx/wb2/sectur/sect_Mensaje_del_Presidente__El_Turismo_como_Prior (accessed February 14, 2007).

11. Cancún was the primary destination for over 3 million tourists. See "Indicadores Turísticos Diciembre 2004," Secretaría de Turismo de Quintana Roo Web site, http://sedetur.qroo.gob.mx/estadisticas/2004/diciembre.php (accessed February 1, 2007).

12. Patricia Alisau, "An expanding resort: Cancún looks forward but honors its past," Entrepreneur.com, April 2005, http://www.entrepreneur.com/tradejournals/article/print/131896 (accessed December 9, 2008).

13. In 2005, over 20 million foreigners visited Mexico. They spent approximately $11 billion. Jo Tuckman, "Mexico Counts Wilma Cost in Lost Dollars and Beaches," *The Guardian,* October 27, 2005, http://environment.guardian.co.uk/climatechange/story/0,,1849393,00.html (accessed January 31, 2007).

14. The federal government established FONDEN in 1996 to aid communities affected by natural disasters.

15. Barnard R. Thompson, "Cancún and Mexico's Maya Riviera Resurrected."

16. "Ofrece el Gobierno Federal apoyos para la reconstrucción de Quintana Roo," *Boletín de Prensa,* No. 117, Secretaría de Turismo, October 28, 2005, http://www.sectur.gob.mx/wb2/sectur/sect_Boletin_117__Ofrece_el_Gobierno_Federal_apoyo (February 14, 2007).

17. Chris Welsch, "Cancún Renewed," *Star Tribune,* December 2, 2006.

18. The actual cost of rebuilding Cancún's sand-stripped beaches was $20 million. This project was performed by the Mexican subsidiary (Mexicana de Dragados S.A. de C.V.) of the Belgian international dredging company, Jan de Nul.

19. FONATUR provided $22 million, while the presidential office pledged $10 million. "Boletín Informativo 123/05," FONATUR, November 5, 2005, http://www.visitemexicoprensa.com.mx/files/informativo/fonatur/bolprensafonatur/05/noviembre/marctex%20bol031105.htm (accessed February 5, 2007).

20. The federal government has pledged 300 million pesos in aid, while the municipal government has pledged 150 million pesos. Raimon Rosado, "Obras por 300 mdp para remodelar calles y avenidas: 2007, año de obra pública," *Diario de Quintana Roo,* December 6, 2006, http://www.yucatan.com.mx (accessed December 8, 2006).

21. Chris Welsch, "Cancún Renewed."

22. Personal communication, architect Ricardo Alvarado Guerrero.

23. Personal communication, Lic. Jorge Fregoso Toledo. These numbers are an estimate because the municipal government was unable to collect data on this out-migration.

24. Due to the heat and the expense, windows in migrants' homes primarily consist of metal bars and window screens to protect against mosquitoes, but they rarely include shutters or glass panels.

25. Personal communication, Lic. Jorge Fregoso Toledo.

26. Victor Ballinas, "Cancún, convertida en ciudad fantasma."

27. Personal communication, Lic. Bertha Valderrama Iturbe.

28. "El turismo como prioridad nacional," Message by President Felipe Calderón Hinojosa.

29. Ibid.

30. Ibid.

31. Including both direct and indirect jobs, tourism accounts for one in ten jobs in Mexico. It accounts for 5 percent of direct jobs. See "El turismo como prioridad nacional," message by President Felipe Calderón Hinojosa.

32. Personal communication, Lic. Jorge Fregoso Toledo.

33. Tajamar was originally called Malecón Cancún, but due to a legal challenge over branding, the name of this project was changed. For a description of Puerto Cancún, see http://www.puertocancun.com/english/index.html.

34. Personal communication, architect Ricardo Alvarado Guerrero.

35. Interview with President Vicente Fox and Yucatán's governor, Patricio Patrón Laviada, Reunion de Evaluación, Tízimin, Yucatán, October 24, 2005. See http://www.reliefweb.int/rw/rwb.nsf/0/9a5b2f39a755b99cc12570a500498c0c?OpenDocument&Click= (accessed February 14, 2007).

36. In response to Hurricane Emily, the government provided campesinos with a one-time subsidy of 600 pesos per hectare.

37. Within the first three months of 2006, the monthly licensing fees for home-based grocery stores increased twice, from 700 pesos to 2,300 pesos. These businesses are also required to pay an annual licensing fee and additional fees every two months to the ayuntamiento.

## Epilogue

1. In September 2000, President Vicente Fox announced plans for a new development project in southern Mexico. Funded by the Inter-American Development Bank (IDB), the Plan Puebla Panamá (PPP) was intended to foster economic growth and facilitate the integration of Mexico's poor southern states (Chiapas, Campeche, Yucatán, Quintana Roo, Puebla, Guerrero, Veracruz, Tabasco, and Oaxaca) and struggling Central American countries into the global economy. The PPP proposed to develop the infrastructure (e.g., roads, dams, airports, etc.) necessary to attract private investment to this region. However, critics pointed out that the PPP allocated more funds to the construction of roads and dams and the installation of electrical cables (82 percent of budget) than it did to the development of social and health services (2.9 percent of budget) for the communities that will be affected, and in some instances displaced, by these projects. For a discussion of the PPP's budget, see Wendy Call, "Resisting the Plan Puebla-Panama," *Citizen Action in the Americas,* no. 2, September 2002, Interhemispheric Resource Center. http://www.americaspolicy.org/citizen-action/series/02-ppp_body.html. Lack of funding and opposition from NGOs, indigenous communities, grassroots organizations, and state governors forced the Mexican government to declare a moratorium on the PPP in 2002. See Miguel Packard, "The Plan Puebla-Panama Revived: Looking Back to See What's Ahead." Americas Program, Interhemispheric Resource Center, http://www.americaspolicy.org, (accessed February 13, 2007). The PPP was resurrected in 2004 and now includes Colombia as a participant. In December 2008, IDB increased its financial support for this project through its Fund for Infrastructure Integration. On June 28, 2008, it changed its name to the Proyecto de Integración y Desarrollo de Mesóamerica (or Proyecto Mesoamérica). For more information, see http://www.planpuebla-panama.org and the IDB's Web page, http://www.iadb.org. For a list of the organizations opposed to the PPP, see http://www.americaspolicy.org/citizen-action/series/02-ppp_body.html (accessed February 13, 2007).

# Bibliography

## Archives

ACK   Archivo de la Comisaría de Kuchmil, Kuchmil, Yucatán, Mexico
AGEY  Archivo General del Estado de Yucatán, Mérida, Yucatán, Mexico
AMBJ  Archivo del Municipio de Benito Juárez, Cancún, Quintana Roo, Mexico
SRAY  Archivo de la Secretaría de Reforma Agraria del Estado de Yucatán,
      Mérida, Yucatán, Mexico

## Works Cited

Abu-Lughod, Lila. 1990. The romance of resistance: Tracing the transformations of power through Bedouin women. *American Ethnologist* 17 (1): 41–55.

Acevedo Rodrigo, Ariadna. 2004. Struggles for citizenship? Peasant negotiations of schooling in the Sierra Norte de Puebla, Mexico, 1921–1933. *Bulletin of Latin American Research* 23 (2): 181–97.

Adler, Patricia A., and Peter Adler. 2004. *Paradise laborers: Hotel work in the global economy.* Ithaca, N.Y.: ILR Press.

Adler, Rachel. 2004. *Yucatecans in Dallas, Texas: Breaching the border, bridging the distance.* New York: Allyn and Bacon.

Aguilar Padilla, Héctor. 1988. *La educación rural en México.* Mexico: Secretaría de Educación Pública.

Alarcón, Norma. 1981. Chicana's feminist literature: A re-vision through Malintzin/ or Malintzin: Putting flesh back on the object. In *This bridge called my back,* ed. Cherríe Moraga and Gloria Anzaldúa, 182–90. New York: Kitchen Table Press.

———. 1989. Traduttora, traditora: A paradigmatic figure of Chicana feminism. *Cultural Critique* 13:57–87.

Alonso, Ana María. 1992. Work and *gusto:* Gender and re-creation in a north Mexican pueblo. In *Worker's expressions: Beyond accommodation and resistance,* ed. John Calagione, Doris Francis, and Daniel Nugent, 164–85. Albany: State University of New York Press.

Alvarez Barret, Luis. 1971. Origenes y evolución de las escuelas rurales en Yucatán. *Revista de la Universidad de Yucatán* 13 (78): 26–51.

Anderson, Benedict. 1983. *Imagined communities: Reflections on the origin and spread of nationalism.* London: Verso.

Anderson, E. N. 2005. *Political ecology in a Yucatec Maya community.* Tucson: University of Arizona Press.

Anzaldúa, Gloria. 1987. *Borderlands/la frontera: The new mestiza.* San Francisco: Aunt Lute Books.

Appadurai, Arjun. 1986. *The social life of things.* New York: Cambridge University Press.

———. 1990. Disjuncture and difference in the global cultural economy. *Public Culture* 2 (2): 1–24.

———. 1991. Global ethnoscapes: Notes and queries for a transnational anthropology. In *Recapturing anthropology: Working in the present,* ed. Richard G. Fox, 191–210. Santa Fe: School of American Research Press.

———. 1996. *Modernity at large: Cultural dimensions of globalization.* Minneapolis: University of Minnesota Press.

Appendini, Kristin. 1992. *De la milpa a los tortibonos: La restructuración de la política alimentaria en México.* Mexico: El Colegio de México/UNRISD.

———. 1998. Changing agrarian institutions: Interpreting the contradictions. In *The transformation of rural Mexico: Reforming the ejido sector,* ed. W. A. Cornelius and D. Myhre, 25–38. La Jolla, Calif.: Center for U.S.–Mexican Studies.

Archer, Margaret S., and Jonathan Q. Tritter. 2000. *Rational choice theory: Resisting colonization.* London: Routledge.

Arditti, Rita. 1999. *Searching for life: The grandmothers of the Plaza de Mayo and the disappeared children of Argentina.* Berkeley: University of California Press.

Ariès, Philippe. 1962. *Centuries of childhood,* trans. Robert Baldick. London: Jonathan Cape.

Arizpe, Lourdes. 1975. *Indígenas en la ciudad de México: El caso de las "Marías."* Mexico: Sep/Setentas.

———. 1981. Relay migration and the survival of the peasant household. In *Why people move: Comparative perspectives on the dynamics of internal migration,* ed. Jorge Balán, 187–210. Paris: The UNESCO Press.

Artiz, Cecile Shay. 1986. Ideology and land reform policies in postrevolutionary Mexico: 1915–1965. Ph.D. diss., Rice University.

Baitenmann, Helga. 1997. Rural agency and state formation in postrevolutionary Mexico: The agrarian reform in central Veracruz (1915–1992). Ph.D. diss., New School for Social Research.

———. 1998. The Article 27 reforms and the promise of local democratization in central Veracruz. In *The transformation of rural Mexico: Reforming the ejido sector,* ed. Wayne A. Cornelius and David Myhre, 105–23. La Jolla, Calif.: Center for U.S.–Mexican Studies.

Baños Ramírez, Othon. 1989. *Yucatán: Ejido Sin Campesinos.* Mérida, Yucatán, Mexico: Universidad Autónoma de Yucatán.

——. 1996. *Neoliberalismo, reorganización y subsistencia rural. El caso de la zona henequenera de Yucatán: 1980–1992.* Mérida, Yucatán, Mexico: Universidad Autónoma de Yucatán.

Bartell, Ernest J. 2001. Opportunities and challenges for the well-being of children in the development of Latin America: An overview. In *The child in Latin America: Health, development, and rights,* ed. E. J. Bartell and A. O'Donnell, xiii–xxxi. Notre Dame: University of Notre Dame.

Basch, Linda, Nina Glick Schiller, and Cristina Szanton Blanc, eds. 1994. *Nations unbound: Transnational projects, postcolonial predicaments, and deterritorialized nation-states.* Basel, England: Gordon and Breach.

Behar, Ruth. 1990. Rage and redemption: Reading the life story of a Mexican marketing woman. *Feminist Studies* 16 (2): 223–58.

——. 1993. *Translated woman: Crossing the border with Esperanza's story.* Boston: Beacon Press.

Berger, Dina. 2006. *The development of Mexico's tourism industry: Pyramids by day, martinis by night.* New York: Palgrave Macmillan.

Berkley, Anthony Robert. 1998. Remembrance and revitalization: The archive of pure Maya. Ph.D. diss., University of Chicago.

Berzunza Pinto, Ramón. 1965/1981. *Guerra social en Yucatán.* Mérida, Yucatán, Mexico: Ediciones del Gobierno del Estado.

Bonfil Batalla, Guillermo. 1996. *Mexico profundo: Reclaiming a civilization,* trans. Philip A. Dennis. Austin: University of Texas Press.

Bosselman, Fred P. 1978. *In the wake of the tourist: Managing special places in eight countries.* Washington, D.C.: Conservation Foundation.

Botey, Carlota. 1998. Mujer rural: Reforma agraria y contrarreforma. In *Tiempo de crisis, tiempo de mujeres,* ed. Josefina Aranda, Carlota Botey, and Rosario Robles, 95–154. Oaxaca: Universidad Autónoma Benito Juárez de Oaxaca; Centro de Estudios de la Cuestión Agraria Mexicana, A.C.

Bourdieu, Pierre. 1984. *Distinction: A social critique of the judgment of taste,* trans. Richard Nice. Cambridge: Harvard University Press.

Bourgois, Philippe. 1995. *In search of respect: Selling crack in el barrio.* Cambridge: Cambridge University Press.

Boyer, Christopher. 2003. *Becoming campesinos: Politics, identity, and agrarian struggle in postrevolutionary Michoacán, 1920–1935.* Stanford, Calif.: Stanford University Press.

Brannon, Jeffrey T. 1991. Conclusion: Yucatecan political economy in broader perspective. In *Land, labor, and capital in modern Yucatán: Essays in regional history and political economy,* ed. Jeffrey T. Brannon and Gilbert M. Joseph, 243–49. Tuscaloosa: University of Alabama Press.

Breglia, Lisa. 2006. *Monumental ambivalence: The politics of heritage.* Austin: University of Texas Press.

Brennan, Denise. 2004. *What's love got to do with it? Transnational desires and sex tourism in the Dominican Republic.* Durham, N.C.: Duke University Press.

Brenner, Suzanne. 1998. *The domestication of desire: Women, wealth, and modernity in Java.* Princeton, N.J.: Princeton University Press.

Bricker, Victoria. 1981. *The Indian Christ, the Indian king: The historical substrate of Maya myth and ritual.* Austin: University of Texas Press.

Bricker, Victoria, Eleuterio Po'ot Yah, and Ofelia Dzul de Po'ot. 1998. *A dictionary of the Maya language as spoken in Hocabá, Yucatán.* Salt Lake City: University of Utah Press.

Brown, Denise Fay. 1999. Mayas and tourists in the Maya World. *Human Organization* 58 (3): 295–304.

Bunster, Ximena, and Elsa M. Chaney. 1989. *Sellers and servants: Working women in Lima, Peru.* Granby: Bergin & Garvey.

Burawoy, Michael. 1976. The functions and reproduction of migrant labor: Comparative material from Southern Africa and the United States. *American Journal of Sociology* 81 (5): 1050–87.

Burns, Allan F. 1983. *An epoch of miracles: Oral literature of the Yucatec Maya.* Austin: University of Texas Press.

Butler, Judith. 1990. *Gender trouble: Feminism and the subversion of identity.* New York: Routledge.

Cabezas, Amalia. 2004. Between love and money: Sex, tourism, and citizenship in Cuba and the Dominican Republic. *Signs: Journal of Women in Culture and Society* 29 (4): 987–1015.

———. 2008. Tropical blues: Tourism and social exclusion in the Dominican Republic. *Latin American Perspectives* 35 (3): 21–36.

Cacho, Lydia. 2005. *Los demonios del Edén.* Mexico: Grijalbo.

Calavita, Kitty. 1992. *Inside the state: The Bracero Program, immigration, and the I.N.S.* New York: Routledge.

Candelaria, Cordelia. 1980. La Malinche, feminist prototype. *Frontiers* 5 (2): 1–6.

Cardiel Coronel, Cuauhtémoc. 1989. Cancún: Turismo, subdesarrollo social y expansión sectario religiosa; *Cuadernos de la Casa Chata* (Centro de Investigaciones y Estudios Superiores en Antropología Social) 6:1–143.

Cardoso, Fernando Henrique, and Enzo Faletto. 1979. *Dependency and development in Latin America,* trans. Marjory M. Urquidi. Berkeley: University of California Press.

Carmack, Robert M., ed. 1988. *Harvest of violence: The Maya Indians and the Guatemalan crisis.* Norman: University of Oklahoma Press.

Carr, Barry. 2008. Issues and agendas in writing the tourism history of Mexico (1940–2008): A comparison of the Acapulco and Cancún development paths. Paper presented at the Tourism Studies Working Group Symposium "Tourism, History, and Mexico," University of California, Berkeley (November 7).

Castañeda, Quetzil. 1996. *In the museum of Maya culture: Touring Chichén Itzá.* Minneapolis: University of Minnesota Press.

———. 2001. The aura of ruins. In *Fragments of a golden age: The politics of culture in Mexico since 1940,* ed. Gilbert M. Joseph, Anne Rubenstein, and Eric Zolov, 452–467. Durham: Duke University Press.

———. 2004. "We are *not* indigenous!" An introduction to the Maya identity of Yucatán. *Journal of Latin American Anthropology* 9:36–63.

Castellanos, M. Bianet. 2003. Gustos and gender: Yucatec Maya migration to the Mexican Riviera. Ph.D. diss., University of Michigan.

———. 2007. Adolescent migration to Cancún: Reconfiguring Maya households and gender relations in Mexico's Yucatán peninsula. *Frontiers* 28 (3): 1–27.

———. 2008. Constructing the family: Mexican migrant households, marriage, and the state. *Latin American Perspectives* 35 (1): 64–77.

———. 2009a. Building communities of sentiment: Remittances and emotions among Maya migrants. *Chicana/Latina Studies* 8 (1): 36–67.

———. 2009b. Cancún and the *campo:* Indigenous migration and tourism development in the Yucatán Peninsula. In *Holiday in Mexico: Critical Reflections on tourism and tourist encounters,* ed. Dina Berger Koecher and Andrew G. Wood, 241–64. Durham, N.C.: Duke University Press.

———. 2010. Don Teo's expulsion: Property regimes, moral economies, and ejido reform. *Journal of Latin American and Caribbean Anthropology* 15 (1): 144–69

Castillo Cocom, Juan. 2004. Lost in Mayaland. *Journal of Latin American Anthropology* 9:179–98.

Chamberlain, Robert Stoner. 1948. *The conquest and colonization of Yucatán, 1517–1550.* Publication 582. Washington, D.C.: Carnegie Institute of Washington.

Chaney, Elsa, and Mary García Castro, eds. 1989. *Muchachas no more: Household workers in Latin America and the Caribbean.* Philadelphia: Temple University Press.

Chant, Sylvia. 1991. *Women and survival in Mexican cities: Perspectives on gender, labour markets, and low-income households.* Manchester, England: Manchester University Press.

———. 1992. Tourism in Latin America: Perspectives from Mexico and Costa Rica. In *Tourism and less developed countries,* ed. David Harrison, 85–101. London: John Wiley & Sons.

Chase, Jacquelyn. 2002. Introduction: The spaces of neoliberalism in Latin America. In *The spaces of neoliberalism: Land, place and family in Latin America,* ed. Jacquelyn Chase, 1–21. Bloomfield, Conn.: Kumarian Press.

Chavez, Leo R. 1992. *Shadowed lives: Undocumented immigrants in American society.* Fort Worth: Harcourt Brace College Publishers.

Child, Brenda. 1998. *Boarding school seasons: American Indian families, 1900–1940.* Lincoln: University of Nebraska.

Chin, Elizabeth. 2001. *Purchasing power: Black kids and American consumer culture.* Minneapolis: University of Minnesota Press.

Chivers, T. 1973. The proletarianisation of a service worker. *Sociological Review* 21:633–56.

Clancy, Michael. 1996. Export-led growth strategies, the internationalization of services, and Third World development: The political economy of Mexican tourism, 1967–1992. Ph.D. diss., University of Wisconsin–Madison.

———. 1999. Tourism development: Evidence from Mexico. *Annals of Tourism Research* 26:1–20.

———. 2001. *Exporting paradise: Tourism and development in Mexico.* New York: Pergamon.

Cline, Howard Francis. 1948. The sugar episode in Yucatán, 1825–1850. *Inter-American Economic Affairs* 1 (4): 79–100.

Cobb, Daniel M., and Loretta Fowler, eds. 2007. *Beyond red power: American Indian politics and activism since 1900.* Santa Fe, N.M.: School of Advanced Research Press.

Collier, George. 1994/1999. *Basta! Land and the Zapatista rebellion in Chiapas.* Oakland, Calif.: First Food.

Collins, Jane L. 2003. *Threads: Gender, labor, and power in the global apparel industry.* Chicago: University of Chicago Press.

Comaroff, John L., and Jean Comaroff. 2001. On personhood: An anthropological perspective from Africa. *Social Identities* 7 (2): 267–83.

Conover, Ted. 1987. *Coyotes.* New York: Vintage Books.

Cooper, Frederick, and Randall Packard, eds. 1997. *International development in the social sciences: Essays on the history and politics of knowledge.* Berkeley: University of California.

Cornelius, Wayne A., David Fitzgerald, and Pedro Lewin Fischer, eds. 2007. *Mayan journeys: The new migration from Yucatán to the United States.* San Diego: University of California, San Diego and Lynne Reinner Publishers.

Cornelius, Wayne A., and David Myhre, eds. 1998. *The transformation of rural Mexico: Reforming the ejido sector.* La Jolla, Calif.: Center for U.S.–Mexican Studies.

Cortellese, Claudio, Alberto Bucardo, Federico de Arteaga, Javier Cayo, and Antonio Gaspar. 2006. *Economic reactivation after a natural disaster: Support for small business.* Donors Memorandum on Mexico (ME-M1019), Inter-American Development Bank and Multilateral Investment Fund.

Cos-Montiel, Francisco. 2001. Sirviendo a las mesas del mundo: Las niñas y niños jornaleros agrícolas en México. In *La infancia vulnerable de México en un mundo globalizado,* ed. Norma del Río Lugo, 15–38. Mexico: Universidad Autónoma Metropolitana, UNICEF.

Cothran, Dan A., and Cheryl Cole Cothran. 1998. Promise or political risk for Mexican tourism. *Annals of Tourism Research* 25 (2): 477–97.

Crabtree, John. 2003. Impact of neo-liberal economics on Peruvian peasant agriculture in the 1990s. In *Latin American peasants,* ed. Tom Brass, 131–61. London: Frank Cass.

Dachary, Alfredo César, and Stella Maris Arnaiz Burne. 1998. *El Caribe mexicano: Una frontera olvidada.* Chetumal: Universidad de Quintana Roo, Fundación de Parques y Museos de Cozumel.

D'Aubeterre Buznego, María Eugenia. 2000. *El pago de la novia: Matrimonio, vida conyugal y prácticas transnacionales en San Miguel Acuexcomac, Puebla.* Zamora, Michoacán: El Colegio de Michoacán, Benemérita Universidad Autónoma de Puebla, Instituto de Ciencias Sociales y Humanidades.

Dávila, Arlene. 2001. *Latinos, Inc.: The marketing and making of a people.* Berkeley: University of California Press.

Davis, Mike. 2006. *Planet of Slums.* New York: Verso.

Dawson, Alexander S. 2004. *Indian and nation in revolutionary Mexico.* Tucson: University of Arizona Press.

Deere, Carmen Diana, and Magdalena León. 2002. Individual versus collective land rights: Tensions between women's and indigenous rights under neoliberalism. In *The spaces of neoliberalism: Land, place and family in Latin America,* ed. Jacquelyn Chase, 53–86. Bloomfield, Conn.: Kumarian Press.

De Genova, Nicholas. 2005. *Working the boundaries: Race, space, and illegality in Mexican Chicago.* Durham, N.C.: Duke University Press.

de Janvry, Alain, Gustavo Gordillo, and Elisabeth Soudalet. 1997. *Mexico's second agrarian reform: Household and community responses, 1990–1994.* La Jolla, Calif.: Center for U.S.-Mexican Studies; University of California, San Diego.

de la Cadena, Marisol and Orin Starn, eds. 2007. *Indigenous experience today.* New York: Berg.

Díaz Polanco, Hector. 1997. *Indigenous peoples in Latin America: The quest for self-determination.* Boulder, Colo.: Westview Press.

Diego Quintana, Roberto S. 1995. El paradigmo neoliberal rural y las reformas agrarias en México. *Cuadernos Agrarios: Neoliberalismo y el campo* 5 (11/12): 13–26.

Douglas, Mary, and Baron Isherwood. 1979/1996. *The world of goods: Towards an anthropology of consumption.* London: Routledge.

Duarte Duarte, Ana Rosa. 2006. Espíritu de lucha: Cuerpo, poder y cambio sociocultural. Ph.D. diss., Universidad Autónoma Metropolitana, Unidad Iztapalapa.

Durand, Jorge, and Douglas S. Massey. 2004. *Crossing the border: Research from the Mexican Migration Project.* New York: Russell Sage Foundation.

Echeverría V., Pedro. 1993. *Educación pública: México y Yucatán.* Mérida, Yucatán, Mexico: Universidad Autónoma de Yucatán.

Ehrenreich, Barbara. 2001. *Nickel and dimed: On (not) getting by in America*. New York: Owl Books.

Eiss, Paul K. 2000. Redemption's archive: Revolutionary figures and Indian work in Yucatán, Mexico. Ph.D. diss., University of Michigan.

———. 2004 Deconstructing Indians, reconstructing patria: Indigenous education in Yucatán from the *Porfiriato* to the Mexican Revolution. *Journal of Latin American Anthropology* 9 (1): 119–50.

Elias, Norbert. 1978/2000. *The civilizing process*. Oxford: Basil Blackwell.

Elmendorf, Mary. 1976. *Nine Mayan women: A village faces change*. New York: Schenkman.

Enloe, Cynthia. 1989. *Bananas, beaches, and bases: Making feminist sense of international politics*. Berkeley: University of California Press.

Escobar, Arturo. 1995. *Encountering development: The making and unmaking of the Third World*. Princeton, N.J.: Princeton University Press.

Fabian, Johannes. 1983. *Time and the other: How anthropology makes its object*. New York: Columbia University Press.

Fallaw, Ben. 1995. Peasants, caciques, and camarillas: Rural politics and state formation in Yucatán, 1924–1940. Ph.D. diss., University of Chicago.

———. 2001. *Cardenás compromised: The failure of reform in postrevolutionary Yucatán*. Durham, N.C.: Duke University Press.

———. 2004. Rethinking Mayan resistance: Changing relations between federal teachers and Mayan communities in eastern Yucatán, 1929–1935. *Journal of Latin American Anthropology* 9 (1): 151–78.

———. 2008. Bartolomé García Correa and the politics of Maya identity in postrevolutionary Yucatán, 1911–1933. *Ethnohistory* 55 (4): 553–78.

Farriss, Nancy M. 1984. *Maya society under colonial rule: The collective enterprise of survival*. Princeton, N.J.: Princeton University Press.

Faust, Betty Bernice. 1998. *Mexican rural development and the plumed serpent: Technology and Maya cosmology in the tropical forest of Campeche, Mexico*. Westport, Conn.: Bergin & Garvey.

Ferguson, James. 1997. Anthropology and its evil twin: "Development" in the constitution of a discipline. In *International development in the social sciences: Essays on the history and politics of knowledge,* ed. Frederick Cooper and Randall Packard, 150–75. Berkeley: University of California.

———. 1999. *Expectations of modernity: Myths and meanings of urban life on the Zambian Copperbelt*. Berkeley: University of California Press.

———. 2006. *Global shadows: Africa in the neoliberal world order*. Durham, N.C.: Duke University Press.

Fernández-Kelly, María Patricia. 1983. *For we are sold, I and my people: Women and industry on Mexico's northern frontier*. Albany: State University of New York Press.

Fink, Leon. 2003. *The Maya of Morganton: Work and community in the nuevo new south.* Chapel Hill: University of North Carolina Press.

Finn, Janet L. 1998. *Tracing the veins: Of copper, culture, and community from Butte to Chuquicamata.* Berkeley: University of California Press.

Fischer, Stanley, and Rudiger Dornbusch. 1983. *Economics.* New York: McGraw-Hill Book Co.

Fixico, Donald. 2000. *The urban Indian experience in America.* Alburquerque: University of New Mexico Press.

Fortuny Loret de Mola, Patricia. 2004. Transnational hetzmek': Entre Oxcutzcab y San Pancho. In *Estrategias identitarias: Educación y la antropología histórica en Yucatán,* ed. Juan A. Castillo Cocom and Quetzil E. Castañeda, 225–54. Mérida, Yucatán, Mexico: Universidad Pedagógica Nacional; The Open School of Ethnography and Anthropology; Secretaría de Educación del Estado de Yucatán.

Foucault, Michel. 1977/1995. *Discipline & punish: The birth of the prison.* New York: Vintage Books.

Fox, Jonathan, and Gaspar Rivera-Salgado, eds. 2004. *Indigenous Mexican migrants in the United States.* La Jolla, Calif.: University of California, San Diego, Center for Comparative Immigration Studies and Center for U.S.–Mexican Studies.

Frank, Andre Gunder. 1967. *Capitalism and underdevelopment in Latin America: historical studies of Chile and Brazil.* New York: Monthly Review Press.

Freeman, Carla. 2000. *High tech and high heels in the global economy.* Durham, N.C.: Duke University Press.

Freidrich, Paul. 1986. *The princes of Naranja: An essay in an anthrohistorical method.* Austin: University of Texas Press.

Fritscher Mundt, Magda. 1995. Las políticas del maíz en el salinismo. *Cuadernos Agrarios* 5 (11/12): 45–58.

Frye, David. 1996. *Indians into Mexicans: History and identity in a Mexican town.* Austin: University of Texas Press.

Gabbert, Wolfgang. 2004a. *Becoming Maya: Ethnicity and social inequality in Yucatán since 1500.* Tucson: University of Arizona Press.

———. 2004b. Of friends and foes: The Caste War and ethnicity in Yucatán. *Journal of Latin American Anthropology* 9:90–118.

Galarza, Ernesto. 1964. *Merchants of labor: The Mexican bracero story.* Charlotte, N.C.: McNally and Loftin.

García Canclini, Néstor. 1993. *Transforming modernity: Popular culture in Mexico.* Austin: University of Texas Press.

———. 2001. *Consumers and citizens: Globalization and multicultural conflicts,* trans. George Yúdice. Minneapolis: University of Minnesota Press.

García Castro, Mary. 1989. What is bought and sold in domestic service? The case of Bogotá: A critical review. In *Muchachas no more: Household workers in Latin*

*America and the Caribbean,* ed. Elsa Chaney and Mary García Castro, 105–26. Philadelphia: Temple University Press.

Gaskins, Suzanne. 2003. From corn to cash: Change and continuity within Mayan Families. *Ethos* 31 (2): 248–73.

Gill, Christopher Joseph. 2001. The intimate life of the family: Patriarchy and the liberal project in Yucatán, Mexico, 1860–1915. Ph.D. diss., Yale University.

Gillingham, Paul. 2006. Ambiguous missionaries: Rural teachers and state facades in Guerrero, 1930–1950. *Mexican Studies/Estudios Mexicanos* 22 (2): 331–60.

Gledhill, John. 1995. *Neoliberalism, transnationalization, and rural poverty: A case study of Michoacán, Mexico.* Boulder, Colo.: Westview Press.

Gmelch, George. 2003. *Behind the smile: The working lives of Caribbean tourism.* Bloomington: University of Indiana Press.

Goldkind, Victor. 1965. Social stratification in the peasant community: Redfield's Chan Kom reinterpreted. *American Anthropologist* 67:863–84.

Gonzáles, Sylvia. 1980. Chicana evolution. In *The third woman: Minority women writers of the United States,* ed. Dexter Fisher, 418–22. Boston: Houghton Mifflin.

González Navarro, Moisés. 1970. *Raza y tierra: La Guerra de Castas y el henequén.* Mexico: Colegio de México.

Gordon, Avery. 1997. *Ghostly matters: Haunting and the sociological imagination.* Minneapolis: University of Minnesota.

Greaves, Cecilia L. 1999. Entre la teoría educativa y la práctica indigenista: La experiencia en Chiapas y la Tarahumara (1940–1970). In *Educación rural e indígena en Iberoamérica,* ed. Pilar Gonzalbo Aizpuru. Mexico: El Colegio de México.

Green, Donald S. and Ian Shapiro. 1994. *Pathologies of rational choice theory: A critique of applications in political science.* New Haven, Conn.: Yale University Press.

Greene, Alison C. 2001a. Cablevision(nation) in rural Yucatán: Performing modernity and *Mexicanidad* in the early 1990s. In *Fragments of a golden age: The politics of culture in Mexico since 1940,* ed. Gilbert Joseph, Anne Rubenstein, and Eric Zolov, 415–51. Durham: Duke University Press.

———. 2001b. Working girls, Cancun style: Reconfiguring private and public domains in practice. *Anthropology of Work Review* 22:7–13.

Greensfelder, Ben. 2003. *Yucatán.* Oakland, Calif.: Lonely Planet Publications.

Gregory, Steven. 2007. *The devil behind the mirror: Globalization and politics in the Dominican Republic.* Berkeley: University of California Press.

Grewal, Inderpal, and Caren Kaplan. 1994. Introduction: Transnational feminist practices and questions of postmodernity. In *Scattered hegemonies: Postmodernity and transnational feminist practices,* ed. Inderpal Grewal and Caren Kaplan, 1–33. Minneapolis: University of Minnesota Press.

Grimes, Kimberly M. 1998. *Crossing borders: Changing social identities in southern Mexico.* Tucson: University of Arizona Press.

Grindal, Bruce T., and Frank A. Salamone, eds. 1995/2006. *Bridges to humanity: Narratives on friendship and anthropology.* Prospect Heights, Ill.: Waveland Press.

Grindle, Merilee. 1986. *State and countryside: Development policy and agrarian politics in Latin America.* Baltimore, Md.: Johns Hopkins University Press.

Guardino, Peter F. 1996. *Peasants, politics, and the transformation of Mexico's national state: Guerrero, 1800–1857.* Stanford, Calif.: Stanford University Press.

Guarnizo, Luis Eduardo, and Michael Peter Smith. 1998. The locations of transnationalism. In *Transnationalism from below,* ed. Michael Peter Smith and Luis Eduardo Guarnizo, 3–34. Comparative Urban and Community Research, vol. 6. London: Transaction Publishers.

Gupta, Akhil, and James Ferguson. 1992. Beyond "culture": Space, identity, and the politics of difference. *Cultural Anthropology* 7 (1): 6–23.

Gutmann, Matthew. 1996. *The meanings of macho: Being a man in Mexico City.* Berkeley: University of California Press.

Harvey, David. 2005. *A brief history of neoliberalism.* Oxford: Oxford University Press.

Harvey, Neil. 1998. *The Chiapas rebellion: The struggle for land and democracy.* Durham, N.C.: Duke University Press.

H. Ayuntamiento Benito Juárez. 2002. *Memorias 1999–2002. H. Ayuntamiento Benito Juárez, Profra. Sonia Magaly Achach Solís, Presidente Municipal, Abril 2002.* Cancún, Mexico: Pixel Press, S.A. de C.V.

Hastrup, Kirsten and Karen Fog Olwig. 1997. Introduction and cultural sites: Sustaining a home in a deterritorialized world. In *Siting culture: The shifting anthropological object,* ed. Karen Fog Olwig and Kirsten Hastrup, 1–38. London: Routledge.

Hernández Castillo, Rosalva Aída., ed. 1998. *La otra palabra: Mujeres y violencia en Chiapas, antes y después de Acteal.* Mexico: CIESAS.

———. 2001. *Histories and stories from Chiapas: Border identities in southern Mexico.* Austin: University of Texas Press.

Hernández Murrillo, Ricardo, and Marjorie Thacker. 1992. *Diagnóstico de salud y nutrición en albergues escolares para niños indígenas.* Mexico: Fideicomiso para la Salud de los Niños Indígenas de Mexico.

Hervik, Peter. 1999. *Mayan people within and beyond boundaries: Social categories and lived identity in Yucatán.* Amsterdam: Harwood.

Hiernaux Nicolas, Daniel. 1989. Mitos y realidades del milagro turístico: "Cancún." In *Teoría y praxis del espacio turístico,* ed. Daniel Hiernaux Nicolas, 109–20. Mexico: Universidad Autonóma Metropolitana-Xochimilco.

———. 1999. Cancún bliss. In *The tourist city,* ed. Dennis R. Judd and Susan S. Fainstein, 124–39. New Haven, Conn.: Yale University Press.

Hiernaux Nicolas, Daniel, and Manuel Rodríguez Woog. 1991. Tourism and absorption of the labor force in Mexico. In *Regional and sectoral development in*

*Mexico as alternatives to migration,* ed. Sergio Díaz-Briquets and Sidney Weintraub, 313–29. Boulder, Colo.: Westview Press.

Hochschild, Arlie Russell. 1983. *The managed heart: Commercialization of human feeling.* Berkeley: University of California Press.

Hodgson, Dorothy L. 2001. Of modernity/modernities, gender, and ethnography. In *Gendered modernities: Ethnographic perspectives,* ed. Dorothy L. Hodgson, 1–23. New York: Palgrave.

Hondagneu-Sotelo, Pierrette. 1994. Regulating the unregulated? Domestic workers' social networks. *Social Problems* 41 (1): 50–64.

———. 2001. *Dómestica: Immigrant workers cleaning and caring in the shadows of affluence.* Berkeley: University of California Press.

Ibarra, María de la Luz. 2003. Buscando la vida: Mexican immigrant women's memories of home, yearning, and border crossings. *Frontiers* 24 (2/3): 261–81.

Iglesias Prieto, Norma. 1997. *Beautiful flowers of the maquiladora: Life histories of women workers in Tijuana,* trans. Michael Stone and Gabrielle Winkler. Austin: University of Texas Press.

INEGI (Instítuto Nacional Estadístico, Geográfico e Informático). 1999. *Encuesta Nacional de la Dinámica Demográfica 1997: Panorama Sociodemográfico Quintana Roo.* Mexico: INEGI.

———. 2000a. *Cuaderno Estadístico Municipal, Edición 1999: Benito Juárez, Estado de Quintana Roo.* Mexico: INEGI.

———. 2000b. *Mexico hoy.* Mexico: INEGI.

———. 2001. *XXII Censo General de Población y Vivienda.* Mexico: INEGI.

———. 2006. *Resultado definitivos del II conteo de población y vivienda 2005 para el estado de Quintana Roo.* Comunicado No. 109/06 (May 24). Chetumal, Quintana Roo, Mexico: Instítuto Nacional Estadístico, Geográfico e Informático.

Instituto Nacional Indigenista (INI). 1994. *Instituto Nacional Indigenista, 1989–1994.* Mexico: INI, SEDESOL.

Jelin, Elizabeth. 1977. Migration and labor force participation of Latin American women: The domestic servants in the cities. *Signs* 3:129–41.

Jonas, Susanne. 1991. *The battle for Guatemala: Rebels, death squads, and U.S. power.* Boulder, Colo.: Westview Press.

Joseph, Gilbert. 1982/1995. *Revolution from without: Yucatán, Mexico, and the United States, 1880–1924.* Durham, N.C.: Duke University Press.

Juárez, Ana María. 2001. Four generations of Maya marriages: What's love got to do with it? *Frontiers* 22 (2): 131–53.

———. 2002. Ecological degradation, global tourism, and inequality: Maya interpretations of the changing environment in Quintana Roo, Mexico. *Human Organization* 61 (2): 113–24.

Karjanen, David. 2008. Gender, race, and nationality in the making of Mexican migrant labor. *Latin American Perspectives* 35 (1): 51–63.

Karttunen, Frances. 1983/1992. *An analytical dictionary of Nahuatl.* Norman: University of Oklahoma Press.

Katzman, David M. 1981. *Seven days a week: Women and domestic service in industrializing America.* Urbana: University of Illinois Press.

Kearney, Michael. 1991. Borders and boundaries of state and self at the end of empire. *Journal of Historical Sociology* 4 (1): 52–74.

———. 1996. *Reconceptualizing the peasantry: Anthropology in global perspective.* Boulder, Colo.: Westview Press.

Kintz, Ellen. 1998. The Yucatec Maya frontier and Maya women: Tenacity of tradition and tragedy of transformation. *Sex Roles* 39 (7/8): 589–601.

Klein, Naomi. 2002. *No logo: No space, no choice, no jobs.* New York: Picador.

Kramer, Karen L. 2005. *Maya children: Helpers at the farm.* Cambridge, Mass.: Harvard University Press.

Kray, Christine A. 2006. Resistance to what? How? Stalled social movements in Cancun. *City and Society* 18 (1): 66–89.

Kroeber, Alfred L. 1939. *Cultural and natural areas of native North America.* Berkeley: University of California Press.

Lave, Jean. 1988. *Cognition in practice: Mind, mathematics, and culture in everyday life.* Cambridge: Cambridge University Press.

Levitt, Peggy. 2001. *The transnational villagers.* Berkeley: University of California Press.

Lewis, Oscar. 1959. *Five families: Mexican case studies in the culture of poverty.* New York: Basic Books.

Lewis, Stephen E. 2006. The nation, education, and the "Indian problem" in Mexico, 1920–1940. In *The eagle and the virgin: Nation and cultural revolution in Mexico, 1920–1940,* ed. Mary Kay Vaughan and Stephen E. Lewis, 176–95. Durham. N.C.: Duke University Press.

Limón, José E. 1994. *Dancing with the devil: Society and cultural poetics in Mexican American south Texas.* Madison: University of Wisconsin Press.

Little, Walter. 2004. *Mayas in the marketplace. Tourism, globalization, and cultural identity.* Austin: University of Texas Press.

Lomawaima, K. Tsianina. 1994. *They called it prairie light: The story of Chilocco Indian School.* Lincoln: University of Nebraska Press.

Lomnitz, Claudio. 2001. *Deep Mexico, silent Mexico: An anthropology of nationalism.* Minneapolis: University of Minnesota Press.

Lomnitz, Larissa. 1977. *Networks and marginality: Life in a Mexican shantytown.* New York: Academic Press.

Lowe, Donald M. 1995. *The body in late-capitalist U.S.A.* Durham: Duke University Press.

Lowe, Lisa, and David Lloyd. 1997. Introduction to *The politics of culture in the shadow of capital,* ed. Lisa Lowe and David Lloyd, 1–32. Durham, N.C.: Duke University Press.

Lowell, Lindsay, and Rodolfo de la Garza. 2000. The developmental role of remittances in U.S. Latino communities and in Latin American countries. Inter-American Dialogue, Tomás Rivera Policy Institute.

Loyo Bravo, Engracia, ed. 1985. *La casa del pueblo y el maestro rural mexicano.* Mexico: Secretaría de Educación Pública.

Loyo Bravo, Engracia. 1996. Los centros de educación indígena y su papel en el medio rural (1930–1940). In *La educación rural e indígena en Iberoamericana,* coord. Pilar Gonzalbo Aizpuru and Gabriela Ossenbach, 139–59. Mexico: El Colegio de México.

Lozano Ascencio, Fernando. 1993. *Bringing it back home: Remittances to Mexico from migrant workers in the United States.* Monograph Series 37. San Diego: Center for U.S.–Mexican Studies, University of California at San Diego.

Lugo, Alejandro. 1990. Cultural production and reproduction in Ciudad Júarez, Mexico: Tropes at play among maquiladora workers. *Cultural Anthropology* 5:173–96.

Madeley, John. 1992. *Trade and the poor: The impact of international trade on developing countries.* New York: St. Martin's Press.

Madsen Camacho, Michelle. 1996. Dissenting workers and social control: A case study of the hotel industry in Huatulco, Oaxaca. *Human Organization* 55 (1): 33–40.

———. 2000. The politics of progress: Constructing paradise in Huatulco, Oaxaca. Ph.D. diss., University of California at Irvine.

Mahler, Sarah J. 1998. Theoretical and empirical contributions toward a research agenda for transnationalism. In *Transnationalism from below,* ed. Michael Peter Smith and Luis Eduardo Guarnizo, 64–100. London: New Brunswick Publishers.

Maldonado Torres, Eduardo. 2000. El Caribe mexicano hacia el siglo XXI. In *Diacrónica del Caribe mexicano: Una historia de Quintana Roo y Cancún,* ed. Eduardo Maldonado Torres, 143–255. Mexico City: Universidad Autónoma Metropolitana-Azcapotzalco.

Malinowski, Bronislaw. 1922/1961. *Argonauts of the western Pacific: An account of Native enterprise and adventure in the archipelagos of Melanesian New Guinea.* New York: E. P. Dutton.

Malkin, Victoria. 2004. "We got to get ahead": Gender and status in two Mexican migrant communities. *Latin American Perspectives* 31 (5): 75–99.

Mallan, Chicki. 1994. *Yucatán Peninsula handbook.* Chico, Calif.: Moon Publications, Inc.

Mallon, Florencia E. 1995. *Peasant and nation: The making of postcolonial Mexico and Peru.* Berkeley: University of California Press.

Martí, Fernando. 1991. *Cancún, fantasy of bankers: The construction of a tourism city from base zero,* trans. Jule Siegel. Mexico: Litho Offset Andina.

Martos Sosa, Lorena. 1994. Projecting the past to the present: The historical knowledge of a Mayan people. Ph.D. diss., Stanford University.

———. 1996. Recasting the historic gaze. In *Gender dimensions in education in Latin America,* ed. Nelly P. Stromquist. Washington, D.C.: Inter-American Council for Integral Development, Organization of American States.

Massey, Doreen. 1994. *Space, place, and gender.* Minneapolis: University of Minnesota Press.

Mauss, Marcel. 1954/1990. *The gift: The form and reason for exchange in archaic societies.* New York: Norton.

McCrea, Heather L. 2002. Diseased relations: Epidemics, public health, and state formation in nineteenth-century Yucatán, Mexico. Ph.D. diss., State University of New York at Stony Brook.

McDonald, James H. 1999. The neoliberal project and governmentality in rural Mexico: Emergent farmer organization in the Michoacán highlands. *Human Organization* 58 (3): 274–84.

Miller, Daniel. 1987. *Material culture and mass consumption.* Oxford, England: Basil Blackwell.

———. 1995. Consumption studies as the transformation of anthropology. In *Acknowledging consumption,* ed. Daniel Miller, 264–95. London: Routledge.

———. 1998. *A theory of shopping.* Ithaca, N.Y.: Cornell University Press.

Mills, Mary Beth. 1997. Contesting the margins of modernity: Women, migration, and consumption in Thailand. *American Ethnologist* 24 (1): 37–61.

———. 1999. *Thai women in the global labor force: Consuming desires, contested selves.* New Brunswick, N.J.: Rutgers University Press.

Mintz, Sidney W. 1985. *Sweetness and power.* New York: Viking.

———. 1998. The localization of anthropological practice: From area studies to transnationalism. *Critique of Anthropology* 18 (2): 117–33.

Mintz, Sidney W., and Eric R. Wolf. 1950. An analysis of ritual co-parenthood (compadrazgo). *Southwestern Journal of Anthropology* 6:341–68.

Modiano, Nancy. 1973. *Indian education in the Chiapas highlands.* New York: Holt, Rinehart and Winston.

Montes de Oca, Rosa Elena. 1977. The state and the peasants. In *Authoritarianism in Mexico,* ed. José Luis Reyna and Richard S. Wiener, 47–63. Philadelphia: Institute for the Study of Human Issues.

Moraga, Cherríe. 1983. *Love in the war years: Lo que nunca pasó por los labios.* Boston: South End Press.

Morgan, Lynne. 1990/1992. When/does life begin? A cross-cultural perspective on the personhood of fetuses and young children. In *Talking about people: Readings in contemporary cultural anthropology,* ed. William A. Haviland and Robert J. Gordon, 28–38. Mountain View, Calif.: Mayfield Publishing.

Morley, Sylvanus G., and George W. Brainerd. 1946/1983. *The ancient Maya.* Revised by Robert J. Sharer. Stanford, Calif.: Stanford University Press.

Mummert, Gail. 1994. From *metate* to *despate:* Rural Mexican women's salaried labor and the redefinition of gendered spaces and roles. In *Women and the Mexican countryside, 1850–1990,* ed. Heather Fowler-Salamini and Mary Kay Vaughn, 192–209. Tucson: University of Arizona Press.

———. 2000. In fields not their own: Commercial agriculture in Ario de Rayón, Michoacán. In *Strategies for resource management, production, and marketing in rural Mexico,* ed. Guadalupe Rodríguez Gómez and Richard Snyder, 7–30. La Jolla, Calif.: Center for U.S.–Mexican Studies, University of California, San Diego.

Myhre, David. 1998. The Achilles' heel of the reforms: The rural finance system. In *The transformation of rural Mexico: Reforming the ejido sector,* ed. W. A. Cornelius and D. Myhre, 39–65. La Jolla, Calif.: Center for U.S.–Mexican Studies.

Nadal, Marie Jose. 1995. Un ejemplo de deconstrucción, reconstrucción genérica en el proceso de integración de las mujeres campesinas al desarrollo. In *Género y cambio social en Yucatán,* ed. Luis Alfonso Ramírez Carrillo, 75–102. Mérida, Yucatán, Mexico: Universidad Autónoma de Yucatán.

Napolitano, Valentina. 2002. *Migration, mujercitas, and medicine men: Living in urban Mexico.* Berkeley: University of California Press.

Nash, Dennison. 1989. Tourism as a form of imperialism. In *Hosts and guests: The anthropology of tourism,* ed. Valene Smith, 37–52. Philadelphia: University of Pennsylvania Press.

Nash, June. 1970. *In the eyes of the ancestors: Belief and behavior in a Maya community.* New Haven, Conn.: Yale University Press.

———. 1995. The reassertion of indigenous identity: Mayan responses to state intervention in Chiapas. *Latin American Research Review* 30 (3): 7–41.

———. 2001. *Mayan visions: The quest for autonomy in an age of globalization.* New York: Routledge.

———. 2007. Consuming interests: Water, rum, and Coca-Cola from ritual propitiation to corporate expropriation in highland Chiapas. *Cultural Anthropology* 22 (4): 621–39.

Nash, June, and María Patricia Fernández-Kelly. 1983. Introduction to *Women, men, and the international division of labor,* ed. June Nash and María Patricia Fernández-Kelly, vii–xv. Albany: State University of New York Press.

Nash, June, ed. 1993. *Crafts in the world market: The impact of global exchange on middle American artisans.* Albany: State University of New York Press.

Ngai, Pun. 2005. *Made in China: Women factory workers in a global workplace.* Durham, N.C.: Duke University Press.

Niezen, Ronald. 2000. *Spirit wars: Native North American religions in the age of nation building*. Berkeley: University of California Press.

Nordstrom, Carolyn, and Antonius C. G. M. Robben, eds. 1996. *Fieldwork under fire: Contemporary studies of violence and culture*. Berkeley: University of California Press.

Nugent, Daniel, and Ana María Alonso. 1994. Multiple selective traditions in agrarian reform and agrarian struggle: Popular culture and state formation in the ejido of Namiquipa, Chihuahua. In *Everyday forms of state formation: Revolution and the negotiation of rule in modern Mexico*, ed. Gilbert M. Joseph and Daniel Nugent, 209–246. Durham, N.C.: Duke University Press.

Nuijten, Monique. 2003. *Power, community and the state: The political anthropology of organisation in Mexico*. London: Pluto Press.

O'Dougherty, Maureen. 2002. *Consumption intensified: The politcs of middle-class daily life in Brazil*. Durham, N.C.: Duke University Press.

Oehmichen Bazán, Cristina. 2001. Mujeres indígenas migrantes en el proceso de cambio cultural. Analisis de las normas de control social y relaciones de género en la comunidad extraterritorial. Ph.D. diss., Universidad Nacional Autónoma de México.

Ong, Aihwa. 1987. *Spirits of resistance and capitalist discipline: Factory women in Malaysia*. Albany: State University of New York.

Osbahr, Henry, and Roger Few. 2006. *Linking climate change adaptation and disaster risk management for sustainable poverty reduction: Mexico country study*. Report for Vulnerability and Adaptation Resource Group, European Commission.

Packard, Miguel. 2004. The Plan Puebla-Panama revived: Looking back to see what's ahead. Americas Program, Interhemispheric Resource Center. http://www.americaspolicy.org (accessed February 13, 2007).

Padilla, Mark. 2007. *Caribbean pleasure industry: Tourism, sexuality, and AIDS in the Dominican Republic*. Chicago: University of Chicago Press.

Palma López, Armando. 1998. El reto de las misiones culturales hacia el siglo XXI. Paper presented at the Primer encuentro regional, académico, cultural y literario de Misiones Culturales. Guerrero, Mexico: Secretaría de Educación.

Pancake, Cherri M. 1991. Communicative imagery in Guatemalan Indian dress. In *Textile traditions of Mesoamerica and the Andes: An anthology*, ed. M. Blum Schevill, J. C. Berlo, and E. B. Dwyer, 45–62. Austin: University of Texas Press.

Park, Lisa Sun-Hee. 2005. *Consuming citizenship: Children of Asian immigrant entrepreneurs*. Stanford, Calif.: Stanford University Press.

Parry, Jonathan P., and Maurice Bloch, eds. 1989. *Money and the morality of exchange*. Cambridge: Cambridge University Press.

Patch, Robert. 1976. La formación de estancias y haciendas en Yucatán durante la colonia. *Boletín de la escuela de ciencias antropológicas de la Universidad de Yucatán* 19:41–61.

Pattullo, Polly. 1996/2005. *Last resorts: The cost of tourism in the Caribbean.* London: Cassell.

Paz, Octavio. 1985. *The labyrinth of solitude,* trans. Lysander Kemp, Yara Milos, and Rachel Phillips-Belash. New York: Grove Press.

Pérez, Gina. 2004. *The near northwest side story: Migration, displacement, and Puerto Rican families.* Berkeley: University of California Press.

Pineda, Baron L. 2006. *Shipwrecked identities: Navigating race on Nicaragua's Mosquito Coast.* New Brunswick, N.J.: Rutgers University Press.

Pinto González, Wilbert. 1998. La Unidad Agrícola Industrial para la Mujer Campesina en la zona henequenera de Yucatán. In *Rehaciendo las diferencias: Identidades de género en Michoacán y Yucatán,* ed. Gail Mummert and Luis Alfonso Ramírez Carrillo, 241–68. Zamora: El Colegio de Michoacán, Universidad Autónoma de Yucatán.

Portes, Alejandro. 2001. Introduction: The debates and significance of immigrant transnationalism. *Global Networks* 1 (3): 181–93.

Portes, Alejandro, and Rubén G. Rumbaut. 1996. *Immigrant America: A portrait.* Berkeley: University of California Press.

Postero, Nancy. 2007. *Now we are citizens: Indigenous politics in postmulticultural Bolivia.* Stanford, Calif.: Stanford University Press.

Pribilsky, Jason. 2001. *Nervios* and "Modern Childhood": Migration and shifting contexts of child life in the Ecuadorian Andes. *Childhood* 8 (2): 251–73.

Puig Casauranc, J. M. 1928. El mejoramiento de los maestros y de las comunidades rurales. In *Las misiones culturales en 1927: Las escuelas normales,* 1–8. Mexico: SEP.

Purnell, Jennie. 1999. With all due respect: Popular resistance to the privatization of communal lands in nineteenth-century Michoacán. *Latin American Research Review* 34 (1): 85–121.

Rabinow, Paul. 1977. *Reflections on fieldwork in Morocco.* Berkeley: University of California Press.

Ramos Díaz, Martín. 2001. *Niños mayas, maestros criollos: Rebeldía y educación en los confines del trópico.* Mexico: Universidad de Quintana Roo, Fundación Oasis, Gobierno del Estado de Quintana Roo.

Rappaport, Joanne. 1990. *The politics of memory: Native historical interpretation in the Columbian Andes.* Cambridge: Cambridge University Press.

———. 2005. *Intercultural utopias: Public intellectuals, cultural experimentation, and ethnic pluralism in Colombia.* Durham, N.C.: Duke University Press.

Re Cruz, Alicia. 1996. *The two milpas of Chan Kom: A study of socioeconomic and political transformation in a Maya community.* Albany: State University of New York Press.

———. 1996. The thousand and one faces of Cancún. *Urban Anthropology* 25 (3): 283–310.

————. 1998. Maya women, gender dynamics, and modes of production. *Sex Roles* 39: 573–87.

————. 2003. Milpa as an ideological weapon: Tourism and Maya migration to Cancún. *Ethnohistory* 50 (3): 489–502.

Redclift, Michael. 2005. "A convulsed and magic country": Tourism and resource histories in the Mexican Caribbean. *Environment and History* 11:83–97.

Redfield, Robert. 1941. *The folk culture of the Yucatán.* Chicago: University of Chicago Press.

————.1950 *A village that chose progress: Chan Kom revisited.* Chicago: University of Chicago Press.

Redfield, Robert, and Alfonso Villa Rojas. 1934/1990. *Chan Kom: A Maya village.* Prospect Heights, Ill.: Waveland Press.

Reed, Nelson. 1964. *The Caste War of Yucatán.* Stanford, Calif.: Stanford University Press.

Reguillo, Rossana, and Marcial Godoy Anativia, eds. 2005. *Ciudades translocales: Espacios, flujo, representación.* Mexico: Instituto Tecnológico y de Estudios Superiores de Occidente; Social Science Research Council.

Rejón Patrón, Lourdes. 1998. Mujer maya, mujer bordadora: Las cooperativas de artesanas en el oriente yucateco. In *Rehaciendo las diferencias: Identidades de género en Michoacán y Yucatán,* ed. Gail Mummert and Luis Alfonso Ramírez Carrillo, 269–91. Zamora: El Colegio de Michoacán, Universidad Autónoma de Yucatán.

Restall, Matthew. 2004. Maya ethnogenesis. *Journal of Latin American Anthropology* 9:64–89.

Richter, Linda K. 1997. The politics of heritage tourism development: Emerging issues for the new millenium. In *Contemporary issues in tourism development,* ed. Douglas G. Pearce and Richard W. Butler, 108–26. New York: Routledge.

Rodaway, Paul. 1994. *Sensuous geographies: Body, sense, and place.* London: Routledge.

Rofel, Lisa. 1999. *Other modernities: Gendered yearnings in China after socialism.* Berkeley: University of California Press.

Romero, Mary. 1992. *Maid in the U.S.A.* New York: Routledge.

Rosaldo, Renato. 1989. *Culture and truth: A remaking of social analysis.* Boston: Beacon Press.

Roseberry, William M. 1994. *Anthropologies and histories: Essays in culture, history, and political economy.* New Brunswick, N.J.: Rutgers University Press.

Rothstein, Frances Abrahamer. 1992. What happens to the past? Return industrial migrants in Latin America. In *Anthropology and the global factory,* ed. Frances Abrahamer Rothstein and Michael L. Blim, 33–46. New York: Bergin & Garvey.

————. 2005. Challenging consumption theory: Production and consumption in Central Mexico. *Critique of Anthropology* 25 (3): 279–306.

Rouse, Roger C. 1989. Mexican migration to the United States: Family relations in the development of a transnational migrant circuit. Ph.D. diss., Stanford University.

———. 1991. Mexican migration and the social space of postmodernism. *Diaspora* 1 (1): 8–23.

———. 1992. Making sense of settlement: Class transformation among Mexican migrants in the United States. In *Towards a transnational perspective on migration: Race, class, ethnicity, and nationalism reconsidered,* ed. Nina Glick Schiller, Linda Basch, and Cristina Blanc-Szanton, 25–52. New York: New York Academy of Sciences.

———. 1995. Questions of identity: Personhood and collectivity in transnational migration to the United States. *Critique of Anthropology* 15 (4): 351–80.

Roys, Ralph L. 1933/1967. *The book of Chilam Balam of Chumayel.* Norman: University of Oklahoma Press.

———. 1957. *The political geography of the Yucatán Maya.* Washington, D.C.: Carnegie Institution of Washington.

———. 1972. *The Indian background of colonial Yucatán.* Norman: University of Oklahoma Press.

Rugeley, Terry. 1996. *Yucatán's Maya peasantry and the origins of the Caste War.* Austin: University of Texas Press.

Rus, Jan. 1994. The "Comunidad Revolucionaria Institucional": The subversion of Native government in highland Chiapas, 1936–1968. In *Everyday forms of state formation: Revolution and the negotiation of rule in modern Mexico,* ed. Gilbert M. Joseph and Daniel Nugent, 265–300. Durham, N.C.: Duke University Press.

Rus, Jan, Rosalva Aída Hernández Castillo, and Shannan L. Mattiace, eds. 2003. *Mayan lives, Mayan utopias: The indigenous peoples of Chiapas and the Zapatista rebellion.* Oxford, England: Rowman and Littlefield Publishers.

Rutz, Henry J., and Benjamin S. Orlove, eds. 1989. *The social economy of consumption.* Monographs in Economic Anthropology, no. 6. Lanham, Md.: University Press of America; Society for Economic Anthropology.

Sahlins, Marshall D. 1976. *Culture and practical reason.* Chicago: University of Chicago Press.

———. 1972. *Stone age economics.* Chicago: Aldine-Atherton, Inc.

Saldaña-Portillo, María Josefina. 2003. *The revolutionary imagination in the Americas and the age of development.* Durham, N.C.: Duke University Press.

Salzinger, Leslie. 2003. *Genders in production: Making workers in Mexico's global factories.* Berkeley: University of California Press.

Saragoza, Alex. 2001. The selling of Mexico: Tourism and the state, 1929–1952. In *Fragments of a golden age: The politics of culture in Mexico since 1940,* ed. Gilbert M. Joseph, Anne Rubenstein, and Eric Zolov, 91–92. Durham, N.C.: Duke University Press.

Sassen, Saskia. 1994. *Cities in a world economy.* Thousand Oaks, Calif.: Pine Forge Press.

Sawyer, Suzana. 2004. *Crude chronicles: Indigenous politics, multinational oil, and neoliberalism in Ecuador.* Durham, N.C.: Duke University Press.

Sayer, Derek. 1991. *Capitalism and modernity: An excursus on Marx and Weber.* London: Routledge.

Scase, Richard. 1992. *Class.* Minneapolis: University of Minnesota Press.

Scott, James C. 1976. *The moral economy of the peasant: Rebellion and subsistence in Southeast Asia.* New Haven, Conn.: Yale University Press.

———. 1985. *Weapons of the weak: Everyday forms of peasant resistance.* New Haven, Conn.: Yale University Press.

Sennett, Richard, and Jonathan Cobb. 1972. *The hidden injuries of class.* New York: Vintage Books.

Sherman, Rachel. 2005. Producing the superior self: Strategic comparison and symbolic boundaries among luxury hotel workers. *Ethnography* 6:131–58.

———. 2007. *Class acts: Service and inequality in luxury hotels.* Berkeley: University of California Press.

Sierra, Augusto Santiago. 1973. *Las misiones culturales (1923–1973).* Mexico: Secretaría de Educación Pública, Setentas.

Smart, Alan, and Josephine Smart. 1998. Transnational social networks in interactions between Hong Kong and China. In *Transnationalism from below,* ed. Michael Peter Smith and Luis Eduardo Guarnizo, 103–29. London: New Brunswick Publishers.

Smith, Robert C. 1998. Transnational localities. In *Transnationalism from below,* ed. Michael Peter Smith and Luis Eduardo Guarnizo, 196–238. London: New Brunswick Publishers.

———. 2005. *Mexican New York: Transnational lives of new immigrants.* Berkeley: University of California Press.

Stack, Carol. 1974. *All our kin: Strategies of survival in a black community.* New York: Harper Torchbooks.

Stavenhagen, Rodolfo. 1986. Collective agriculture and capitalism in Mexico: A way out or a dead end? In *Modern Mexico: State, economy, and social conflict,* ed. Nora Hamilton and Timothy F. Harding, 262–85. Beverly Hills, Calif.: Sage Publications.

Steedman, Carolyn Kay. 1986/1997. *Landscape for a good woman: A story of two lives.* New Brunswick, N.J.: Rutgers University Press.

Stephen, Lynn. 1997. *Women and social movements in Latin America: Power from below.* Austin: University of Texas Press.

———. 1998. Interpreting agrarian reform in two Oaxacan ejidos: Differentiation, history, and identities. In *The transformation of rural Mexico: Reforming the ejido sector*, ed. Wayne A. Cornelius and David Myhre, 125–43. La Jolla, Calif.: Center for U.S.–Mexican Studies.

———. 2002. *Zapata lives! Histories and cultural politics in southern Mexico.* Berkeley: University of California Press.

———. 2006. Los nuevos desaparecidos y muertos: Immigration, militarization, death and disappearance on Mexico's borders. Paper presented at the American Anthropological Association Meetings, San Jose, California, November 17.

———. 2007. *Transborder lives: Indigenous Oaxacans in Mexico, California, and Oregon.* Durham, N.C.: Duke University Press.

Stephens, Sharon. 1995. Introduction: Children and the politics of culture in "late capitalism." In *Children and the politics of culture*, ed. S. Stephens, 3–48. Princeton, N.J.: Princeton University Press.

Strathern, Marilyn. 1988. *The gender of the gift: Problems with women and problems with society in Melanesia.* Berkeley: University of California Press.

Strickon, Arnold. 1965. Hacienda and plantation in Yucatán: An historical-ecological consideration of the folk-urban continuum in Yucatán. *América Indígena* 25:35–63.

Sullivan, Paul. 1989. *Unfinished conversations: Mayas and foreigners between two wars.* Berkeley: University of California Press.

Tancer, Robert S. 1975. *Tourism in the Americas: Some governmental initiatives.* Tempe: Center for Latin American Studies, Arizona State University.

Tarrío, María, Cristina Steffen, and Luciano Concheiro. 1995. La modernización en crisis: análisis de la evolución de los principales productos agroalimentarios— Un balance de la política salinista para el campo. *Cuadernos Agrarios* 5 (11/12): 27–43.

Taylor, Diana. 1997. *Disappearing acts: Spectacles of gender and nationalism in Argentina's "Dirty War."* Durham, N.C.: Duke University Press.

Terán, Silvia. 1983/1994. *La platería en Yucatán.* Mérida, Yucatán, Mexico: Dirección General de Culturas Populares y Casa de las Artesanías del Estado de Yucatán.

Thompson, E. P. 1967. Time, work-discipline, and industrial capitalism. *Past and Present* 38 (1): 56–97.

———. 1971. The moral economy of the English crowd in the eighteenth century. *Past and Present* 50 (February): 76–136.

Thompson, Richard A. 1974. *The winds of tomorrow: Social change in a Maya town.* Chicago: University of Chicago Press.

Tiano, Susan. 1994. *Patriarchy on the line: Labor, gender, and ideology in the Mexican maquila industry.* Philadelphia: Temple University Press.

Torres, Rebecca Maria, and Janet D. Momsen. 2005a. Gringolandia: The construction of a new tourist space in Mexico. *Annals of the Association of American Geographers* 95:314–35.

———. 2005b. Planned tourism development in Quintana Roo, Mexico: Engine for regional development or prescription for inequitable growth? *Current Issues in Tourism* 8 (4): 259–85.

Tsing, Anna Lowenhaupt. 1993. *In the realm of the diamond queen: Marginality in an out-of-the-way place.* Princeton, N.J.: Princeton University Press.

Tuirán, Rodolfo. 1996. Las trayectorias de vida familiar en México: Una perspectiva histórica. In *Hogares, familias: Desigualdad, conflicto, redes solitarias y parentales,* 7–14. Mexico: Sociedad Mexicana de Demografía.

Turner, Victor. 1967/1989. Betwixt and between: The liminal period in *Rites de Passage.* In *The forest of symbols: Aspects of Ndembu ritual,* 93–111. Ithaca, N.Y.: Cornell University Press.

Underiner, Tamara L. 2004. *Contemporary theatre in Mayan Mexico: Death-defying acts.* Austin: University of Texas Press.

Urrea, Luis Alberto. 2005. *The devil's highway: A true story.* New York: Back Bay Books.

Urry, John. 1990. *The tourist gaze: Leisure and travel in contemporary societies.* London: Sage.

———. 1999. Sensing the city. In *The tourist city,* ed. Dennis R. Judd, and Susan S. Fainstein, 71–86. New Haven, Conn.: Yale University Press.

Van Bramer, Sharon. 1997. Cancun flashback: How it all began. In *The everything pages: Cancun, Cozumel, Mayan Corridor, Mexico,* 6–8. Cancún, Quintana Roo: Telephone Directory Company, S.A. de R.L. de C.V.

van Gennep, Arnold. 1960. *The rites of passage.* Chicago: University of Chicago Press.

Vaughan, Mary Kay. 1982. *The state, education, and social class in Mexico, 1880–1928.* Dekalb: Northern Illinois University Press.

———. 1997. *Cultural politics in revolution: Teachers, peasants, and schools in Mexico, 1930–1940.* Tucson: University of Arizona Press.

———. 2006. Nationalizing the countryside: Schools and rural communities in the 1930s. In *The eagle and the virgin: Nation and cultural revolution in Mexico, 1920–1940,* ed. Mary Kay Vaughan and Stephen E. Lewis, 157–75. Durham, N.C.: Duke University Press.

Veblen, Thorstein. 1967. *The theory of the leisure class.* New York: Penguin Books.

Velasco Ortiz, Laura. 2005. *Mixtec transnational identity.* Tucson: University of Arizona Press.

Villa Rojas, Alfonso. 1945. *The Maya of east central Quintana Roo.* Publication 559. Washington, D.C.: Carnegie Institution of Washington.

———. 1978. *Los elegidos de Dios: Etnografía de los Mayas de Quintana Roo.* Mexico: Instituto Nacional Indigenista.

———. 1980. La imagen del cuerpo humano según los mayas de Yucatán. *Anales de Antropología* 2:31–47.

———. 1985. *Estudios etnológicos: Los mayas.* Mexico: Universidad Nacional Autónoma de México.

Villagómez, Gina, and Wilbert Pinto. 1997. *Mujer maya y desarrollo rural en Yucatán.* Mérida, Yucatán, Mexico: Ediciones de la Universidad Autónoma de Yucatán.

Villanueva, Alma. 1985. La chingada. In *Five poets of Aztlán,* ed. Santiago Daydí-Tolson. Binghampton, N.Y.: Bilingual Review Press.

Viquiera, Juan Pedro. 1997. *Indios rebeldes e idólatras: Dos ensayos históricos sobre la rebelión india de Cancuc, Chiapas, acaecida en el año de 1712.* Mexico: CIESAS.

Warman, Arturo. 1976. *Y venimos a contradecir.* Mexico City: Casa Chata.

———. 1985. *Estrategias de sobrevivencia de los campesinos mayas.* Mexico: Universidad Nacional Autónoma de México.

Warren, Jonathan W. 2001. *Racial revolutions: Antiracism and Indian resurgence in Brazil.* Durham, N.C.: Duke University Press.

Warren, Kay. 1998. *Indigenous movements and their critics.* Princeton, N.J.: Princeton University Press.

Watanabe, John M., and Edward F. Fischer, eds. 2004. *Pluralizing ethnography: Comparison and representation in Maya cultures, histories, and identities.* Santa Fe, N.M.: School of American Research Press.

Wells, Alan, and Gilbert M. Joseph. 1996. *Summer of discontent, seasons of upheaval: Elite politics and rural insurgency in Yucatán, 1876–1915.* Stanford, Calif.: Stanford University Press.

Wilk, Richard R. 1989. Houses as consumer goods: Social processes and allocation decisions. In *The Social Economy of Consumption,* ed. Henry J. Rutz and Benjamin S. Orlove, 297–322. Monographs in Economic Anthropology, no. 6. Boulder, Colo.: Westview Press.

Williams, Brackette F. 1991. *No stain on my name, war in my veins: Guyana and the politics of cultural struggle.* Durham: Duke University Press.

Williams, Brett. 1988. *Upscaling downtown: Stalled gentrification in Washington, D.C.* Ithaca, N.Y.: Cornell University Press

———. 2004. *Debt for sale: A social history of the credit trap.* Philadelphia: University of Pennsylvania Press.

Wilson, Tamar Diana. 2008. Economic and social impacts of tourism in Mexico. *Latin American Perspectives* 35 (3): 37–52.

Wolf, Diane Lauren. 1992. *Factory daughters: Gender, household dynamics, and rural industrialization in Java.* Berkeley: University of California Press.

Wolf, Eric. 1966. *Peasants.* Englewood Cliffs, N.J.: Prentice-Hall, Inc.

———. 1982. *Europe and the people without history.* Berkeley: University of California Press.

Zapata, Francisco. 2005. *Tiempos neoliberales en México.* Mexico: El Colegio de México.

Zavella, Patricia. 1987. *Women's work and Chicano families: Cannery workers of the Santa Clara Valley.* Ithaca, N.Y.: Cornell University Press.

Zelizer, Viviana A. 1994. *The social meaning of money.* New York: Basic Books.

# Index

Abu-Lughod, Lila, 105
abusado (abuse, take advantage of):
   risk faced by women of being
   sanctioned for being too abusadas,
   154–57; use of, 151
acculturation of indigenous communities, 48
Acevedo Rodrigo, Ariadna, 45, 46,
   191n.20
Adler, Patricia A., 81, 198n.25
Adler, Peter, 81, 198n.25
Adler, Rachel, xxxiii, xxxv
adolescence: adolescent migration in
   global era, 75–76; beginning of,
   for boys and girls, 68; economic
   contribution to rural household
   in, 75; entry into labor market in,
   motivation for, 116–17; expenses
   in, 70; going to Cancún to spend
   summer working as marker of, 66,
   144–45; relationship between right
   to self-expression, consumption,
   and parental demands in, 117–18;
   responsibilities in, 67–68. See also
   youth migration
adult education, 37, 39–41
adventure tourism, 197n.17
aggressiveness, 151. See also chingón/a
   (aggressive and astute)
agrarian communities: population of,
   xxxiv
agrarian crisis, 28–31; displacement

due to, xviii; education as solution
   to, 56; hunger facing Maya families
   and, 55–56
agrarian reform, xl, 19, 24–35, 42;
   agrarian code of 1940, 191n.16;
   agrarian crisis, xviii, 28–31, 55–56;
   under Cárdenas administration,
   24–25, 29, 191n.19; delineation and
   formalization of boundaries of
   rural communities, 24; dissolution
   of, 180; ejido as community, 26–28,
   42; new Agrarian Law of 1992,
   31–35; postrevolutionary, 24–26
agriculture: milpa, xix, 7, 12, 13, 17,
   30, 43, 56, 60, 61, 188n.3; subsidies,
   for losses from Hurricane Wilma,
   175–76; subsistence farming, xxxiv,
   4–9, 29–30; sub-subsistence farming, 29, 34, 192n.23; swidden (slash-
   and-burn), 20, 25, 27
Aguilar Padilla, Héctor, 49, 50
aguinaldo (Christmas bonus), 120
Alarcón, Norma, 150, 202n.7
albergues escolares (elementary boarding schools), 49, 50, 51–52
alcohol: reduction/absence of remittances ascribed to, 137–38
Alemán Váldes, Miguel, xxviii, 186n.15
Alisau, Patricia, 203n.12
Alonso, Ana María, 24, 25, 192n.31
alternative modernities, xxiv, xxv
Alvarado, Salvador, 45–46, 50

Cardiel Coronel, Cuauhtémoc, 197n.9, 202n.5

Cardoso, Fernando Henrique, 142

Caribbean, tourism in: leakages in import costs associated with, 173; receipts as percent of gross domestic product in, 172

Carmack, Robert M., 186n.7

Carr, Barry, 84

Carrillo Puerto, Felipe, 46–47, 50

Casa del Estudiante Indígena (House of Indigenous Student) program, 47

Casa del Pueblo school system, 35

casa escuela (boarding school), 43, 49, 50, 52

Caso, Alfonso, 48

Castañeda, Quetzil, xxvi, xxxviii, 173, 186n.14, 188n.29

Castellanos, M. Bianet, 10, 74, 180, 191n.21, 200n.17, 200n.22, 201n.24, 202n.5

Caste War of 1847, 1, 11, 18, 190n.5, 190n.7, 190n.9, 201n.24, 202n.6; epoch of slavery before, 19–22; life in southeastern Yucatán disrupted by, 22; time of *libertad* after, 22–24

Castillo Cocom, Juan, 188n.29

Catholic Church, 20, 21

cattle ranching, 29

Cayo, Javier, 165

cell phones, use of, 107–8, 109, 129, 131; parental demands communicated by, 136

cenote (sinkhole), 1, 5, 11, 188n.4

Centros Coordinadores Indigenistas (Coordinating Indigenous Centers, or CCI), 49–50, 51

Centros de Educación Indígena (Center for Indigenous Education, or CEI), 47–48, 193n.6–7

Chamberlain, Robert Stoner, 20

Chaney, Elsa, 105

Chan Kom, Maya community of, xxi, xxvi, xxxv, 23, 145, 194n.21

Chan Sahkay (village pseudonym), 24, 34; Cultural Missions in, 38; ejido grant of, 27, 30

Chant, Sylvia, 84, 88, 90

charter flights to Cancún, 85

Chase, Jacquelyn, 32

Chavez, Leo R., 201n.2

Chiapas: Maya peoples in, xxv; population, 188n.28

Chichén Itzá, Pisté community neighboring, xxvi

Child, Brenda, 54, 59

childhood: altered conceptions of, 58–62

children's labor, Maya, 194n.15; education and loss of, 57; family's reliance on, 51; responsibilities, 194n.17. *See also* adolescence; youth migration

Chin, Elizabeth, 112, 113

Chingada, La, 148

chingaderas (bullshit, acts of mischief and treason), 149, 161

*chingar* (to fuck, to be brave, to be beautiful), 147–50, 152; gendered and sexualized origin of, 148, 149–50; La Chingada, 148; usage of term, 147–48, 152

chingón/a (aggressive and astute): becoming, xli–xlii, 141, 146–62, 181; becoming too chingón, 152–58; being despierto and, 147, 150, 151, 181; challenging capitalism's inequities, 158–60; chingón as working class macho, 148–50; limits of progress and, 160–62; "logic of the absurd" encompassed in, 152; reference to power, 150

Chivers, T., 104

**M. BIANET CASTELLANOS** is assistant professor of American studies at the University of Minnesota.